THE DARLINGS OF WAPPING WHARF LAUNDERETTE PRESENT..

quite naturally
the small faces
A DAY-BY-DAY GUIDE TO THE CAREER OF A POP GROUP

KEITH BADMAN & TERRY RAWLINGS
WITH KEN SHARP, KENT BENJAMIN & JOHN HELLIER

This book is dedicated to Kay Marriott
and to the memory of Steve.

The Darlings of Wapping Wharf Launderette would like to give a big service wash thank you to all the people who helped get "Quite Naturally" finally completed after years of set-backs.

Paul Weller for his initial help and enthusiasm and Kenney Jones for originally trying to get the book out

Martin Costello (and all at 'Complete Music')
Mark Waine ('Red Snapper Design')
Jimmy Winston
Doug McLauchlan (for invaluable archive material)
Mandi O'Connor (for her wonderful 'Small Faces' collection)
Paul McEvoy
Tony Gale
Glen Marks at Rex
John Bloomfield
Roch "the Mod" Vidal (for some great pictures)
Andy Neill
Kathleen and Sheila (the original 'Small Faces' fan)
Jenny Gaylor
Wendy & Heather of the "Oldham Chronicle"
John Reed and all at "Record Collector" magazine
Stephen Rouse
Jason Hobbs
Peter Chalcraft
Henry Scott Irvine

KEITH BADMAN WOULD LIKE TO THANK THE FOLLOWING FILM, TV & RADIO ARCHIVES:
Neil Sommerville (BBC)
Len Brown & John Piper (Granada ITV)
Leonard Karlson (April TV - Sweden)
Rolf B. Tiesler (Radio Bremen - Germany)
HR Media (Germany)
Peter Whitehead (Lorimer Films)
BVL Enterprises
BRTN (Belgium)
Dick Clark Media Archives (USA)

KEN SHARP & KENT BENJAMIN WOULD LIKE TO THANK:
Jody Denberg & Ed Mayberry of KGSR-FM in Austin, Texas and
Terri Sharp

plus the grateful assistance of:
Steve Marriott, Ian & Kim McLagan, Ronnie & Susan Lane and Kenney Jones without whom....................

AND A VERY SPECIAL THANK YOU TO:
Steve Marriott's mum, Kay, for her most invaluable memories, help and use of her priceless photographs - we hope we've done you proud.
John Hellier, for his invaluable collection, assistance and unlimited access to his "Small Faces Information Library". The greatest source of information on the group, anywhere in the world!

Published in Great Britain by "Complete Music Publications" 1997.
ISBN 095172066X. All rights reserved.

PHOTOGRAPHIC CREDITS:
Rex Features: pages 4, 31, 34, 56, 73, 76, 77, 78, 79, 122.
Redferns: pages 97.
Roch Vidal (France): pages 40, 48, 49, 52, 54, 55, 62, 75, 80, 82, 83, 84, 85, 91, 102, 104, 105.
John Hellier (Wapping Wharf archive): pages 5, 7, 9, 13, 14, 15, 19, 43, 44, 46, 47, 51, 69, 97, 98, 101, 106, 112, 114, 171, 172.
David Wedgebury: pages 6, 21, 22, 23, 24, 27, 28, 30, 35, 41.
Terry Rawlings: pages 2, 89.
Doug McLauchlan: pages 88, 102.
Mandi O'Connor: 85, 86, 87, 165.
Trevor French: pages 119.
Pictorial Press: pages 18, 99, 100.

Book design and layout Terry Rawlings and Mark Waine.
Cover design Terry Rawlings and Paul McEvoy.

A Writing Wrongs Book 1997
© Complete Music Publications

Special thanks to all the Small Faces.

Steve Marriott with Terry Rawlings London, 1982

contents

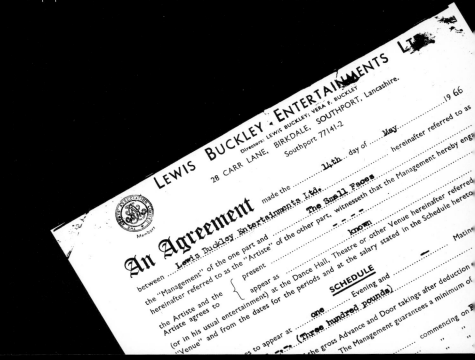

introduction

by Ian McLagan

The early years of the Small Faces were exciting and often hilarious times in our lives, and it knocks me out to read about the renewed interest in the band. It proves that the excitement still comes across, and although millions of dollars have been stolen from us over the years, the recent settlement with the current owners of our recording rights has meant that we are

finally in a position to get something back for all the hard work and fun that we had.Hopefully, these interviews etc. will give you an idea what it was all about, but if you still want more, then I hope you'll read my book, tentatively titled, 'Autobiography Of A Short Arse', when it's released in 1997. I think you'll enjoy the sneaky look behind the curtains, the peep around the dressing room door and the glimpse between the sheets that it offers.
In the meantime, I'll let you dig in to this little lot.

See ya,
Ian McLagan

foreword

by Jimmy Winston

In the words of that famous old Rock and Rolling - psychedelic - street poet of many moons ago (the old bard himself) William Shakespeare - "If music be the food of love, play on". If there is anything in music's great history that actually says if something worked then- continue's to work and if it really made some kind of statement of its time onwards and forwards until our time, it is simply that the music "Plays on!"

What still pleases me deep down in the old heart department is that regarding the Small Faces and my own bands thereafter, is that the essence seems to have worked and "Plays On" and still seems to work even now. Right from the early original tracks that I co-wrote and performed on with the SF right through the band's evolution, somehow something came through that the fans could see - hear and feel and has kept them in touch with the HEART of the band all this time. That's a great buzz in itself.

Anyway, enough of this MODAPHONIC (new word, just invented it!) banter. The show must go on. I've had a great time writing - playing - recording for over 37 years now and as long as you learn to take the very rough with the silky smooth along life's magical highway, it's a great industry to be a part of. Many sharks along the way unfortunately in music's mystical ocean. But no doubt if we all wish hard enough, they (who know who they are) anyway, will get their big fat 'rip-off' bums bitten fairly and squarely according to the great laws of rip-off 'karma'.

Anyway, enough of that. Must not waste space on the unworthy. Maybe I should write a book soon and put a few wrongs to right, so to speak. I must admit that it really does irritate the soul to hear all the misappropriate bullshit that the 'wally brigade' has continued to pass on down the line. (But that's another thing!)

So onwards and upwards. I do believe that good books (like this one, of course) plus accurate stories - journalists who take the trouble to find out the truth before they print it, and don't stoop to conquer from one anothers mistakes, generally to do a good job to help keep the music on the road, so to speak. And as some of these are good fans anyway, they all work to weave the fabric of continuance. Keep up the good work lads! One to mention here is John Hellier who runs the SF fanzine. He's done so much excellent work on the magazine that it's a wonder that he's got any time left at the end of the day for anything else! A real 22 carat fan! Rock on to the "Darlings Of Wapping Warf Launderette". You're doing a grand job!

It's also great to see DECCA RECORDS waking up to wonderland and re-releasing all the early Small Faces material on CD, which I'm very glad to say I'm on! Who knows, maybe I'll even get paid at last for all the blood, sweat and tears (not forgetting the music). As the wonderful Forrest Gump said "What goes around, comes around". Nice one!

Another nice touch recently was the Small Faces convention at the Ruskin Arms Pub on the 26th of January 1997. I was invited over by the fanzine 'modaphonics' and was asked to play a couple of numbers. A very strange experience after all this time! Remember I lived in the pub for twelve years and that was 29 years ago. (WHAT!!!!) I played a couple of acoustic numbers (more of my recent stuff) just to keep the old hand in. Great audience! Great buzz! It was a good turn out. Fans there from 16 to 60. What longevity! The music lives on and on! What more can you ask for?

One last thing before I go. The strangest experience happened for me after the SF convention, when I took my son and his mate for a 'rock and roll' regulation curry in the Indian restaurant that is now part of the Ruskin Arms Pub. When I lived in the Pub it was an off-licence and next to the off-licence was my bedroom. Anyway, now it's a curry shop and lo and behold here we are sitting in an Indian restaurant that used to be my bedroom. Then it dawned on me that this was, of course, the space where my band THE REFLECTIONS and then the FUMBS used to rehearse and, not only that, I wrote the tracks "Real Crazy Apartment/Snow White" etc in this very room! Now I'm thinking "My bed used to be there........and many more kaleidoscopic implausibles that happened in that space........" Goodness, what a real crazy apartment this all is!

Anyway, enough said for now. Sit back - relax - take a nice long drink or whatever else gets you up to the 'higher faculties'. Hope you enjoy the book, and remember the old saying: "It's nice to be nice!"

All the best
JW (March 24th 1997)

there were but four small faces (well five actually)

Steve Marriott

Born: January 30th 1947

Educated: Sandringham secondary modern.

The early years:

Placed first in the "Talent" competition during 'The Uncle Ken Show' at Jaywick Sands on June 18th 1958. One year later, he again was placed first in the "Children's Talent Contest" during 'The Uncle Ken Show' at Jaywick, Clacton-on-Sea on June 19th 1959.

Performed in groups such as:

* "The Mississippi Five", whilst at school.
* "Coronation Kids", they were described as 'Saturday Morning Picture's Kids'.
* "Wheels", who regularly performed Buddy Holly numbers.
* "Frantics", who performed a cross-section of numbers by The Shadows and Shane Fenton.
* "Moonlights", circa 1963, specialising in R & B numbers.

Steve's next big group, 'Steve Marriott's Moments' came about at the start of 1964. A detailed listing of the group and their 1964, eighty-one date concert tour can be found starting on the third entry for that year.

Steve's first big wish in life was to become either a groom or a vet, but that all changed In 1960, when his mother Kay noticed the advert in "The Sketch" casting for youngsters to replace the original cast in the West End stage play of Lionel Bart's "Oliver" at the New Theatre in St Martin's Lane, London. At Steve's audition he performed firstly the Connie Francis No.1 hit from 1958 "Who's Sorry Now" and then Buddy Holly's 1957 hit "Oh! Boy". This was most unusual, considering all auditionees were meant to perform only one song! During his year long run in "Oliver" at the West End, playing one of the fourteen children in the workhouse and thieves kitchen scenes, he would regularly leave his C3A class at Manor Park's 'Sandringham School' and within hours be up on stage. Following his performances each night, Steve, then only fourteen years

of age, would be met by either Kay or his father William. His payment per week was £8, of which a third of that was put by towards buying a new guitar. He was given 5 shillings a week pocket money. The show was recorded for posterity on a "World Records Club" Original Cast Recording album (TP 151), and contained three tracks ("Consider Yourself/I'd Do Anything" & "Be Back Soon") sung by Steve.

Following his departure from 'Oliver', Steve appeared, in another stage West End production, this time in the role of 'Tootles', one of the 'Lost Boys' in the Italia Conte stage production of 'Peter Pan' at the 'Astoria' in Charing Cross Road. Then for a few weeks only, in the role of the young pop-star Art Joyful in the BBC radio series "Mrs. Dale's Diary" starring alongside the 1930's music-hall singer and dancer Jessie Matthews, who had only recently taken over the role of Mrs. Dale herself. The long-running serial naturally concerned the day-to-day life and activities of Mrs. Dale. Other BBC radio roles followed including a bit part in the play "Don't Get Caught Freddy". Steve also showed his talents as an 'agony aunt' alongside the late Marjorie Proops on Radio Luxembourg's Sunday night letters show, transmitted at 10:00pm. Steve's part in the show was to read out letters sent in by listeners and Marjorie (one of the world's most famous 'agony aunts' who wrote regularly for "The Daily Mirror") would give her solutions to the problems. Another uncredited role for the young Steve at this time was as a voice over for the TV commercial '1001' carpet cleaner.

Ronnie Lane

Born: April 1st 1946. Plaistow, East London.

Educated: Lister Technical College in Plaistow.

The early years:

Left school to work on the 'roll-a-penny' stall at the fairground.

He was introduced to Kenny by his brother Stan. Worked

with Kenny at 'Selmers Amplifiers' in High Holborn, London WC1 (the musical instrument factory) as testers. Played in various groups (also with Kenny) such as firstly The Pioneers, which included a line-up of Alan Hunt on bass, Ben Chimes on organ and a guy called Steve on guitar. Alan Hunt continued with Ronnie and Kenny when, in 1964 they formed The Outcasts. They added to the line-up Terry Newman on guitar and a guy called George on lead vocals.

Kenny Jones

Born: September 16th 1948. Stepney, East London
Educated: St, George's in the East and Stepney Green Senior School.
The early years:
After leaving school, Kenny was briefly an Army Cadet and then, in 1963, was introduced to Ronnie by his brother Stan. (See Ronnie for further details.)

Jimmy Winston

Born: Jimmy Langwith, April 21st 1943. (The year was later changed to 1945 on the instructions of Don Arden.)
Educated: Stratford Green Secondary Modern.
The early years:
After leaving school he worked for a couple of years as a lighterman on the River Thames before earning a scholarship to attend the 'E15' Drama School (for two and a half years) which was first based in Stratford, London E15, and then later moved to Debden in Essex. To earn extra money, he worked as a compere/singer in his parents pub the 'Ruskin Arms'. Like Steve, Jimmy would also get work as an actor, such as in the TV film called "Silent Evidence" and in a cinema film entitled "Two Left Feet". But just as he was completing his time at drama school in 1965, and about to get himself an agent, Steve and Ronnie walked into the 'Ruskin Arms', and the rest, as you say, is history!
Following, his departure from the Small Faces and the music industry in general, he appeared in the musical "Hair" and recorded two singles. Later he got a bit part in the Gerry Anderson sci-fi programme "UFO" (the episode was called "Sub-Smash") and in the 1980's, appeared in an episode of "Dr Who". Jimmy made a special guest appearance, performing on stage with his own compositions, at the first ever "Small Faces Convention" held at the 'Ruskin Arms' public house on Sunday January 26th 1997.

Ian "Mac" McLagan

Born: May 12th 1945 in Hounslow, Middlesex. (The year was later changed to 1946, again on the instructions of

Steve with his pre-Moments group The Frantics

Educated: Spring Grove Grammar School, in Hounslow, Middlesex.
The early years:
Performed in bands such as 'The Muleskinners' (a Twickenham based R & B combo). Their lead singer was Terry Brennan, who had previously played with Eric Clapton and Manfred Mann's Tom McGuinness in The Roosters. Later, in 1964, Mac played with Boz, (AKA the Norwich based Boz Burrell) in his backing group 'The Boz People'.

1963

MARCH
Steve Marriott releases the single "Give Her My Regards" backed by "Imaginary Love", written by Steve. (Decca F 11619). The single features Marriott giving an unintentionally hilarious impression of Adam Faith.

SATURDAY OCTOBER 5th
A management agreement between Stephen Marriott, of 9, Daine's Close, Manor Park, London and Tony Calder of 4, Norfolk Road, Shirley, Southampton, remained unsigned due to Steve's father William being unhappy with the arrangements.

then we'll begin - 1964

SATURDAY MARCH 14th

The "Record Mirror" reports that four record labels are in a race to sign youngster Steve Marriott, who has recently been offered the lead in a new musical play.

SATURDAY MARCH 21st

The "Record Mirror" reports, one week later, that "I Cried" will be the second Steve Marriott single and hints at a romance between Steve and fellow Decca artiste Adrienne Poster (who would later change her surname to Posta). Steve had first met Adrienne while they were both at the 'Italia Conti Drama School'.

"STEVE MARRIOTT'S MOMENTS".

Formed following the demise of 'The Moonlights' at the end of 1963, the 'Moments' (who were briefly managed by 'High Numbers/Who' boss Pete Meadan) began rehearsals at the start of the year in the disused "Uplands Tea-Room" in Billett Lane, Chadwell Heath, East London. Following two months of rehearsing, "Steve Marriott's Moments", occasionally joined by Adrienne Poster, (who would duet with Steve on The Beatles cover 'Twist & Shout' as the group's encore), set off on a seven month (81 date) tour around the country. Such was their popularity from the tour, a fanzine entitled "Beat '64" was created and a fan club for the group was set up by Anne Marshall, who ran the club from her home in Uphall Road, Ilford in Essex. What follows is the first published breakdown of that Moments' tour. (Their repertoire largely consisting of Beatles and Stones covers.)

SATURDAY MARCH 28th

The group perform their first concert at the 'Cellar Club' in Kingston, London.

WEDNESDAY APRIL 1st

The 'Corn Exchange' in Rochester.

SATURDAY APRIL 4th

The 'Blue Moon' in Cheltenham.

SUNDAY APRIL 5th

The 'Star' in Croydon.

THURSDAY APRIL 9th

The 'Wykeham Hall' in Romford, Essex.

TUESDAY APRIL 14th

The 'Palais' in Ilford, Essex.

WEDNESDAY APRIL 15th

The 'Assembly Rooms' in Tunbridge Wells.

THURSDAY APRIL 16th

The 'Corn Exchange' in Bristol. Tonight the group plays support to Gene Vincent.

TUESDAY APRIL 21st

A return appearance at the 'Cellar Club' in Kingston.

FRIDAY APRIL 24th

The 'Star' in Croydon.

SUNDAY APRIL 26th

The first of three gigs at the 'Willow Rooms' in Romford, Essex supporting 'Scrooge & The Misers'. The frontman for the group was lead-singer Pete Harper, whom Steve often cited as being "one of his biggest influences". Incidentally, both the 'Moments' and 'Scrooge & The Misers' were both represented by the agent "Kenneth Johnson Promotions" of Earlham Grove in London E7.

MONDAY APRIL 27th

The 'Flamingo Club' in London, supporting Zoot Money.

TUESDAY APRIL 28th

The 'Co-Op' Hall, in Grays, Essex.

THURSDAY APRIL 30th

The '100 Club', at 100 Oxford Street, London, supporting The Graham Bond Organisation.

FRIDAY MAY 1st

The 'Wilton Hall' in Bletchley.

SUNDAY MAY 3rd
The second of three gigs at the 'Willow Rooms' in Romford, Essex. Again supporting 'Scrooge & The Misers'.

MONDAY MAY 4th
The 'Florida Club' in Brighton, Sussex.

TUESDAY MAY 5th
Another appearance at the 'Cellar Club' in Kingston.

WEDNESDAY MAY 6th
The 'Mercury Theatre' in Notting Hill, London.

SATURDAY MAY 9th
The 'Dreamland' centre in Margate, Kent.

SUNDAY MAY 10th
The third and final gig at the 'Willow Rooms' in Romford, Essex supporting 'Scrooge & The Misers'.

MONDAY MAY 11th
The 'Blue Moon' in Cheltenham, supporting Mose Allison.

WEDNESDAY MAY 13th
Another performance at the 'Cellar Club' in Kingston.

SATURDAY MAY 16th
A return appearance at the 'Wykeham Hall' in Romford.

SUNDAY MAY 17th
The 'Flamingo Club' in London, supporting Georgie Fame.

THURSDAY MAY 21st
The 'Star' in Croydon.

FRIDAY MAY 29th
The '100 Club' at 100, Oxford Street, London, supporting The Action.

SATURDAY MAY 30th
The 'Market Hall' in Redhill.

MONDAY JUNE 1st
Another appearance at the 'Cellar Club' in Kingston.

TUESDAY JUNE 2nd
The 'Leyton Baths' in London, supporting John Mayall.

WEDNESDAY JUNE 3rd
The 'St. Mathews Hall' in Ipswich.

SATURDAY JUNE 6th
The 'Birdcage' in Portsmouth.

TUESDAY JUNE 9th
'St. Augustines' in Hoddesdon.

SUNDAY JUNE 14th
'Discs-A-GoGo' in Bournemouth.

MONDAY JUNE 15th
The 'Concorde' in Southampton.

TUESDAY JUNE 16th
The 'Crawdaddy Club' in Richmond.

FRIDAY JUNE 19th
The 'Community Centre' in Southall.

SUNDAY JUNE 21st
'Cooks Ferry Inn', Edmonton in London.

WEDNESDAY JUNE 24th
'Ealing College', London.

THURSDAY JUNE 25th
The 'Bluesville Flamingo' in Manor House, London.

FRIDAY JUNE 26th
The 'Crazy E Club', London.

TUESDAY JUNE 30th
The 'Embassy' in Northampton.

SUNDAY JULY 5th
The group return to the 'Cellar Club' in Kingston.

MONDAY JULY 6th
Another performance at the '100 Club', at 100, Oxford Street, London supporting the T-Bones.

WEDNESDAY JULY 8th
The 'Locarno' in Basildon, Essex supporting The Mike Cotton Sound.

SATURDAY JULY 11th

The 'White Hart' in Brentwood, Essex.

TUESDAY JULY 14th

The 'Blue Indigo Club' in Southampton.

FRIDAY JULY 17th

A return appearance at the 'Cooks Ferry Inn' in Edmonton, London.

MONDAY JULY 20th

Another appearance at the 'Cellar Club' in Kingston.

FRIDAY JULY 24th

The group support The Animals at 'The Attic Club' at 1A, High Street, in Hounslow, Middlesex. Tickets were 7/6 in advance or 8/6 on the door. The manager of the club Bill Channell decided to record tonight's show on a portable tape recorder. The tape survived until Steve found fame in the Small Faces two years later, where upon it vanished and has never been seen since.

SATURDAY JULY 25th

The 'Pontiac' in Putney, London.

SUNDAY JULY 26th

The 'Flamingo' in London, supporting The Cheynes.

MONDAY JULY 27th

The 'Beat City' in London.

TUESDAY JULY 28th

A most historic night in the history of the Small Faces when Steve's band play at the 'Albion' public house in Rainham, Essex. Also on the bill that night was The Outcasts, featuring a bass guitarist by the name of Ronnie Lane.

SUNDAY AUGUST 2nd

'St. Justine's Hall' in West Wickham.

MONDAY AUGUST 3rd

The 'Star' in Croydon.

THURSDAY AUGUST 6th

The 'Wykeham Hall' in Romford, Essex.

SATURDAY AUGUST 8th

The 'Crawdaddy Club' in Richmond.

SUNDAY AUGUST 9th

'The Attic' Club at 1A, High Street in Hounslow, Middlesex. The show is billed as "raving R & B".

TUESDAY AUGUST 11th

Another performance at 'The Attic' Club at 1A, High Street, in Hounslow, Middlesex. The show starting at 7:30pm, with the tickets costing 3/6.

FRIDAY AUGUST 14th

'Coronation Hall' in Ramsgate.

TUESDAY AUGUST 18th

The group return to 'The Attic' Club in Hounslow.

MONDAY AUGUST 24th

The 'Golders Green Refectory' in London.

TUESDAY AUGUST 25th

The 'Orchid' in Purley.

FRIDAY SEPTEMBER 4th

The 'Bluesville' in Ipswich.

FRIDAY SEPTEMBER 11th

The group travel North for three dates in the Midlands. The first being at the 'Sherwood Rooms' in Nottingham.

SATURDAY SEPTEMBER 12th

A performance at 'Leeds University'.

SUNDAY SEPTEMBER 13th

A performance at 'Manchester University'.

TUESDAY SEPTEMBER 15th

A return performance at 'The Attic' Club in Hounslow. The show starting at 7:30pm, with tickets costing 3/6.

SATURDAY SEPTEMBER 19th

The 'Palais' in Peterborough, supporting chart stars The Nashville Teens.

TUESDAY SEPTEMBER 22nd

The group return to the 'Cellar Club' in Kingston.

WEDNESDAY SEPTEMBER 23rd

The 'Pontiac' in Putney, London.

SATURDAY SEPTEMBER 26th
The 'Ilford Baths', supporting again Zoot Money.

SUNDAY SEPTEMBER 27th
Another performance at 'The Attic' Club in Hounslow, Middlesex.

SUNDAY OCTOBER 4th
The 'Goldhawk Rooms' in Shepherds Bush, London.

WEDNESDAY OCTOBER 7th
The 'Cellar Club' in Kingston.

SUNDAY OCTOBER 11th
The 'Flamingo' in London supporting Zoot Money.

SATURDAY OCTOBER 17th
The 'Lotus' in Forest Gate, London.

SUNDAY OCTOBER 18th
The 'Blue Moon' in Cheltenham.

SATURDAY OCTOBER 24th
The 'Pontiac' in Putney, London.

TUESDAY OCTOBER 27th
The group return to 'The Attic' Club in Hounslow, Middlesex for their final concert.

OCTOBER
Steve Marriott's Moments release (in America only) the single "You Really Got Me/Money, Money" (World Artists WA 1032). The A-side being a cover of The Kinks track from earlier that year.

NOVEMBER
The November edition of the fanzine dedicated to 'Steve Marriott's Moments' entitled "Beat '64" is compiled by a member of David Bowie's 'Manish Boys'. Stuart Tuck, who runs the 'Kensington Youth Centre' becomes increasingly impressed with the Moments, and recommends them to his friend Maurice King, owner of the 'Starlight Rooms' off Oxford Street, in London. Ironically, it was this month that the other band members threw Steve out of the group!

DECEMBER
Maurice King invites the Moments to perform a couple of Sunday afternoon sessions at his 'Starlight Rooms' club, but as Steve is now a solo act, he accepts the invitation anyway and travels there alone. During the two slots (on December 8th and 15th), Steve performs with the group 'Johnny Be Great & The Quotations'. who incidentally, the following year, would feature a new drummer by the name of Phil Collins. During Steve's short residency at the club, he would come into contact with the singer Elkie Brooks for the first time.

MONDAY DECEMBER 2nd
A contract is drawn up between 'Contemporary Records'

house to see Jimmy playing with the resident band. Steve asks if he could get up and play harmonica with them, which he did. Following the the gig, Jimmy invites the two of them back to his home, above the Ruskin Arms public house in Stratford, East London where they invite him to join their new band. He immediately accepts and they sit up all night getting drunk and discussing their future in the pop business. A first rehearsal is planned for Wednesday.

WEDNESDAY JANUARY 27th

The line-up comprising of Steve on Ronnie's 'Gretsch' guitar, Ronnie on his new 'Harmony' Bass, Kenny on drums and Jimmy on keyboards assemble at the 'Ruskin Arms' in High Street North, Manor Park, East London. (The pub could be used for free, as Jimmy's parents owned it). Kenny remembers that first session:

Steve taught Jimmy a couple of notes that went 'Da Dah, Da Dah, Da Dah' which was "Whatcha Gonna Do About It", and Jimmy got the flavour for it, and he went straight away and bought a huge 'Leslie' cabinet. So he was in".

The rehearsals, mainly featuring Jimmy Reed and James Brown covers, would continue, off and on, for over three months.

FEBRUARY

First the music press announce that the new Steve Marriott single on Decca, "Tell Me" (a cover of the Stones song), backed by "Maybe" will be available soon via Ronnie Vaughn Managements, and then, shortly afterwards, Decca announce that they have rejected the single. There was no catalogue number assigned to the release, and, contrary to belief, no acetates/test pressings were made. But this misfortune did bring Steve into contact with the Stones manager Andrew Oldham. This led Steve to being asked to play harmonica on various 'Andrew Loog Oldham Orchestra' projects, such as those by Jennie & The Redheads, Bo & Peep and Cleo.

MARCH

Steve, not entirely happy with the rehearsals with Lane, Jones and Winston that are currently taking place, replies to an advert in the 'Melody Maker' where the band The Lower Third are requesting for a lead singer. Steve's audition did not go well and the vacancy was later taken by David Jones (AKA David Bowie). Jones was apparently chosen due to his resemblance to Yardbirds lead singer Keith Relf.

THURSDAY MAY 6th

The group, still without a name, comprising a line-up of Marriott, Lane, Jones and Winston are invited by Stuart Tuck to perform their very first gig at the Kensington Youth Centre in East Ham. It was also during this night that their name came about. Steve's girlfriend Annabella, (who was introduced to Steve by Jimmy) having caught sight of the four of them standing together in front of the stage, remarked "Cor, ain't you got small faces?". This name was ideal. 'Face' was a term for a high-profile 'mod-about-town', and 'small' coming from their height. Steve, Ronnie and Kenny all stood under 5 foot 6 inches. "Except Jimmy", as Kenny pointed out, "who was too tall!"

A regular haunt for Steve and Ronnie to talk about their future plans at this time, over cups of coffee and brown sauce rolls, was at the 'Giaconda Cafe' in Denmark Street, London W1. It was here, later this month, that they decided to turn professional.

FRIDAY MAY 7th

The owner of the 'Kensington Youth Centre' Stuart Tuck invites them back the following night to play another (unpaid) gig. He is greatly impressed, and invites them to play at his wedding reception tomorrow.

SATURDAY MAY 8th

The Small Faces give their third public performance (the second using the name) for the wedding party of Stuart Tuck in Loughton, Essex. Steve had been living in a flat with Mick O' Sullivan and friends from acting school, and this afternoon he invited Stuart to hold their reception in their home. As the group's equipment was already at the flat (Ronnie and Kenny would occasionally stop over and rehearse) Steve, Ronnie and Kenny needed no persuasion to get up and perform for the wedding party. As the evening wore on, a panic occurred when the bride jumped out of the first floor balcony! Meanwhile, Stuart Tuck sensed that the group were destined for better things and put another phone call through to Maurice King, who was keen to see the Small Faces and invited the group down to London to perform two Sunday afternoon slots in his club. The first would be next Sunday, May 16th.

MONDAY MAY 10th to SATURDAY MAY 15th

Excited by the prospects in London, the group rehearse throughout the week at both the 'Kensington Youth Centre' and the 'Ruskin Arms' Public House. On Tuesday May 11th and Thursday May 13th, the group perform two (unpaid) gigs in front of the pub regulars.

SUNDAY MAY 16th

The Small Faces travel down to London to perform the two afternoon shows at the 'Starlight Rooms'. Maurice King, seeing the group for the first time, was greatly impressed. He, in turn, puts a phone call through to a friend of his up North in Sheffield. His name was Peter Stringfellow, and he ran a venue called the 'Mojo Club'. He agrees to let the group perform the following weekend on Saturday May 22nd.

THURSDAY MAY 20th

The Small Faces (Marriott, Lane, Jones and Winston) climb into a black 'Maria' van (owned by Jimmy's brother Frank) this morning and are driven North to Manchester by their roadie, an acquaintance of Steve, named 'Terry The Egg'. That evening, the group play their first Northern gig at the 'Twisted Wheel' R & B club at Brazennose Street, off Albert Square in Manchester. Their performance occurred in the 7:30 to 11:00pm slot. During the Small Faces concert, a local villain 'borrowed' their van for an hour. When it was returned, it was full up with leather coats. Unbeknown to the group, the van had been used to assist in a local robbery! (Steve, Ronnie and Kenny all received a leather coat as thanks for lending their van!!)

FRIDAY MAY 21st

The next Northern gig occurred at a working man's club in Sheffield, but their performance only lasted three James Brown numbers before the manager, disgusted by their performance, threw them out, telling them to "Piss Off!" The group on a walkabout then stumble upon the trendy blues 'Esquire Club' in Sheffield. They persuade the management to let them play an evening performance. Due to the place being packed out with Mods, their set went down a storm.

SATURDAY MAY 22nd

The group really take off when they play at Peter Stringfellow's 'Mojo Club' (upon the recommendation of Maurice King) in Sheffield. It was the biggest club they had played at this point.

SUNDAY MAY 23rd

Ronnie, Kenny and Jimmy return to London that afternoon, while Steve makes his way back to his flat in Loughton, Essex.

SATURDAY MAY 29th

Steve Marriott is one of the artists appearing at the NME stand during the 'Variety Club Star Gala' concert at the Battersea Park Festival Gardens. Steve was pictured as he signed autographs for charity. That night, the Small Faces travel to the 'Cavern In The Town' Club at 5, Leicester Place, just off Leicester Square in hope of getting a gig. Steve and 'Terry The Egg' were instrumental in speaking to the Irish manager. They pleaded insistently for a chance to play, but hit problems when they announced to him they only know five numbers. "Can you do two more?", he asked. They agreed. This was done by repeating, and slightly ad-libbing two numbers from their set. The Small Faces performance that night went down tremendously well, and when the manager saw the crowd's reaction, invited them back the following Saturday, with a chance of a brief residency. Amongst the packed audience that night were the singer Elkie Brooks and Maurice King. Following their final performance, King, thinking of taking the group under his wing, approaches the band and enquires of their current management status. Steve cheekily asks him if they could use his 'Starlight Rooms' again, this time to rehearse. King agrees, and asks them "This Monday, how does that suit you?."

MONDAY MAY 31st

As planned, the group rehearse this afternoon at Maurice King's 'Starlight Rooms' club. By chance, a friend of King, Pat Meehan visits the club for a social visit and watches the group rehearse. Their performance greatly impresses him and eagerly, upon returning to his Carnaby Street office, tells his employer of the group he has just witnessed. His employer was one Don Arden. Arden makes attempts to get Steve Marriott's telephone number. Firstly he contacts King, who doesn't have it, and then he rings the manager of the 'Cavern In The Town', where he is offered Steve's home number. He phones there later, where he speaks to Steve's mother Kay.

Following the rehearsal, Steve returns to his flat in Loughton.

TUESDAY JUNE 1st

Steve, as usual, phones home once a week via a public call box, where he is told by his mother Kay that a man by the name of Don Arden is trying to contact him. Excitedly, Steve rings Ronnie (again via the call box) to inform him of Arden's interest. In turn, Steve rings Arden's office to speak to him directly. Unfortunately, he was not in the office, but Steve tells his assistant Pat Meehan that they are both invited to come and see the group perform at the 'Cavern In The Town' on Saturday night (June 5th).

FRIDAY JUNE 4th

During the day, Ronnie travels over to Loughton in Essex to stay with Steve at his flat. But tragedy strikes when Steve and Ronnie, following a night out in Loughton, are set upon by six skinheads from Tottenham, North London in a van, carrying bottles and wood with protruding nails. Steve and

the audience that night were Don Arden and his assistant Pat Meehan. At the end of the show, Arden approached the group and invited them to his Carnaby Street office on Monday (June 7th) to discuss a management deal. Also in the audience that night was The Who's manager Kit Lambert, who also showed an interest in the Small Faces.

MONDAY JUNE 7th

The Small Faces (Marriott, Lane, Jones and Winston)

Ready, Steady, Go!

Ronnie, with their faces pouring with blood, make their way to "Woodford Hospital". Which, unbeknown to them was a 'Maternity Hospital'!! The attack, not personally aimed at either Steve or Ronnie, was by way of revenge following a group of boys from Loughton who had recently badly beaten-up lads in Tottenham.

SATURDAY JUNE 5th

Steve and Ronnie, with their faces covered in stitches, black eyes and fat lips, are picked up in the black Maria van by Terry The Egg, Kenny and Jimmy, en route to their first 'billed' performance at the 'Cavern In The Town' at 5, Leicester Place, off Leicester Square in London. Among

assemble at 10:00am in Arden's 52-55, Carnaby Street offices where he makes them an offer:

"Now listen, you can have a straight wage, or a percentage". Kenny remembers what happened next. "We (the Small Faces) went outside (the office) and said 'We ain't stupid, we want a wage and a percentage!'. We went back in and told him. So he said 'Ok, I'll give you twenty pounds a week and you can have a percentage of the records, plus a shopping account in every clothes shop in Carnaby Street".

They shook hands, and were promised that contracts would be drawn up by the following Thursday (June 10th). The group went out to celebrate in the nearest pub. So confident that the Small Faces would sign for him, Arden arranged their first gig under his management for the following Thursday (June 10th - see entry).

Ronnie later gave his views of having accounts in Carnaby Street and living on twenty pounds a week.
"We were like a bunch of old women at the jumble sale; when we walked into a shop, some of the stuff we never even wore. We lived on the road and all the expenses were paid for. In actual fact, we often had money left over from that twenty quid, and we were out of our boxes most of the time."

THURSDAY JUNE 10th
The Small Faces (along with their respective parents) sign a three-year management contract with Don Arden's 'Contemporary Records'. Their subsequent meteoric rise to fame at the end of 1965 raised many eyebrows. But years later, in 1972, Arden revealed that all was not as it seemed.

"They came to me as three hungry scarecrows from London's East End." Arden said, "I raised them in three months to £200 a night stardom with a fashionable house in Pimlico with a maid, housekeeper and chauffeur-driven limousine".

Arden then revealed his secret. "Hyping", he replied, adding "the secret of their success and mine, was a sleazy trick of the trade known as 'hyping.' Dead easy if you're in the know, and not over-fussy about your methods. I just paid thousands of pounds to "fix" some of the hit charts supposedly compiled from the sales returns of record shops. I knew that for certain sums, any record I was associated with could be elevated to the charts."

"It got to be a habit. I paid out anything from £150 to £500 a week to people who manipulated the charts and who in turn shared the cash with people organising other charts so again for bills

as to ensure they tallied. For instance, if I had a record at No.18 in one, they would see to it that the same record appeared as either 16 or 17 or thereabouts, in the others. Neat little swindle, wasn't it? Of course, the Small Faces had no idea what went on."

"But with the connections I had with television we fixed

the Faces up with appearances on some well-known programmes. In a month the record ("Whatcha Gonna Do About It") was in the top twenty. Accounts were opened for them at all the best boutiques in London. They bought shirts by the dozen, shoes by the score and their cupboards bulged with countless suits. My company (Contemporary Records) were entitled to 25 per cent of their earnings, but we never really had a chance to collect. As the money came in, so it went out again for bills, and just to prove that the 'Al Capone' of the pop world has a soft spot, let me tell you I felt these kids should have at least one year of enjoying the very best in life. After all, they had been very hungry in their time."

Now with the group under his control, Arden informs them that he has arranged their first gig under him for later that night at the 'Wykeham Hall' in Romford Essex. As planned, the group perform at the hall, but following the conclusion of their performance, the promoter Ron King, a business friend of Arden's, informs them that he is refusing to pay them. Naturally, the group ask why not, to which King

replied, "Because you played too fuckin' loud!"

SATURDAY JUNE 12th
The second 'billed' performance at the 'Cavern In The Town' at 5, Leicester Place, London.

SATURDAY JUNE 19th
The third 'billed' performance at the 'Cavern In The Town' at 5, Leicester Place, London.

From the Faces' 5 track session on August 28th (reel no. TLO 535/691) he copied:

*"Jump Back" (duration - 1' 40", 7th item on reel one)
*"Whatcha Gonna Do About It?" (duration - 2' 15", 8th item on reel two)
*"Think" (duration - 3' 35", 4th item on reel two).

These three tracks were mastered onto a 7 1/2 IPS 7" reel, and immediately dispatched across London. (see entry for Tuesday September 28th for review.)

THURSDAY SEPTEMBER 16th

Fifty-seven days after Pat Meehan of the 'Contemporary Record Co. Ltd" sent "Top Of The Pops" producer Johnny Stewart an advance copy of the single "Whatcha Gonna Do About It?" (see entry for Wednesday July 21st 1965) the group are invited to perform the song on the top BBC pop-music show. Recordings are carried out at Studio 2 at the Television Centre in Wood Lane, London, where, following a brief afternoon rehearsal, the group perform a 'lip-synched' version of the song "Whatcha Gonna Do About It?" in the transmission broadcast

live on BBC1 between 7:25 and 8:00 that night. The show, hosted by Jimmy Savile, also featured in the studio, The Hollies, Manfred Mann and The Silkie. While Herman's Hermits, Sonny (minus Cher), The Walker Brothers and The Rolling Stones all appeared by way of 'previously recorded' VT inserts and both Donovan and Nini Rosso appeared in specially shot 35mm film sequences. (The show ran to 34 minutes, 35 seconds.) Incidentally, for this, and the next "Top Of The Pops" appearance on Thursday September 30th, (see entry) the group were paid all of £47-5 shillings-0 pence!!

FRIDAY SEPTEMBER 17th

Due to Arden's persistent phone-calls to his friends in the media, the Small Faces are hurriedly slotted into making their debut on tonight's edition of Rediffusion Television's pop programme "Ready Steady Go!" Following an extremely brief afternoon rehearsal in Studio One at the Wembley Studios, 128, Wembley Park Drive in London, the group perform a live version of "Whatcha Gonna Do About It" in the live transmission across some of the ITV network that night between 6:08 and 6:59pm. The show, hosted as usual by Cathy McGowan, also featured

performances by Dusty Springfield, the Hollies and Gary Lewis & The Playboys. At the end of the Small Faces set, Steve went down into the audience and danced with the girls. (This sight was caught by the TV cameras.) RSG! host Cathy McGowan said about Steve, "He is quite a one, he's a real little mod!" Meanwhile, Ian McLagan, who is at home preparing himself for a night out on the town in Hounslow, Middlesex, is called downstairs by his father to watch the Small Faces appearance on television.

WEDNESDAY SEPTEMBER 22nd
The group travel to Nottingham, to perform two concerts at 'The Dungeon'. Meanwhile on this day, Contemporary records sign an exclusive three-year release deal with Decca Records.

THURSDAY SEPTEMBER 23rd
Two performances at the 'Public Hall' in Epping.

FRIDAY SEPTEMBER 24th
Two performances at the 'Market Hall' in Trowbridge.

SATURDAY SEPTEMBER 25th
Two performances at the 'Blue Spot' in Brighton.

SUNDAY SEPTEMBER 26th
Two concerts at the 'Bromel' in London.

TUESDAY SEPTEMBER 28th
The trial tape of the Small Faces BBC radio recording on August 23rd (see relevant entry) compiled by producer Brian Willey on Monday September 13th (see entry for full details) is heard by a three-man 'Talent Selection Group' that afternoon at the "BBC Auditions Room" in Hanover Square. Only the first three of the five tracks are put under scrutiny. (ie."Jump Back"/"Whatcha Gonna Do About It" and "Think".)

The results from each panelist were as follows:

"Driving imaginative sound, - very commercial sound, - choice of material very much the same in tempo and feel".

"A very good R & B group in the style of "The Who". They get an authentic 'back to the jungle' sound with lots of mood."

"Pop-art I suppose this is called. A group riding in the wake of "The Who". It's efficient and capable enough and the lead voice is commercial."

A resounding "Yes" from the judges, with the positive results confirmed by chief judge J. E. Grant. The panelists' final comment was: "A very good driving pop R & B group".

The BBC would reply to the Small Faces regarding the trial on October 5th (See entry).

THURSDAY SEPTEMBER 30th
The group make their second appearance on BBC TV's "Top Of The Pops", again at studio 2 of the BBC TV Centre, Wood Lane in London. Following the customary afternoon camera rehearsals, the group mime again to the record "Whatcha Gonna Do About It?" (this time 'spun' by 'jockette' Samantha Juste) in the 92nd edition, transmitted live on BBC1 between 7:25 and 8:00 that evening. The show, hosted by David Jacobs, also featured musical contributions by Ken Dodd, Andy Williams, Peter Paul & Mary, The Hollies, Billy Joe Royal, Herman's Hermits, The Searchers and Sandie Shaw. (The programme was never recorded.)

OCTOBER
The 'Starbeat' column in latest "Rave" reveals: "The Small Faces have two very excellent unpaid publicists working for them in America - namely Sonny Bono and Cler LaPiere!"

"We met both Sonny and Cher while working on our first "Thank Your Lucky Stars", lead guitarist Steve Marriott informed me. "When I saw their gear my immediate reaction was that they were another pair of flash Yanks!"

"I was so wrong. You couldn't wish for a nicer couple. They told us they really dug our music and wanted to take back records and photographs to show people in America. Naturally, we parceled them up with a good big bundle and we've had two letters from them asking for more material".

"Cher's sister Georgianne asked our guitarist Jimmy Winston back to their Knightsbridge flat for coffee and we all met up again on 'Ready Steady Go!' just before they left for America. They seem to like us because we were young and doing something new. Do you need to ask what we think of them?'

The same issue of "Rave" features a review of the Faces' latest "Whatcha Gonna Do About It" in the 'Charts : Where The Action Is' section. The single was at no.6 in the "Rave's Top 6- For The Trend Treatment":

"Here's a success story if you like and a lesson for other

perform live the songs "Whatcha Gonna Do About It" and "What's The Matter Baby" which are included in the transmission that day. As with their previous BBC session, the group received a £30.00 fee, and Jimmy is again credited as "James Winstone". (The £30.00 fee would remain that way right up until April 9th 1968 - see entry.) Later that night, the group travelled to Bournemouth to perform two shows at the 'Pavilion'.

SATURDAY OCTOBER 23rd
Two shows at the 'Gaiety Ballroom' in Ramsgate, Kent.

SATURDAY OCTOBER 30th
Two shows at the 'Town Hall' in Grantham.

SUNDAY OCTOBER 31st
The group travel to Stockport, to perform two shows at the 'Manor Lounge'. This would be Jimmy Winston's final appearance with the group. During the weekend's stay in the hotel, Steve, Ronnie and Kenny go to great lengths in avoiding Winston, clearly embarrassed by the fact that he is to sacked but, as to yet, he has not been told.

In what transpired to be a totally bizarre twist of events, it was during that weekend that Steve, Ronnie and Kenny flicked through 'Beat Instrumental' and found a picture of 'Mac' incorrectly credited to Boz of the 'Boz People'. Still thinking of a replacement for Jimmy, Ronnie asks Arden to call Boz ('Mac') and find out what he was doing. Meanwhile, Ian 'Mac' McLagan who is now on the verge of quitting the music business altogether, finds the van that the 'Boz People' used for gigging has broken down coming back from Scotland. The van was repaired but kept breaking down on the motorway. When they eventually reached London they were caught in several traffic jams and broke down again on the North Circular overpass. Mac had had enough, got out and decided to thumb a lift home. Later that night, feeling depressed, he went to see his girlfriend Irene who lived in Manor Park. The evening ended when he returned home to Hounslow where he bumped into Phil Weatherburn, his neighbour Gillian's cousin. He asked Mac "How is your band?" "Rotten, I just quit!" was Mac's stern reply. "Why don't you join the Small Faces?" Phil suggested.

NOVEMBER
"Beat Instrumental" carries an article entitled 'Faces In The Valley', which concerns the recording (in the second week of October at Central Sound Studios in London, with the now departed Winston) of the songs for the forthcoming film, provisionally titled, "Diamonds For Danger".

MONDAY NOVEMBER 1st
Ian "Mac" McLagan receives a phone call at 10am from Don Arden inviting him to his Carnaby Street office, where he is offered a job. He is invited to a meeting at 12 noon. Mac takes a tube into London and goes to Arden's office in Carnaby Street above 'John Michael's' shop. He waits in the waiting room and wonders what group he will be asked to join. At 5pm Arden calls him into his office where he sits with Arden's assistants Pat Meehan and Ron King. Arden enquires of his current wages and informs him that the group he'll be joining, on a month's probation, is the Small Faces. "You're to tell no-one, ok? Right, be back here at 6 o'clock sharp." Mac, in a daze, leaves the office and finds himself in 'The Ship' on Wardour Street where he orders himself a packet of crisps and a pint of bitter. At 6 o'clock Mac returns to Carnaby Street where he meets the other Small Faces for the first time. They all got on extremely well. The four were then driven to the 'Russell Square Hotel' in the west end where they got to know each other better and ordered drinks on the room service. The rest of the night was spent with Mac answering questions about himself. He revealed later that he was ready to quit the music business the previous day. "My wage packet got smaller and smaller each week" Mac commented "I was sick of careering up and down the country humping my gear about. We broke down on the road back from Scotland that night and I promised myself that night was the last straw, then I got a call from Don Arden".

Mac went on to recall his first meeting with Messrs Marriott, Lane and Jones in Arden's office that afternoon (Monday November 1st). "When I met the other Faces, it was like looking at a mirror of myself- I couldn't believe it, we all looked alike. Plonk (Lane) and Steve might have been brothers. It was about the first time that I've ever counted myself lucky to be small because, apart from needing a new organist, I fitted the group image of being little!"

TUESDAY NOVEMBER 2nd
The day begins with 'Mac' having a haircut (Small Faces style) and joining Steve, Ronnie and Kenny in Carnaby Street as they dress him out in the latest clothes. (On the account, of course.) Later that night he is presented with a "Fender Telecaster" guitar ready for tonight show. Ian "Mac" Mclagan would make his debut (albeit miming the

Winston and his Reflections wait for early opening time at the Borough fruit and veg market, SE London.

guitar part on "I've Got Mine") with the Small Faces at the Lyceum in the Strand, London for the Radio Luxembourg programme "Ready Steady Radio". Unfortunately, Jimmy also turned up, not realising that he was no longer in the group. The evening lasted between 7:30 and 11:30pm but the Small Faces only appeared for the benefit of the radio broadcast which occurred live on Radio Luxembourg between 9:45 and 10:00pm and then again between 10:30 and 10:45pm.

WEDNESDAY NOVEMBER 3rd
Ian "Mac" McLagan makes his 'playing' debut with the Small Faces during their concerts at Swindon's 'Locarno Ballroom'. Following the concert, Marriott reveals to a "Beat

Instrumental" journalist that "Mac's Hammond really slew me, it did something to me inside. It's a wonderful sound. I was so moved I could have cried".

FRIDAY NOVEMBER 5th
Decca release the single "I've Got Mine/It's Too Late" (Decca F 12276), and with it, a quarter page advert in the NME. The paper also reviews the single, but this does not help sales, and the record fails to chart.

SATURDAY NOVEMBER 6th
Two performances at the 'Imperial' in Nelson. Meanwhile, today's "Boyfriend" magazine features Steve, alongside a doctor, a psychologist and a fashion expert in the "Girls

Advisory Bureau" column, and the Small Faces, alongside The Walker Brothers are chosen to appear in the 'Pilot' programme for the new Rediffusion pop-music show "IOGA", a replacement for "Ready Steady Go!" The show never materialises and "Ready Steady Go!" continues on ITV for another year.

SUNDAY NOVEMBER 7th

Two performances at the 'Odeon' in Colchester. The promoter for the shows Arthur Howes, in the NME 'tailpieces' the following Thursday (November 12th) is quoted as saying he was "disappointed with poor attendances for Animals-Small Faces-Beryl Marsden Colchester shows on Sunday".

TUESDAY NOVEMBER 9th

Two performances at the 'Winter Gardens' in Cleethorpes.

WEDNESDAY NOVEMBER 10th

Ian "Mac" McLagan makes his BBC TV debut with the group, when they appear on the seventh edition of the popular children's 'Friday tea-time' entertainment show "Crackerjack", hosted by Leslie Crowther and Peter Glaze. Rehearsals take place from 1:30pm at the Television Centre, and then from 4:00pm, (in front of an hysterical young crowd, many of which were sitting with their fairly restrained parents), record two tracks "Whatcha Gonna Do About It?" and "I've Got Mine". The songs are broadcast, along with guitar legend Bert Weedon, in the edition transmitted between 5:00 and 5:44pm two days later on Friday November 12th. Following the taping, the group give two performances at the 'Town Hall' in Aylesbury.

THURSDAY NOVEMBER 11th

Two performances at the 'Locarno Ballroom' in Swindon.

FRIDAY NOVEMBER 12th

The Small Faces (who had already appeared on the BBC show "Crackerjack" 35 minutes earlier- see entry for November 10th) appear on the TV again, this time making a live appearance on "Ready Steady Go!" in Studio One at the Wembley studios of Rediffusion, performing "I've Got Mine"again with Mac playing the 'Fender' guitar .The show also featured an 'International' line-up of Wilson Pickett, Johnny Hallyday, The Sorrows, The Nashville Teens and Marc Bolan (who was making his TV debut). The show, hosted by Keith Fordyce and Cathy McGowan, is transmitted that night between 6:08 and 6:59pm across some of the ITV network.

Following the broadcast, the group give two performances at the 'Wimbledon Palais'.

SATURDAY NOVEMBER 13th

Two performances at the 'Rhodes Centre' in Stortford. Meanwhile, the Small Faces (alongside such pop contemporaries as The Who, The Action, Jonathan King's Hedgehoppers Anonymous and Beryl Marsden) feature in a 'Melody Maker' article entitled "Next Generation - A Melody Maker Guide To The New Groups And Singers Who Could Be The Next Pop Sensations".

SUNDAY NOVEMBER 14th

The group travel to Birmingham, for two shows at the 'Plaza and Ritz'.

TUESDAY NOVEMBER 23rd

Two performances at the Stonecross Hall, Harlow New Town in Essex.

THURSDAY NOVEMBER 25th

Two shows at the 'Empire', situated in the 'Neath & Glen Ballroom', in Llanelly.

FRIDAY NOVEMBER 26th

Two performances at the 'Mariner Ballrooms' in Morecombe.

SATURDAY NOVEMBER 27th

Two performances at the 'Astoria' in Rawtenstall.

SUNDAY NOVEMBER 28th

Two performances at the 'Odeon' in Guildford with The Walker Brothers.

TUESDAY NOVEMBER 30th

Two performances at the 'Starlight' in Herne Bay.

DECEMBER

"Beat Instrumental" carries a feature entitled 'A New Small Face' which includes an interview with newcomer Ian "Mac" McLagan. During the interview he naturally talks about the other members of the Small Faces, adding that he ".....likes their approach. Their ideas are so fresh and of course, they are all immersed in their music. They have their very own brand of material. If they get any outside stuff from records, it soon gets an arrangement which makes it Small Faces' property".

He goes on to add that he likes the sound which surrounds him on stage, where he (and his Hammond L.102 organ) sit very near one of Ronnie's bass speakers cabinets, adding "He uses a very trebly sound. I like it, it's very different".

Amongst the revelations of the article, was that the very first song they ran through with Mac was the Booker T. track "Comin' Home". Steve (Marriott) later commented that he ".......didn't like to expect too much but I was really knocked back (during the session), he was so good!!"

The same issue features Marriott, posing with his 'Gretsch Tennessean' guitar, in the "Beat Instrumental Portrait Gallery".

Meanwhile, the NME publish the results of the 14th Annual International Popularity Poll. The Small Faces are voted at No.6 in the 'Best New Group' category (behind The Seekers, Walker Brothers, The Yardbirds, The Who and The Fortunes).

The Small Faces also feature in NME news stories, where

it is announced that singer/comedian Kenny Lynch has written the group's next single "Sha La La Lee", due for release on January 7th 1966 and the film in which they make their big-screen debut, now re-titled "Dateline Diamonds", will be released on the Rank Cinema circuit on December 26th, alongside Norman Wisdom's latest "The Early Bird". Four tracks by the group will released on an LP at the same time.

Meanwhile, another article appears on the group in the latest issue of 'Rave', entitled "Now They're The Big Faces". Dawn James met the group to find out more about their 'fantastic rise to fame'.

"Plonk (Ronnie Lane) collapsed onto a chair so surely that it crushed even under his featherweight".

"'I'm late because I went shopping," he gasped. "So sorry, but I can't keep away from Carnaby Street."

"Take it easy boy," Ian McLagan urged, "everything is under control." Plonk has enormous hazel eyes, dark brown hair and a skinny body. He is a sort of leader of The Small Faces (Steve Marriott, vocal and lead guitar; Ian McLagan, organ and rhythm guitar; Kenny Jones, drums.)

"We call him Plonk because he plonks instead of plinks on his bass," said Kenny, helpfully.

The Small Faces have been given every plug in the business. Their first record, 'Whatcha Gonna Do About it' went sailing merrily up the charts, and the group established themselves. They hail from the East End of Soho and Mayfair with a fresh honesty, a cockney sense of humour, and the ability to stand outside themselves and laugh. They were only too ready to assure me that they are not musically knowledgeable.

"Listen, luv", said Steve Marriott, perching on the desk. "We don't know a flat from a sharp, on paper. Our whole success has been a big giggle to the rest of the lads and me. It was a gay, phenomenal accident."

He paused, chuckled at the thought of it, and said, "We all met in a pub one night by accident, and got talking, and Plonk said he wanted to start a group, just for the fun of experimenting with sounds. He said that he had already asked Kenny Jones to join him. Kenny was already with another group and is the only real musician amongst us.

Plonk suggested that Jimmy (Jimmy Winston, their organist who recently left) should join them. He was a bit bothered. "I'd like to, but I can't play organ," he said. "I can't play lead guitar", said I. "I can't play Bass," said Plonk. So he said he'd be pleased to have a go."

Once they started practising they found they had the right musical feeling and were able to make good sounds from ear. Although about two weeks ago Jimmy Winston left and Ian 'Mac' McLagan took his place.

"We sometimes made up tunes as we went along, but somehow they meant something. We could see something in them," Steve explained. "Within a few weeks we had learned some authentic tunes, and were offered a date at the 'J860 Club' in the East End. By some turn of fate, we were offered a date at 'The Cavern', Leicester Square, and we went down a bomb. They asked us back for five weeks running." Eight eyes watched me wide, still amazed at their luck, and thrilled at the outcome of it."

"During one of the nights at 'The Cavern', the man who is now our agent heard us, and signed us up immediately. We told him we were very new to pop, but he said it didn't matter. It was the sound he cared about and the audience reaction."

"We do some crazy things on stage," Plonk said, "and they are never planned, they just happen."

Listening to The Small Faces explaining their great success in the entertainment business in such a light-hearted manner, it became clearer why their records sell. Like them, their records are bright and sensitive and honest.

But not only do they have some refreshing ideas about musical sounds, they can also talk about life and values. They dress like mods, but they don't feel the label 'mod' is quite right.

"What does fashion matter anyway?" asked Ian suddenly. "It's great for the person interested in it, but it doesn't count, does it? Human beings are the things that matter."

The boys have nice manners, are quietly spoken and seem to know exactly what they are, what they want to be, and what they consider important to them.

I asked how important the money they are making is to

their lives now.

"It is important in proportion to other things," Steve said.

"Yes, you're right, Steve." Ian nodded. "It doesn't matter more than good health, and I wouldn't hurt anyone deliberately to acquire more. But it is a good feeling when you have it. My most thrilling experience was opening my bank account. Not from greed, but because it was a step nearer security."

"It would be wonderful to have enough money so you can go to a specialist if you are ill, instead of waiting in the surgery. And to have a comfortable home when you get married, instead of one tiny room."

Steve is eighteen, Ian nineteen, Plonk nineteen and Kenny sixteen. Before they became full-time musicians, Steve had stage parts in 'Oliver' and was on TV. in 'Citizen James' and was on the radio in a play 'Don't Get Caught, Freddy'. Plonk worked in a fairground, Jimmy worked with a local group, and Kenny was at school.

"If we suddenly failed in the pop world we would start where we left off," they said calmly.

Then they looked at their watches, and Plonk got a bit upset again, and they said, "We'll have to go. Terribly sorry, but there is a recording session booked. We are recording a song we wrote-in our heads, of course. We couldn't put it on paper, hope we remember it.................".

And they rushed off.

Incidentally, due to a mix-up in the layout of the article, Ronnie is captioned under a picture of Kenny and vice-versa!

WEDNESDAY DECEMBER 1st
Two performances at the 'Tower Ballroom' in Great Yarmouth.

THURSDAY DECEMBER 2nd

Two performances at the 'Starlight' in Crawley.

FRIDAY DECEMBER 3rd

Two performances at the 'Regency' in Bath.

SATURDAY DECEMBER 4th

Two performances at the 'Pavilion' in Bath.

SUNDAY DECEMBER 5th

Two performances in Leicester at the 'De Montford Hall'.

MONDAY DECEMBER 6th

Two performances at the 'Town Hall' in Torquay.

TUESDAY DECEMBER 7th

Two performances at the 'Civic Hall' in Plymouth.

WEDNESDAY DECEMBER 8th

The group make their debut on Rediffusion/ITV's other (albeit occasional) pop programme "Here Comes The Pops". Appearing again in Studio One at the Rediffusion television studios in Wembley at 2pm, where (following rehearsals) they record a lip-synched version of "I've Got Mine" in a

show also featuring The Walker Brothers and Wilson Picket. The performance would be transmitted across the ITV network later that night between 9:10 and 9:29pm. Following the recording, the group travel to North London to perform two shows at 'Blues Grove' in Tottenham.

THURSDAY DECEMBER 9th

Two performances at 'Austaral', in Sidcup, Kent.

FRIDAY DECEMBER 10th

Two performances at Leicester University.

SATURDAY DECEMBER 11th

Two performances at 'The Baths' in Leyton.

SUNDAY DECEMBER 12th

Two performances at the 'ABC Theatre' in Romford, Essex.

TUESDAY DECEMBER 14th

Two performances at 'Exeter University'.

THURSDAY DECEMBER 16th

The group travel to R.A.F. Cottismore to perform a show at the 'Flying Fox' Club.

FRIDAY DECEMBER 17th

Two performances at the 'Floral Hall' in Morecombe. While the NME today announce that the release of the film (now called) "Dateline Diamonds" has been delayed to next spring, with an accompanying E.P. containing four songs from the film by the Small Faces. (See entry for March 27th 1966 concerning further details on the film.)

SATURDAY DECEMBER 18th

Two performances at the 'Marcam Assembly Rooms' in March, Cambridgeshire.

SUNDAY DECEMBER 19th

Two performances at the 'Embassy' in Peterborough.

WEDNESDAY DECEMBER 22nd

Two performances at the 'Locarno' in Stevenage.

THURSDAY DECEMBER 23rd

Two performances at 'Victoria' in Chesterfield.

FRIDAY DECEMBER 24th

The group play two shows at a special Christmas concert at the 'Wilton Hall' in Bletchley.

SUNDAY DECEMBER 26th

The group (minus Kenny) spend Boxing Day moving their belongings into the £40 a week two storey flats at 22 Westmoreland Terrace, Pimlico, London SW1. Also living there was Mick O' Sullivan and a German housekeeper Liesel. (See entry for February 5th 1966.) One room is given over completely to their Scalextric model motor racing track. "It cost about £80", Steve announced "We race those cars for hours at a time. Plonk is the expert, "The speed that the cars gave, soon disappointed the group. So Ronnie's brother Stan, who was 'good with his hands' came to their rescue. He produced four 'souped up' models with tiny fast engines built inside. This was more to the Small Faces liking! Incidentally, the cars survive to this day, where they have been returned to Stan.

MONDAY DECEMBER 27th

Two shows at the 'Memorial Hall' in Northwich.

TUESDAY DECEMBER 28th

Don Arden arranges a last minute TV appearance, when the group hurriedly appears before the 'Rediffusion' TV cameras for a live appearance on the children's programme 'Five O'Clock Club', hosted by Muriel Young and Wally Whyton. During the live session in studio one at the Rediffusion Studios, the group lip-synch "I've Got Mine". The live broadcast, which also future member of The Moody Blues, Justin Hayward, The Variations, The Zombies, Tommy Quickly and Joy Marshall, plus the 'Five O'Clock Club' regulars such as The Alexis Korner Sextet and the puppets Ollie Beak and Fred Barker, was transmitted across the ITV network between 5:00 and 5:24pm. Following the broadcast, the Small Faces travelled straight on to Stourbridge for another concert performance.

FRIDAY DECEMBER 31st

The Small Faces perform a special 'New Years Eve' concert in Tunbridge Wells.

Right: Wedgbury on location with the band once again was confronted by this strange sight. Aparently the aligators had been sent to the band by a fan who read in a teen mag's profile of Ronnie Lane. He had joked that instead of a conventional pet he would like an aligator!

plaistow to pimlico – 1966

SATURDAY JANUARY 1st

The first concerts of the new year, take place at London's 'Wimbledon Palais'.

WEDNESDAY JANUARY 5th

The Small Faces begin the year with live and TV performances on the Continent, leaving England at London Airport on the morning of January 5th. Over the next six days their short tour takes them to Holland, Belgium and Germany. The first night sees performances in Bussum, Holland.

THURSDAY JANUARY 6th

Performances in Rotterdam, Holland.

FRIDAY JANUARY 7th

The group travel to Belgium, for performances in Gent. Meanwhile, the NME in England, publish their points table for "Chart Successes of 1965". The Small Faces appear at number 77.

SATURDAY JANUARY 8th

Performances in Anderlecht in Belgium.

SUNDAY JANUARY 9th

The group fly to Germany for performances in Frankfurt.

MONDAY JANUARY 10th

The final show of the tour takes place in Munster. The group fly out of Germany immediately following the show, arriving back at London Airport in the early hours of Tuesday 11th.

TUESDAY JANUARY 11th

The Small Faces attend the "Boys and Girls" exhibition at Earls Court in London. Steve posed for photographers on a push bike, Kenny jumped in the cockpit of an RAF mock flight trainer and the group tested their skills on model car racing.

WEDNESDAY JANUARY 12th

The Small Faces perform at the Corn Exchange in Bristol.

THURSDAY JANUARY 13th

The group travel to Worthing, for two performances at The Pavilion.

FRIDAY JANUARY 14th

The latest Decca single "Sha-La-La-La-Lee/Grow Your Own" is released. (No. F 12317). The A-side is co-written by Mort Schuman and the entertainer Kenny Lynch, who can be heard singing backing vocals on the song. Two years later in 1967, Ronnie gave his opinions on the song. "I quite liked 'Sha-La-La-La-Lee', but I didn't like the vocal backings- specifically Lynch's falsetto- which totally spoilt it for me. Apart from that it was quite a good little Saturday night dance record." By now, the group were reasonably pleased with their success. "We were pleased to have some money in our pockets, because we'd driven around for about a year, living in the back of an old black maria." Ronnie continued, "playing for nothing, living on brown sauce rolls. We used to wake up in the morning, look around and think 'my God!' All the windows would be steamed up and there'd be heaps of old socks."

Meanwhile, the group travel to the 'Playhouse Theatre' in London, to record their third BBC radio session, and their second for "The Joe Loss Show", working again with the producer Don George. Arriving at 10:00 am for a rehearsal, then, during the live transmission between 1:00 and 2:00pm, the group perform fourth in the running order "Sha-La-La-La-Lee", returning later to sing "Whatcha Gonna Do About It", then (following an orchestral version of the Beatles' "Day Tripper") perform "Comin' Home Baby". The fourth appearance in the broadcast sees the Small Faces' perform "Woman You Need Love". Incidentally, for the broadcast, Steve used for the first time Mac's "Fender Telecaster" guitar, where 'Humbucker' pick-ups had recently been added.

Following the transmission, the group travel to Gravesend, where they perform two concerts at the 'Co-Operative Hall' in the town centre.

SATURDAY JANUARY 15th

The group travels to Redhill, where they play two shows at the Market Hall.

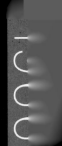

[M]ONDAY JANUARY 17th

[Th]e Small Faces perform two shows at the Town Hall in [Ch]atham, Kent.

[SA]TURDAY JANUARY 22nd

[Th]e 'Record Mirror' reports: 'Pimlico house for the Small [Fac]es'.

[M]ONDAY JANUARY 24th

[Th]e group travel to South Ockenden to perform two concerts [at] the town's 'Youth Centre'.

[TU]ESDAY JANUARY 25th

[Th]e Small Faces cancel their appearance on Radio [Lux]embourg's "Radio Ready Radio".

[W]EDNESDAY JANUARY 26th

[Th]e group travels up to Manchester to appear for the first [tim]e on Granada ITV's prestigious regional news magazine [pro]gramme "Scene At 6:30". The Small Faces, following [brie]f camera rehearsals in studio 3 at the Granada TV [Ce]ntre, record a mimed version of their latest Decca release ["S]ha La La La Lee". (The performance, which included the [live] debut of Steve with Mac's Telecaster, would be included [in] the evening broadcast across the Granada ITV region [on]ly, between 6:31 and 6:59pm.)

[TH]URSDAY JANUARY 27th

[Th]e group return to London in the early hours of the morning [so] that they can fulfil their engagement at the grand opening [of] the 'Carnabees Club' later that night, at 50 Carnaby [Str]eet, London W1. The group were second on the bill to ["To]p of the Pops" presenter Jimmy Savile. The show also [inc]luded the VIP's and James Royal.

[F]RIDAY JANUARY 28th

[Th]e group return to Studio One of Rediffusion Television in [We]mbley to perform a live version of "Sha La La La Lee" on [ITV]'s "Ready Steady Go!" The broadcast, hosted by Cathy [Mc]Gowan, also featured Sandie Shaw and Paul & Barry [Ryan, but was transmitted across] [only part] of the ITV

SATURDAY JANUARY 29th

The group travel to Southport for two concerts at the 'Floral Hall'.

SUNDAY JANUARY 30th

The Small Faces stay over night in Southport then travel to the Alpha Studios in Aston, Birmingham, to record another performance of "Sha La La La Lee", this time for "Thank Your Lucky Stars". The show (transmitted across the ITV network on Saturday February 5th between 5:15 & 5:54pm) was hosted by Jim Dale, and also featured Dusty Springfield, Gerry & The Pacemakers, The King Brothers, Salena Jones, The Uglys, Neil Landon and The Twins.

FEBRUARY

The latest in the Rave "This Is Your Life" series features Kenny giving his opinion on the dilemmas of a youngster who is desperate to be part of the 'in-crowd'. The same February issue features the Small Faces in colour on the back page. Meanwhile NME journalist Keith Altham tells of his first meetings with Steve Marriott back in 1964. "He used to call in my office saying 'I know I'm going to be a big star'. He talked 24 to the dozen."

THURSDAY FEBRUARY 3rd

The group gives two concerts at the Town Hall in Kidderminster.

FRIDAY FEBRUARY 4th

The group travels to Leicester, for two shows at the 'De Montford Hall', in Granville Road, Leicestershire.

SATURDAY FEBRUARY 5th

The day begins with Steve announcing he is worried about their Pimlico house that the group rents. "We reckon it's haunted" he admitted. "First we thought it was the central heating making the noises, but then a tradesman called who said that he lived in the house about twelve years ago. He confirmed our suspicions, and told us all about this old lady who used to live there. She died!!" Meanwhile,

later that night, the group give two shows at the St. Georges [Hall in Hinckley.]

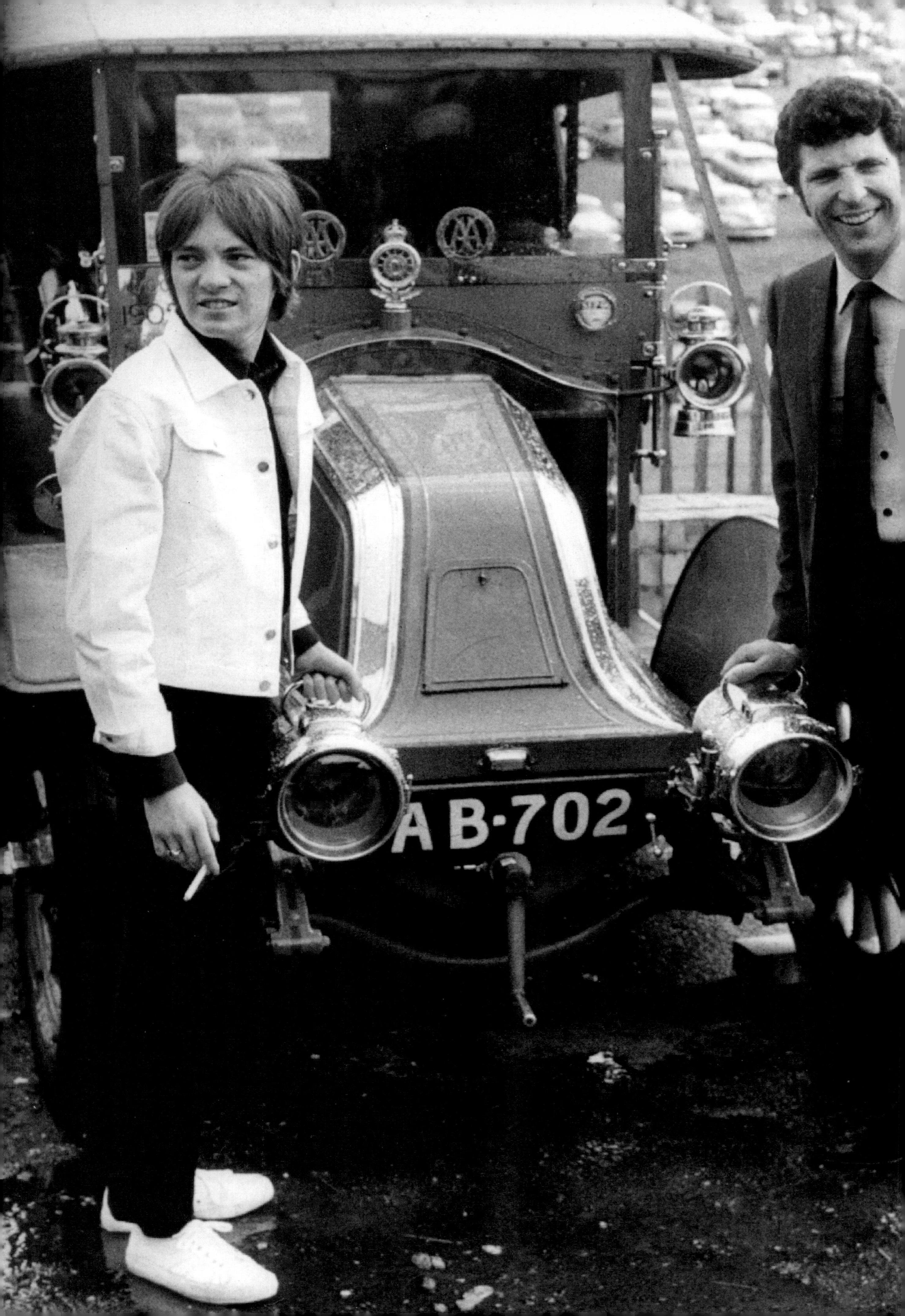
AB-702

THURSDAY FEBRUARY 10th

Following a four day break from work, the group travel to Oldham for two shows at the Astoria Ballroom. Meanwhile "Sha La La La Lee" enters the British Record Charts at No. 40, staying on the chart for 11 weeks, and peaking at No.3.

FRIDAY FEBRUARY 11th

The group perform two shows that night at Southampton University.

SATURDAY FEBRUARY 12th

Two shows that evening, at the 'Bird Cage Club' in Portsmouth.

SUNDAY FEBRUARY 13th

The group travel to Sheffield, and perform two shows that night at the 'Mojo Club'.

THURSDAY FEBRUARY 17th

The Small Faces return to Studio 2, BBC TV Centre in Wood Lane, London to promote their latest release "Sha-La-La-La-Lee" on "Top Of The Pops". Rehearsals took place before the cameras, with the other acts on the show, between 12:00 midday and 6:00pm, with the live transmission taking place between 7:30 and 8:00 on BBC1 that evening. The show, hosted by Alan "Fluff" Freeman, also featured in the studio, The Animals, Lulu, The Mindbenders and The Truth, while The Rolling Stones appeared by way of an 'Ampex' VT insert. (Again, the broadcast was unfortunately not recorded.)

FRIDAY FEBRUARY 18th

The group perform two shows at the 'Gaiety Ballroom' in Grimsby.

SATURDAY FEBRUARY 19th

The Small Faces perform two shows at the 'Imperial Ballroom' in Nelson, while in today's "Melody Maker", it is reported that the group will undertake their first major tour of Britain in the autumn. The tour, organised by Don Arden, will also feature an American artist, rumoured to be Little Richard.

SUNDAY FEBRUARY 20th

The group travel to Manchester, for two shows at the 'Oasis' club in Lloyd Street. While the group are up North, burglars break into their Pimlico home stealing records and clothing.

MONDAY FEBRUARY 21st to FRIDAY FEBRUARY 25th

The Small Faces begin five days of recording at the 'IBC (International Broadcasting Company) Studios, at 35, Portland Place, London W1. The group record original numbers, working for the first time with the producer Mike Leander. Some fruits of their labour will appear as their next single "Hey Girl/Almost Grown" (released on May 6th) and tracks for their first Decca album "Small Faces" (released on May 13th).

(Public appearances during this time included:)
WEDNESDAY FEBRUARY 23rd

Two performances in Stevenage.

THURSDAY FEBRUARY 24th

The group return again to Studio 2 at BBCTV Centre in London to appear for the fifth time on "Top Of The Pops". Naturally, it is to perform the single "Sha-La-La-La-Lee", which is currently standing at No. 7 in the charts. The group take part in camera rehearsals which last between 12:00 and 6:00, and 'lip-synch' the song in the live (7:30 to 8:00) transmission on BBC1. The show was hosted by Peter (Pete) Murray, and also featured musical contributions in the studio by The Hollies, The Walker Brothers and The Mindbenders.

FRIDAY FEBRUARY 25th

The group return for two performances at the old 'Cavern In The Town' in Leicester Place, London. By this time the venue had now been renamed "Latin Quarter". Supporting the group this night was a three piece called 'Safari' featuring one Labi Siffre, who would flavour chart success himself in 1971 and 1972.

SATURDAY FEBRUARY 26th

The group leave London Airport for a brief visit to Paris, France, where tonight they perform at the famous 'Locomotive Club'. That day's 'Melody Maker' carries an article entitled "Night Time Is The Right Time For The Small Faces". The piece concerns the group's regular late-night rehearsals in their Pimlico home.

SUNDAY FEBRUARY 27th

The Small Faces return to England at London Airport that morning and immediately travel to Edgeware in London for a 8:00pm concert at the White Lion Hotel.

MONDAY FEBRUARY 28th

The Small Faces are amongst the guests invited to the opening of the new 'Tiles' Club at 79/89 Oxford Street, where tonight The Animals are the headline act and Radio Caroline DJ Kenny Everett is the resident Disc Jockey.

Promotional flyers for the 'trendy' club announce that they are open daily between 12:00 to 3:00pm and 6:00 to 11:30pm.

MARCH

"Beat Instrumental" carries a short piece in its news section titled "Mike Leander recording Small Faces". The story reports that " A & R man Mike Leander is now the official record producer for all artists within the Don Arden Agency. These include the Small Faces, the Nashville Teens, the Clayton Squares, the New Breed and Jimmy Winston and the Reflections".

TUESDAY MARCH 1st

The group begin the day with a visit to the BBC Paris Studios in Regent Street, London where between 1:00 and 1:55pm they participate in a live studio interview with Keith Fordyce, for the Light Programme radio show "Pop Inn". To complement the interview, the Decca single "Sha-La-La-Lee" was played. (Incidentally, the short interview would later be used as part of a 'BBC Transcription Disc' for use overseas.) Following the session, (for which they were paid 10 guineas), the group take part in a photo shoot at the studios with fellow popsters Dave Berry and Julie Rogers, who also took part in the transmission.

THURSDAY MARCH 3rd

Another live performance, this time a 8:30pm concert at the 'Dorothy Ballroom' in Cambridge.

FRIDAY MARCH 4th

The Small Faces travel to Shrewsbury for a performance at the 'Golden Guitar Club'.

SATURDAY MARCH 5th

An evening performance at the Drill Hall army barracks in Grantham.

SUNDAY MARCH 6th

The Small Faces perform at the 'Sunshine Floor' nightclub in East Durham.

MONDAY MARCH 7th

Police were called in to quell a near riot by Small Faces' fans at the 'Radio London' stand at the "Ideal Home Exhibition". DJ's Mike Lomax and Ed Stewart started their show at 12 midday, and had planned to present pop stars and groups at their stand each day, despite the pleas from the exhibition authorities that they were not to do so. 300 excited fans, in anticipation of the Faces' appearance, began shouting "We Want The Small Faces", even though the authorities had made it clear the group would not be appearing. Disappointed fans began smashing doors, some of which were ripped off their hinges, while others began shouting and pushing other fans. Meanwhile the Small Faces perform this evening at the Community Centre in Watford.

WEDNESDAY MARCH 9th

The group travel to Southampton for a 8:30pm performance at the 'Top Rank' Ballroom.

THURSDAY MARCH 10th

The first of two days of BBC performances, begins with another "Top Of The Pops" appearance in Studio 2 at the BBC TV Centre in London. For the live transmission on BBC1 that evening between 7:30 and 8:00pm, the group mime to the live record of "Sha-La-La-La-Lee" played by 'Disc-girl' Venetia Cunningham. The show, hosted by Alan Freeman, also featured musical appearances by The Yardbirds, The Mindbenders, The Bachelors, Val Doonican, Lou Christie, The Beach-Boys, The Kinks and The Walker Brothers. Following the show, the group perform at London's Streatham 'Locarno'.

FRIDAY MARCH 11th

The day begins with another appearance on BBC radio's "The Joe Loss Show", compered by Tony Hall, arriving at the 'Playhouse Studio' in London to begin the usual 10am rehearsal. For the live transmission (the usual lunch-time 1:00 to 2:00pm slot on the Light Programme) the group performed "Sha-La-La-Lee", "You Really Got A Hold On Me" and "Shake", alongside regulars Joe Loss & His Orchestra, Ross McManus and Larry Gretton.

Later the group performed at the 'Starlite' in Greenford. Meanwhile, fans read about the group in the 'Tail-pieces' section on the latest NME. "....because Arthur Howes wouldn't agree equal billing" the story goes ".......Don Arden refused to allow Small Faces' appearance on Walker

Small Faces at Decca Records press party at Albert Embankment
Bottom: The band with, far left, Decca's Dick Rowe, the man who famously turned the Beatles down!

MONDAY MARCH 28th

Steve journeys to the south-east wing of 'Bush House' in Aldwych, London, WC2, to record two interviews for the BBC 'World Service'. The first being at 12:00 midday, when he was interviewed for the BBC German radio series "Hit '66". (Receiving again the standard BBC interview rate of £5 guineas for his trouble.) Then at 12:15pm, (this time with a different producer) he recorded an interview with Turrie Akerele for his African radio series "Turrie On The Go". (The latter was transmitted on April 7th, by which time the title of the series had now become 'Good Morning With Turrie Akerele.')

During the course of the two interviews, Steve was asked about the "Dateline Diamonds" film, which had just been released.

WEDNESDAY MARCH 30th

Performances at the 'Top Rank' Ballroom in Sunderland.

FRIDAY APRIL 1st

The group perform two concerts at the 'Memorial Hall' in Barry, Glamorgan.

Meanwhile a news item in the NME reports that "The Who, Yardbirds, Small Faces and Crispian St. Peters are among a host of name attractions being negotiated for an open-air pop festival at Lincoln City's Sincil Bank football ground on Whit Monday, May 30th. Others being booked include Dave Dee, Dozy, Beaky, Mick & Tich, The Ivy League, Barron Knights, Georgie Fame and The Kinks".

SATURDAY APRIL 2nd

Despite being penciled in for the show, tonight's edition of "Juke Box Jury" (BBC1 between 5:50 and 6:14pm) goes

Small Faces and Los Lobos

ahead without Steve's assistance. His place is taken by the comedienne Millicent Martin. The Small Faces meanwhile give an evening performances at the 'Latin Quarter' (formerly known as the 'Cavern In The Town') at 5 Leicester Place, just off Leicester Square, in London.

SUNDAY APRIL 3rd

The Small Faces travel to the 'Guildhall' in Portsmouth for two 'Pop '66' concerts with promoter Mervyn Conns and Joe Collins. The line-up also featured David & Jonathan amongst others. Controversy reigned when at the last minute, other acts on the bill, Lou Christie and The Kinks, pulled out to be replaced by The Alan Price Set. The NME (Dated April April 8th) report that there was a "hasty finale" to the conclusion of the first Small Faces concert, due to "struggles between staff and screaming girls". The compere for the shows was Alan Field.

MONDAY APRIL 4th

Two performances at the 'Town Hall' in Chatham, Kent.

TUESDAY APRIL 5th

Two performances at the 'Top Rank' in Doncaster.

WEDNESDAY APRIL 6th

The Small Faces take a break from performances to make their debut on the BBC1 'tea-time' programme for teenagers "A Whole Scene Going". The group return again to Studio 2, at the Television Centre in Wood Lane, London for a 2:30pm rehearsal, which lasts until 6:00pm. For the 14th show in this series (which was transmitted live between 6:30 and 7:00pm), the group mimed to the (as yet unpublished) song "Sorry She's Mine". The programme, which featured the regular hosts of Wendy Varnals and Barry Fantoni, also featured music from Lou Christie, and reports on such matters as an 'American Party' and Winnie The Pooh. Unfortunately, the transmission was not recorded.

Upon returning to their Pimlico home that night, they were alarmed to discover that a mysterious small fire had broken out in their kitchen. Firemen who arrived to put the fire out, put it down to the electric kettle they use which had not been unplugged, and had subsequently burnt itself out.

THURSDAY APRIL 7th

Two performances at the 'City Hall' in Salisbury.

FRIDAY APRIL 8th

The 'Pop '66' tour continues with Crispian St. Peters and

Martha Reeves & The Vandellas at the 'Granada Theatre' in Bedford. Meanwhile, the latest NME "Tailpiece", belatedly reports that "Steve Marriott of 'The Small Faces' had an acting role in the Kenny Lynch/Heinz film 'Live it Up'".

SATURDAY APRIL 9th

The 'Pop '66' package tour reaches Cardiff in Wales, with two shows at the 'Sophia Gardens'.

SUNDAY APRIL 10th

The 'Pop'66' tour reaches the Adelphi Theatre in Slough, but the Small Faces instead play a performance at the 'Belle Vue' in Manchester.

MONDAY APRIL 11th

The Small Faces rejoin 'Pop'66' with two performances at the 'Winter Gardens' in Morecombe.

THURSDAY APRIL 14th

'Pop'66' performances at the 'City Hall' in Newcastle.

FRIDAY APRIL 15th

The Small Faces perform two (non 'Pop'66') performances at the 'Iron Curtain' in Sidcup, Kent.

SATURDAY APRIL 16th

Again two (non 'Pop'66') performances at the 'Golden Torch' in Tunstall. Meanwhile, the group appears in a 'Fabulous' magazine article entitled "Down On The Farm With The Small Faces".

SUNDAY APRIL 17th

The Small Faces rejoin the 'Pop'66' tour with two performances at the 'Hippodrome' in Birmingham.

MONDAY APRIL 18th

The Small Faces travel to Streatham in London for a rather unusual performance at the 'Silver Blades Ice Rink'. The Small Faces concert (non 'Pop'66') takes place between the normal public evening skating session, therefore the 5/6 admission price includes both the concerts and skating. The NME 'Tailpiece' (dated April 29th) reports that the concert attendance beat the previous record attendance at the venue held by Georgie Fame. Following the performance, fans who surged towards the group, injured both Steve and Kenny. Kenny dislocated his shoulder (he visited a 'Harley Street' specialist the next day for a check-up), while Steve was knocked semi-conscious, forcing him to spend two days recovering. Later he was reported as

saying: "Thank goodness they didn't wreck my Camel-hair jacket. I only bought it the other day. It cost £40."

WEDNESDAY APRIL 20th

The group resume their duties with a performance at the 'Tower Ballroom' in Great Yarmouth.

THURSDAY APRIL 21st

Performance at the 'Starlite Ballroom' in Crawley in Sussex.

FRIDAY APRIL 22nd

The group rejoins the 'Pop'66' tour at Leicester's 'De Montford Hall' for two performances.

SATURDAY APRIL 23rd

The Small Faces, along with Crispian St. Peters, The Truth, The Dixie Cups, The Overlanders, Wayne Fontana and The Puppets perform the final 'Pop'66' concerts at the 'Granada' in Walthamstow. Meanwhile, the "Record Mirror" reports that the Small Faces will be appearing with The Nashville Teens and The Clayton Squares for 11 Sunday concerts during the summer, (six Sundays in Blackpool and five Sundays in Great Yarmouth) and 'Fabulous' magazine prints the first of four giant size pin-up's of the Small Faces. The first part is of Kenny.

SUNDAY APRIL 24th

The first of three nights at 'Top Rank Ballrooms'. The first being in Handley, where they perform their usual two concerts.

MONDAY APRIL 25th

Two performances at the 'Top Rank Ballroom' in Brighton.

WEDNESDAY APRIL 27th

Two performances at the 'Top Rank Ballroom' in Cardiff, Wales.

THURSDAY APRIL 28th

Performance at the 'Pavilion' in Worthing, Sussex.

FRIDAY APRIL 29th

Two performances at the the 'Matrix Ballroom' in Coventry.

SATURDAY APRIL 30th

Two performances at the 'Floral Hall' in Southport.

MAY

Kenny Jones passes his driving test in his red 'Mini'. Reports

Small Faces at the Wembley Empire poll winners' concert, 1st May 1966

suggest, he passed with "flying colours!" Meanwhile in the latest issue of 'Rave', Mac takes his turn in playing an 'agony aunt', where he voices his opinions on leaving home. "Is it a wise move to make?", he states, and the Small Faces turn down an offer to appear on the May 8th edition of "Thank Your Lucky Stars".

SUNDAY MAY 1st
The Small Faces make their first appearance at the annual NME Poll Winners Concert at the Empire Pool, Wembley, alongside an all star cast of The Beatles, The Rolling Stones, The Walker Bros.,
Dave Dee, Dozy, Beaky, Mick & Tich, The Spencer Davis Group, The Shadows, The Yardbirds, Cliff Richard, Herman's Hermits, The Seekers, The Fortunes, Roy Orbison, The Overlanders, The Alan Price Set, Cliff Richard, The Shadows, Sounds Incorporated, Dusty Springfield, Crispian St. Peters and The Who.

The Small Faces, introduced by Jimmy Savile, perform, second on the bill in front of twelve thousand screaming fans, "Sha-La-La-La-Lee" and "Whatcha Gonna Do About It", and is included in part one of the ABC Television programme "Poll Winners Concert" transmitted by only some ITV regions, London not being one of them, on Sunday May 8th between 3:50 and 4:59pm. (The main reason why various ITV companies declined to transmit the event was due to the fact that the two main attractions of The Beatles and The Rolling Stones were not filmed due to various disagreements over the PA and contracts.)

Sadly, only part two of "Poll Winners Concert" now survives in the ABC archives.

MONDAY MAY 2nd
Two performances at the 'Carousel' In Farnborough, Kent.

TUESDAY MAY 3rd
The group travels to the 'Playhouse Theatre' in London to record another appearance on "Saturday Club". From 2:00 to 4:30pm (including a brief rehearsal) they record "Come On Children", "Almost Grown", "E Too D", "Hey Girl" and "One Night Stand". The performance is included in the edition transmitted the following Saturday (Light Programme, May 7th between 10:00 and 12:00 midday), alongside The Bachelors, The Ladybirds, The Les Reed Orchestra and The Rockin' Berries, plus the usual host Brian Mathew. Later that night, the group perform at the 'Locarno' in Stevenage, Kent.

FRIDAY MAY 6th

Decca released today the single "Hey Girl/Almost Grown" (Decca F 12393). In the morning, the group makes an appearance outside the 'Lord John' boutique in Carnaby Street, London for the Dutch Tv programme "Fan Club". Unfortunately, filming was held up when hysterical fans found out where the group was appearing. Two police cars were called to break up the session. The Small Faces lip-synched their latest release "Hey Girl", and was included in the transmissions of the programme in Holland and Germany that month. The first album, simply titled "Small Faces" (Decca LK 4790) was also scheduled for release today, but was delayed for one week, due to 'technical problems'. (The recordings for all of the first album taking place at the 'IBC Studios', 35, Portland Place, London W1.)

To coincide with the release of the single, the Small Faces travel again to the studios of Rediffusion to make another live appearance on "Ready Steady Go!" Following a brief 2pm camera rehearsal, the Small Faces perform live in the transmission (between 6:07 & 6:34pm across only some ITV regions) their latest release "Hey Girl". The group also undertook a brief three minute interview with the host Cathy McGowan. The programme also featured music by Wayne Fontana and Patti LaBelle & The Belles. The group stay in London that night, for two performances at the 'Wimbledon Palais'.

SATURDAY MAY 7th

The group perform two concerts at the 'New Century Hall' in Manchester.

SUNDAY MAY 8th

The Small Faces make a rare 'Cabaret' appearance when they perform on the bill at 'Mister Smiths' in South London. The show also included the English singer Craig Douglas, who first hit the British charts in June 1959 with "A Teenager In Love". Steve refers to Craig Douglas as Craig Drugless!

MONDAY MAY 9th

Performance at the 'Top Rank Ballroom' in Cardiff, Wales.

The band performing at a festival in France

WEDNESDAY MAY 11th

Meanwhile the single entered the UK charts at No.16, peaking at No.12 in the NME chart, dated May 25th.

THURSDAY MAY 12th

Two performances at 'Dorothy's' in Cambridge. While "Hey Girl" enters the British singles chart, staying there for 9 weeks, and eventually peaking at No.10.

FRIDAY MAY 13th

The Small Faces appear on TWW's musical comedy pop programme "Discs-A-GoGo" which was transmitted live from TWW Centre, Bath Road, Bristol in Somerset. Following afternoon rehearsals (lasting between 2:00 and 5:00pm) the group perform live "Hey Girl" during the transmission on the ITV station TWW between 7:00 and 7:29pm that night. (TWW standing for 'Television Wales and West'. The Faces' appearance being only seen in those ITV regions.) The show, which also featured musical performances by Neil Christian and The Mindbenders, was hosted by Mike Palin (three years before finding fame as one of the 'Monty Python' team) and Cynthia Pettigrew. Meanwhile, Steve Marriott also appeared in the 'Pop Periscope' spot in the programme, and the Small Faces' path with Palin would cross again on December 10th 1967. (See entry.)

SATURDAY MAY 14th

Two performances at the 'Palais' in Peterborough. The group was also approached today to perform on the May 21st edition of ABC TV Saturday night pop programme "Thank Your Lucky Stars", but pulled out when it was announced they would only be allowed to perform the song "Hey Girl" and no others. The group had insisted on performing "Hey Girl" and one track from the forthcoming album. They were replaced on the show by The Dave Clark Five. Meanwhile, the "Record Mirror" reports that The Small Faces are re-decorating their house in Pimlico to give it an 'antique-cum-modern' look!

SUNDAY MAY 15th

The tour reaches the 'Starlight Ballroom' in Greenford, where they perform two concerts. Steve announces that he has started to carry a whistle on stage. "There's always so much noise" Steve revealed, "a whistle is the only way of getting the attention of the others in the group."

MONDAY MAY 16th

The Small Faces perform at the 'Pavillion' in Bath.

Kent.

JESDAY MAY 17th

e Small Faces perform at the 'Palais' in Ilford, Essex.

EDNESDAY MAY 18th

e Small Faces perform at the 'Top Rank Ballroom' in
istol. Meanwhile the Small Faces album reaches no.3
the NME charts, where it remains for seven weeks.

URSDAY MAY 19th

r the second time in six days, the Small Faces pull out of
op pop TV programme. In a dispute over billing, the
up walk off the set of BBC TV's "Top Of The Pops", at
evision Centre, London, where they were scheduled to
rform "Hey Girl".

IDAY MAY 20th

o performances at the 'Coronation Hall' in Ramsgate,

SATURDAY MAY 21st

Two performances at 'St. George's Hall' in
Hinckley. Meanwhile, the Small Faces grace
the cover of today's 'Fabulous' magazine.

SUNDAY MAY 22nd

The Small Faces, along with The Kinks, The
Alan Price Set, Quiet Five and The Graham
Bond Organisation are scheduled to appear in
a Sunday afternoon gala concert, held at the
ground of Edgeware Town Football Club. But
controversy raged before the show, when
the Kinks pulled out of the concert at the last
minute due to their refusal to "play support to anyone!"
(Promoters had unfortunately arranged for the two groups
to share equal billing.)

MONDAY MAY 23rd

The group perform at the 'Top Rank' Ballroom in Southampton. Marriott would review the events leading up to show in the "One Nighter" column of the June issue of "Rave" revealing:

"I woke up early the day we were going to do the Top Rank Ballroom, Sunderland. Good job too, because we were supposed to set off at 9.0am. After the usual groping about and moaning we got into the car and left Pimlico around ten past. Terry and Bob, the two best road managers in the business, had already left with our gear".

"In the car I couldn't help but wonder what the audience would be like that night. We hadn't played Sunderland before, and it's always a bit worrying going to a new place because audiences vary so much. I decided to stop worrying and just leave it to fate. We stopped once or twice on the route; it's a pretty long haul. Of course, when we went into the transport cafes, we got the usual wise-cracks and whistles: but we're used to them by now".

"We finally arrived in Sunderland at around 6.20pm., so we went for a quick meal and then decided to go straight on to the booking. Trouble was, we didn't really know where it was. We looked around for someone to ask and stopped by a couple of "rocker" types".

"Excuse me, mate, do you know where the Top Rank ballroom is?" They looked at us, then each other, then turning back to us one of them said...........well I can't really print what they said, but it was rather rude. "Charming", said Plonk, "But what can you expect from these 'Elvis Is God' types?'"

"Finally, a little old lady told us how to get there. Funny how we always seem to meet them".

"We drove straight past the ballroom once just to see how many people were outside, and to find out which entrance to use. Eventually we parked and went in through the back. We went straight to the dressing room and began to change. This is always where the nerves start playing you up. Plonk and I grabbed our guitars and started to tune to the 'pitch fork'. I don't think you can trust pipes. It's not a case of two guitarists saying to each other, 'OK, you tune to me.' Because we have the organ, we've got to be in perfect pitch. I was very nervous by that time and I seemed to go deaf, I couldn't get the pitch".

"It's funny, you know, we all show our nerves. Take Kenny for instance, he comes over all exuberant, he runs about punching people and playing on your head with his sticks. Plonk just laughs all the time, you just can't shut him up, he keeps on laughing. Mac goes very very quiet. Won't say a word. Me? Well, I don't know, it's hard to tell what you're like yourself. All I know is that I get very panicky".

They had a revolving stage at this place, so we were able to tune up through the amps once more just before it was time to go on. It was quite a job hearing ourselves backstage because the disc-jockey was churning the old records out at full belt and, in between, he kept trying to work the kids up by saying things like, "In just one minute's time, you're going to be able to see, right here on this stage......".

"At last the records stayed off, the bloke at the side of the stage gave us the thumbs-up, and round we swung into a deafening wall of shouts and screams and hundreds of people clawing the stage. We went straight into "Ooop Oop A Doop" as we were coming round and I got that great feeling that everything was just fine. The amps were giving us a beautiful sound and I was really pleased with my guitar. After "Ooop" we went into "You Need Love", and whoops! All of a sudden the whole crowd came screaming at us. We just ran over the back of the stage, amps were going down, wires tripped us up. We got back to the dressing room and flopped down".

"I thought perhaps that would be the end, just when everything was going so well, too. Bob went out to see what was going on and he came back and told us that the manager had come onto the stage and said, "Right, if you don't all sit down on the floor and behave yourselves you won't be seeing the Small Faces again". Surprisingly enough they did what he said and we went back on stage. It was a scream seeing everybody sitting on the floor, but off we went again".

"We did a few more numbers and everyone seemed to be OK, but when we got to "Sha La La La Lee", they all went mad, they got up and came after us again. We finished up pretty smartish and ran off. Back in the dressing room we patted each other on the back and chatted while we had a good rub down. After that we shifted a good few cokes. Actually we were pretty lucky because none of the girls managed to get backstage. I remember, in Warrington, we came off stage and saw this girl peeping out of the toilet

I told Bob what I'd seen, so he went across, threw
the door, and do you know how many girls came out
ead of that one? Thirty! I counted them. I almost
psed, laughing".

SDAY MAY 24th

group make their return appearance at the
quee'Club, in Wardour Street, London.

NESDAY MAY 25th

group perform in Cambridge today.

RSDAY MAY 26th

ek following the disagreement over their "Top Of The
" billing, the group return to Studio 2 at the BBC TV
re in London, to finally record "Hey Girl" for "Top Of
ops". The mimed performance was transmitted live in
edition broadcast on BBC1 that night between 7:30
3:00. The show, hosted by Jimmy Savile, also featured
Andrews, The Animals, Wayne Fontana, Ken Dodd
The Rolling Stones. This edition also saw the Small
s' BBC appearance fee rise to £78- 15 shillings- 0
e!!

FRIDAY MAY 27th

The group perform at the 'Pier Pavilion' in Morecambe.
Meanwhile, the NME announces the formation of Jimmy
Winston & The Reflections.

SUNDAY MAY 29th

The group travel to Wales, to perform in Rhyl.

MONDAY MAY 30th

The Small Faces, along with The Who, The Kinks, The
Yardbirds, The Alan Price Set, Georgie Fame and Dave Dee,
Dozy, Beaky, Mick & Tich appear in an all-day show at
Lincoln City Football Club.

TUESDAY MAY 31st

The group perform at the 'Top Rank' Ballroom in Newcastle.

WEDNESDAY JUNE 1st

The Small Faces travel north to begin a week of ballroom
dates in Scotland. The first being at the 'New Town Hall'
in Falkirk.

THURSDAY JUNE 2nd

The first date of the Scottish tour takes place at the 'Two
Red Shoes' ballroom at South College Street, Elgin in
Morayshire.

FRIDAY JUNE 3rd

Performance at the 'Raith Ballroom' in Raith. Meanwhile,
the single "Sorry She's Mine/It's Not What You Do (But The
Way That You Do It)" by Jimmy Winston & The Reflections
is released, (Decca F12410) which never charted and sank
without trace. The NME (in the regular "Tailpiece" section)
reports that "A Steve Marriott composition is under
consideration for the Nashville Teens' next release" and
"Tony Calder ('Immediate' partner of Andrew Oldham) once
managed Steve Marriott"...

SATURDAY JUNE 4th

Performance at the 'Olympia' in East Kilbride. The show
was stopped when fans rushed towards the stage knocking
Steve unconscious. Also sent flying was Bill Corbett, the
former Beatles road-manager, who now tours with the Small
Faces.

SUNDAY JUNE 5th

Performance at the 'House Hotel' in Lennox Bank, Balloch.

A pleasant day in Pimlico (The Magic Grotto)

[M]ONDAY JUNE 6th

[Th]e Small Faces return to London during the early hours
[of] the morning.

[W]EDNESDAY JUNE 8th

[Tw]o performances at the 'Top Rank Ballroom' in Doncaster.

[TH]URSDAY JUNE 9th

[Tw]o performances at the 'Locarno' in Streatham, London.

[F]RIDAY JUNE 10th

[Th]e group, with an extremely exhausted Marriott, arrive at
[?]:40am at the studios of the BBC's 'Playhouse Theatre',
[to] record another appearance on "The Joe Loss Show".
[Pro]ducer Don George, a long-time acquaintance of the
[gro]up, asks Steve if he is able to record the show, but was
[re]assured he was fine.

[Fo]r the live 1:00 to 1:50pm transmission on the Light
[Pr]ogramme, (which also included the 'Joe Loss Show'
[re]gulars) the group recorded "Hey Girl", "One Night Stand"
[an]d "Sha-La-La-La-Lee". Following the session, the group
[im]mediately travel to an afternoon recording of "Ready
[St]eady Go!" at the Rediffusion studios in Wembley. But
[du]e to low blood pressure and severe exhaustion, Marriott
[co]llapses and is taken back to his Pimlico home, where
[he] is ordered to rest. The scheduled evening concert at
[th]e 'Top Of The World' in Stafford, is naturally cancelled.

[S]ATURDAY JUNE 11th

[Th]e concert tonight at the 'Pavilion' in Weston-Super-Mare
[is] cancelled.

[S]UNDAY JUNE 12th

[Th]e concert in Kingston, London, is cancelled due to their
[Su]nday engagement in Rhyl, Wales, with The Clayton
[Sq]uares.

[W]EDNESDAY JUNE 15th

[Wi]th Marriott now recovered, the group resume their tour
[wi]th two concerts at the 'Top Rank Ballroom' in Sunderland.

[TH]URSDAY JUNE 16th

[A p]erformance at the 'Locarno Ballroom' in Hull.

[F]RIDAY JUNE 17th

[Tw]o performances at Leicester University, again supported
[by] The Clayton Squares.

SATURDAY JUNE 18th

Two performances at the 'Dreamland Ballroom' in Margate,
Kent.

SUNDAY JUNE 19th

The Small Faces attend 'Radio London's' own trophy
meeting at the Brands Hatch motor racing circuit with The
Walker Bros., The Kinks, Tom Jones, The Pretty Things,
Paul & Barry Ryan, Chris Farlowe, Susan Maughan and
David Garrick. The motor racing was twice suspended when
fans invaded the track. ITN news cameraman Rowan Bulmer
was on hand to capture the event, featuring in the ITN
news that night. (Transmitted between 6:00 and 6:14pm
across the ITV network.) Following the meeting, a dance
is held on the racetrack where they watch the groups
Episode Six, The McCoys, The Crawdaddies and David
Bowie & The Buzz perform. Later, the Small Faces travel
to Bournemouth, for two shows at the 'Pavilion'.

WEDNESDAY JUNE 22nd

The Small Faces again travel to the BBC 'Playhouse Theatre'
in London, this time to record a live appearance on the
Light Programme's "Parade Of The Pops", working with the
producer Ian Scott and compere Denny Piercy. During the
1:00 to 1:50pm lunch-time slot, the group perform "You'd
Better Believe It" and "Hey Girl", alongside the 16-piece
Bob Miller & The Millermen, The Milltones, Dougie Arthur,
Tony Crane, Rosanella and Vince Hill. Later that night, the
group give two performances at the 'Locarno' in Stevenage.

THURSDAY JUNE 23rd

Two performances at the 'Locarno' in Burnley.

SATURDAY JUNE 25th

Today's 'Disc and Music Echo' features guitarist Jeff Beck
discussing the latest hits in the column "Hit Talk". Under the
microscope was the Faces' latest single "Hey Girl", where
Beck is quoted as saying : "I like the jolly part of the Small
Faces record, but I was expecting something a bit different
from them this time". Meanwhile, a quick look at the album
chart reveals that the "Small Faces" album has dropped
from No. 3 to this weeks No.4. That evening sees the group
perform two shows at the 'Pavilion' in Buxton.

SUNDAY JUNE 26th

Two performances at the 'Mojo' Club in Sheffield.

TUESDAY JUNE 28th

An evening performance (7:30 to 11:00pm) at the

'Marquee Club' 90, Wardour Street, in Soho, London, with support band Sands.

WEDNESDAY JUNE 29th

Two performances at the 'Orchid' in Purley.

THURSDAY JUNE 30th

The Small Faces depart for Reykjavik in Iceland for a two day concert tour.

JULY

"Top Of The Pops" Disc-Jockey Alan Freeman interviews the group on the roof for his exclusive "Heart-To-Heart With The Small Faces" article, appearing in the latest edition of 'Rave'.

During the course of the interview, (carried out to a background sound of the Stones' latest album 'Aftermath') Steve revealed they used to live on brown sauce rolls, and that Plonk and Kenny were 'testers' at the big musical instrument factory "Selmers".

FRIDAY JULY 1st

The Small Faces fly directly onto Frankfurt in Germany to begin a six date tour.

SATURDAY JULY 2nd

The Small Faces continue their short German tour with a performance in Cologne. Meanwhile reports are announced in the English music press that the Small Faces will visit America from Monday August 1st, for eleven days of promotional dates and guest appearances, including one or two in New York.

SUNDAY JULY 3rd

The group perform at the 'Jaguar Club' in Herford, Germany with support act on the tour 'The Remo Four'. Incidentally, the admission price for the gig was 8 German Marks!

MONDAY JULY 4th

The group perform in Hanover, Germany. Meanwhile, in England, the BBC write to the group at Pavion Ltd, informing them that due to their increased working relationship with the Corporation, Steve Marriott and the Small Faces have now been given their own 'BBC Index Card'. (Incidentally, the index remained in force until the 23rd of March 1970, when, over a year after they 'officially' broke-up, the card was changed to just 'The Faces'.)

TUESDAY JULY 5th

Performances in Bremen, Germany.

WEDNESDAY JULY 6th

Performance at the 'Star Club' in Hamburg, Germany. Due to their engagement out of the country, the scheduled evening appearance at the 'Locarno' in Stevenage was naturally cancelled.

THURSDAY JULY 7th

The Small Faces arrive back in England, at London Airport this morning. That evening the group play at the 'Dorchester Hotel' in London.

FRIDAY JULY 8th

The group perform at the 'Skyline Ballroom' in Hull.

The Small Faces pose on top of DJ Alan Freeman's London pad

ONDAY JULY 11th

e Small Faces travel to the BBC studios at 1, Kensington
use in Shepherds Bush, to record a 15 minute interview
n Brian Mathew for the series "Pop Profile". The interview
uld form a part of another 'BBC Transcription Disc'. (ie.
use overseas.) They were paid 15 guineas.

ESDAY JULY 12th

eve and Ronnie sign the second of two 'assignment
ntracts' for their music publishing with Don Arden's
ading Music'.

URSDAY JULY 14th

o performances at the 'Palace Ballroom' in Douglas, Isle
Man.

IDAY JULY 15th

e group perform, for a fee of three hundred pounds, at
e 'Palace Ballroom' in Maryport.

ATURDAY JULY 16th

rformance at the 'California Ballroom' in Dunstable,
ton in Bedfordshire.

INDAY JULY 17th

Performance at the 'Beatcomber' in Nottingham.

TUESDAY JULY 19th

Performance at the 'Locarno Ballroom' in Blackburn,
Lancashire.

FRIDAY JULY 22nd

Performance at the 'Ram-Jam' club in Brixton, London.

SATURDAY JULY 23rd

Performance at the 'Locarno Ballroom' in Coventry.

MONDAY JULY 25th

Performance at the 'Key Club' in Plymouth.

THURSDAY JULY 28th

The Small Faces (c/o their 'Pavion Ltd' office at 52/55
Carnaby Street) receive an invitation from 'Rediffusion
Television' to appear on the "Ready Steady Go!" edition to
be transmitted on Friday August 5th. (See entry.) Later this
evening the Small Faces were among 68 stars of stage
screen and television at Radio England's 'The Party of the
Year' held at the Hilton Hotel in London. Guests from the
world of pop also included The Spencer Davies Group, The
Zombies, Manfred Mann, The Moody Blues, Unit 4+2 and

The Action amongst many others.

FRIDAY JULY 29th

The group perform on the first night at the "Sixth National Jazz & Blues Festival', held this year for the first time at Balloon Meadow, Windsor Racecourse. (Moving from it's regular Richmond venue where it had been held since 1961.)

Among the other attractions on this opening night included The Spencer Davis Group, Geno Washington & The Ram Jam Band and Slough-based artist Mark Barry. During it's three night run, other musical artists included The Who (who closed Saturday night) plus 25 other bands and individual performers. Of all the scheduled performers, only The Yardbirds and Chris Farlowe failed to show up. The crowds, who began arriving on the previous Wednesday, were forced to endure diabolical weather and totalled 30,000 per day. Organisers were quick to point out that the reason why the previous years Richmond events attracted, on average, 10,000 fans more, was that this year the country was gripped by World Cup fever!

An all-day ticket cost 12 shillings 6 pence, and were available from the 'Ricky-Tick' club in Barry Avenue, Windsor.

AUGUST

The Small Faces appear on the cover and feature inside the latest issue of the pop-magazine "Rave".

WEDNESDAY AUGUST 3rd

The Small Faces perform at the 'Flamingo' in Redruth.

FRIDAY AUGUST 5th

Decca release the next Small Faces single "All Or Nothing/Understanding" (Decca F 12470). To coincide with its release, the group make another live appearance on Rediffusion Television's "Ready Steady Go!" (Show number 70). Assembling at studio one at Rediffusion Television's Wembley complex for a first camera rehearsal and sound check which lasts between 10:00 and 10:30am, then between 11:00 and 12:00 midday, 'record' sound checks along with the other artists on the show. Following lunch (taken between 1:00 and 2:00pm), the group take part in further camera rehearsals, which last until 6:30pm. After final make-up and line-up checks, the programme is transmitted live (across only some ITV regions) between 7:00 and 7:25pm. The group, fourth in the running order,

perform "Understanding" and then later (in part 2 of the show) return to deliver a wonderful live version of "All Or Nothing". The show, as always, was hosted by Cathy McGowan, featured The Troggs (who topped the bill), Glen Dale, Los Bravos, Kim Fowley and The Breakaways. (Future 'Mrs. McLagan' Sandy Sarjeant, along with Cynthia Pettigrew and Cassandra Mahon appeared again as the resident "RSG!" dancers.) The show was not recorded during the transmission.

Incidentally, during the afternoon camera rehearsals, Steve was annoyed to find out that Los Bravos were receiving a fee of £47-10 shillings, almost £10.00 more than that the Small Faces, were getting. They will reappear on the show in three weeks on August 26th (see entry). Following the programme, the Small Faces travel to the 'Granby Hall' in Leicester for a late night show with The Merseys.

Meanwhile, it is also announced today that Genevieve has been added to the "Swinging '66" Small Faces package tour, which starts on Friday August 12th.

SATURDAY AUGUST 6th

Performances at the 'Imperial Ballroom' in Nelson.

SUNDAY AUGUST 7th

The Small Faces begin their Sunday residency at the South Pier Theatre in Blackpool (jointly promoted by George Cooper

and Larry Parnes). Meanwhile their manager Don Arden flies out to the US to set up a new American distributor for the group.

MONDAY AUGUST 8th

Performances at the 'Pavilion' in Bath.

TUESDAY AUGUST 9th

The group perform at the 'Malvern' Winter Gardens' (the concert at the 'Floral Hall' in Southport being scrapped), and following the concert, travel to Manchester where they stay the night.

WEDNESDAY AUGUST 10th

The Small Faces remain in Manchester, where they travel, that morning, to the studios of Granada/ITV to record the TV programme "Scene At 6:30- Special". ("Scene At 6:30" was the Granada regional week-nightly news/magazine show, where, in the past, acts such as The Beatles, Rolling Stones and The Walker Brothers would perform one or two songs. But tonight, the entire 27 minutes show was devoted to the Small Faces.) The programme is produced by Johnny Hamp, who was responsible for giving The Beatles their first big TV break, and later produced their 1965 TV special "The Music Of Lennon & McCartney".

During this "Scene At 6:30-Special", The Small Faces perform "Understanding", "One Night Stand", "Sha-La-La-La-Lee", "You'd Better Believe It", "Oo-Poo-Pa-doo", "You Need Love", "Hey Girl" and finally "All Or Nothing". During the last song, one of Steve's guitar strings broke, but he carried on performing regardless. The show is transmitted the one and only time (in the Granada ITV region only) on Friday August 12th between 6:30 and 6:59pm. The assistant producer on the programme Rod Taylor described it as "the most exciting spectacular we have made since the one featuring Little Richard".

The group drive back to London later that evening, following a private screening (to Steve and Ronnie) of the special in one of Granada TV's 'viewing rooms'. Thankfully, this

SPECIAL! OUT NOW!

SMALL FACES
All or nothing

45 rpm record   F.12470

The Decca Record Company Limited
Decca House Albert Embankment London S E 1

DECCA

wonderful TV programme still survives but unfortunately NOT in the Granada ITV archives.

THURSDAY AUGUST 11th

Another TV appearance beckons, when the group travel, (for the first time), to Studio G at the BBC studios of Lime Grove to make their eighth appearance on "Top Of The Pops". The group mime their new single "All Or Nothing" in the live BBC1 transmission that evening between 7:30 and 8:00. The show, hosted by David Jacobs, also featured music in the studio by The Alan Price Set, Billy Fury and David & Jonathan. Meanwhile, "All Or Nothing" had entered the British singles chart today, where it stayed for 12 weeks, and eventually becoming their only UK No.1.

Meanwhile, 'Rediffusion Television' requests today (in writing to their Carnaby Street office), another appearance for the group on "Ready Steady Go!" (the edition scheduled for Friday August 26th 1966 - see entry).

FRIDAY AUGUST 12th

The first night of the Radio London (the newest pirate radio station at the time) and 'Pier Vic Ltd' "Swinging '66" nationwide package tour begins with two concerts at the 'Odeon Theatre' in Lewisham, London. Besides the Small Faces, there were also performances by Crispian St. Peters, Lou Christie, Neil Christian, The Limeys and The Koobas. Guesting this night was Wayne Fontana & The Opposition. (Percy Sledge was also tipped for the tour, but remained unsigned.) During the tour, at the conclusion of every song, Steve insisted on doing a 'cross' sign to the audience, because, in Steve's own words, "Mac's keyboards sounded like a Church organ!"

Meanwhile the NME reports first that the Small Faces will begin a nine day tour of Sweden on October 1st.

SATURDAY AUGUST 13rd

The tour reaches the 'Astoria' in Finsbury Park, London, where again, Wayne Fontana & The Opposition guest. Norrie

Drummond unfavourably reports on the concert for the NME (dated August 19th) "....one of the most mediocre pop packages I've seen in a long time" adding "the only sign of life from the half-empty second house audience came when the Small Faces appeared. Despite the fact that they are a lively, colourful group, I don't really think they're ready to top the bill on a major tour!"

SUNDAY AUGUST 14th

The second of six consecutive Sunday dates at the 'South Pier Theatre' at Blackpool.

MONDAY AUGUST 15th

The "Swinging '66" tour reaches the 'Odeon' in Birmingham, where Dave Berry joins the package (replacing Wayne Fontana) and stays to the end of the run.

TUESDAY AUGUST 16th

Two performances at the 'Gaumont' in Sheffield.

WEDNESDAY AUGUST 17th

While "All Or Nothing" enters the NME charts at No. 15, the group travel to Leeds for two performances at the 'Odeon' Theatre.

THURSDAY AUGUST 18th

Following the success of their latest single, the group are forced to return to Studio G at the BBC studios in Lime Grove, Shepherds Bush, London, to perform, for the second time, "All Or Nothing" for inclusion in "Top Of The Pops". (The version in the previous week's show - August 11th-

was transmitted live and not recorded, much to Steve's annoyance!!) But due to their imminent departure to Scotland that night, the group had no option but to arrive at the studios at 12:00 midday, where they 'Ampex' (video-tape) an "insert" clip to be put into that evenings transmission on BBC1 between 7:30 and 8:00pm. The short performance clip (the first time a "Top Of The Pops" performance by the group was preserved) was introduced by Pete Murray, and was preceded by 'studio' musical appearances by Chris Andrews, Manfred Mann and The Alan Price Set. This clip of "All Or Nothing" will be repeated in the 'Top Of The Pops' edition transmitted on Thursday September 15th when the song reaches no.1. (see entry.)

Following the taping (which ended at 2:00pm) the Small Faces faced the long drive to Glasgow for two performances at the 'Odeon' Theatre. Following the conclusion of the Small Faces' second show, Ronnie had to be treated in hospital for concussion after being knocked unconscious when fans besieged the group outside their hotel. Accidentally locked out of the hotel, Ian was taken to the police station for his own protection.

FRIDAY AUGUST 19th
Two performances at the 'Odeon Theatre' in Newcastle. The NME "Tailpiece" reveals that their manager Don Arden had been taken ill and that plans are underway for the Small Faces to visit America for the first time on October 6th for six days.........

SATURDAY AUGUST 20th
Two performances at the 'Odeon Theatre' in Liverpool. Today's 'Melody Maker' features an article entitled "Small Faces Fill The Scream Gap- And They Enjoy It, Too!" Accompanying the story is a picture of Ronnie, with a caption which reads: "We work 26 hours a day". Steve meanwhile issues a statement where he replies to John Lennon's controversial "Beatles are bigger than Jesus Christ" statement. "He was right to think it," Steve said," but not to say it. Religion IS dying in this country. You're being taught science and religion at school.... the two clash. The C of E is so morbid it's dirge."

SUNDAY AUGUST 21st
The regular Sunday night residency at the South Pier in Blackpool.

MONDAY AUGUST 22nd
Two performances at the 'Odeon Theatre' in Manchester.

TUESDAY AUGUST 23rd
Two performances at the 'Capitol Theatre' in Cardiff, Wales.

WEDNESDAY AUGUST 24th
Two performances at the 'Odeon Theatre' in Exeter.

THURSDAY AUGUST 25th
The proposed final night of the "Swinging '66" tour takes place in Southampton at the 'Gaumont Theatre'.

FRIDAY AUGUST 26th
The group take a break from the tour to make another live appearance on Rediffusion Television's "Ready Steady Go!", now on its last legs before the axe fell on the show completely. Working again with director Daphne Shadwell, the group assemble (at 10:00am) in studio one at the Wembley studios of Rediffusion, where they begin live sound recordings between 11:00 and 12:00 midday and first camera rehearsals, between 12:15 and 1:15pm. Following lunch (between 1:15and 2:15pm) the group, as well as other acts on the show, take part in a second, much longer period of camera rehearsals, which run until 6:30pm.

With final make-up being administered from 6:30 to 7:00pm, the group prepares itself for the live transmission (across only some ITV regions) between 7:00 and 7:26pm. The Small Faces opened the show with "One Night Stand", then reappeared (eighth in the running order) to perform again live, "All Or Nothing". The show, hosted by Cathy McGowan, also featured, from America, Sonny & Cher, The Overlanders, The Mindbenders and The Breakaways. (The programme was not recorded during transmission.)

Meanwhile it is reported in the NME 'Tailpiece' today that "The Small Faces had requested a longer spot for The Koobas on the current Radio England tour".

SATURDAY AUGUST 27th
Due to the success of the "Swinging '66" tour, an extra concert takes place at the Boston Gilderdrome in Lincolnshire. Due to a crowd surge during the show, Kenny was injured through flying glass, receiving cuts to his head.

SUNDAY AUGUST 28th
The Small Faces continue their residency at the South Pier in Blackpool.

MONDAY AUGUST 29th
Performance at Hersham Public Hall.

TUESDAY AUGUST 30th
Another appearance on "Saturday Club" means another appearance at the BBC Paris Studios in London. The recordings (including a rehearsal) last between 4:00 and 6:30, and feature "You'd Better Believe it", "All Or Nothing" and "Understanding". The session would be transmitted the following Saturday (September 3rd) between 10:00 and 12:00 midday on the Light Programme, and was, as always, hosted by Brian Matthew. Other artists appearing

on the show included The Spencer Davis Group, The Alan Price Set and Brian Poole & The Tremeloes.

THURSDAY SEPTEMBER 1st
Another live "Top Of The Pops" appearance at Studio G, at BBC's Lime Grove facilities. The group mime their third version of "All Or Nothing", which is included in the transmission on BBC1 that evening between 7:30 and 8:00. The show, hosted by Alan Freeman, also featured musical appearances in the studio by The Seekers, Sandie Shaw and the "Top Of The Pops" orchestra. Following the transmission, the group rush to give a live performance at the 'Public Hall' in Barrow-In-Furness.

FRIDAY SEPTEMBER 2nd
The NME announce that: "The Faces are currently completing their second album for November release.............because of a British engagement, the group are unlikely to be able to accept an offer to appear at the Venice Film Festival next week in support of their British entry. Like The Walker Brothers, the Faces have also had an offer to appear in the new Brigitte Bardot film "Two Weeks In September" which is being considered by their manager Don Arden".

SATURDAY SEPTEMBER 3rd
Two performances at the 'Memorial Hall' in Northwich. While today's 'Melody Maker' features a double dose of Ronnie. Firstly appearing in the 'Blind Date' section where he reviews new releases by James Brown, Sandie Shaw, The Seekers, Spencer Davis Group, Eddy Arnold, Wilson Pickett, Nancy Wilson, The Cymerons, Norma Tanega, Barry Mann and The Who's new release "I'm A Boy", where he describes it as "Yeah, I like it, it must be Pete's", adding, "Can I hear it again?", and secondly in the "The Raver" column on page 2, where a cryptic message appears: "Plonk Lane knocked out by Billy Preston".

SUNDAY SEPTEMBER 4th
The group give the last of their six gig performances at the South Pier in Blackpool.

TUESDAY SEPTEMBER 6th
Two performances at the Agricultural Show in Shepton Mallet.

WEDNESDAY SEPTEMBER 7th
Two performances at the 'Orchid' in Purley.

THURSDAY SEPTEMBER 8th
The Small Faces appear live again on "Top Of The Pops". With a 2:00 to 6:00pm session, (including camera rehearsals) again at Studio G, at Lime Grove. A weary group 'go through the motions' with another mimed performance of "All Or Nothing". The group's lip-synched version of the song (accompanied by the Decca single, played live by 'Disc-Girl' Samantha Juste) would be included in the live transmission (7:30 to 7:59pm) on BBC1 that evening, alongside other musical contributions by David & Jonathan, The Fortunes, The Mamas & the Papas, John Barron, Cliff Bennett & The Rebel Rousers, Manfred Mann, The Searchers, Jim Reeves and The Beatles. The show was hosted by David Jacobs.

FRIDAY SEPTEMBER 9th
Two performances at the 'Gaiety' in Grimsby, meanwhile the latest edition of the NME contains news items which reads: "The Small Faces' new American record distribution deal (a three way agreement between Don Arden's 'Contemporary Records', 'Decca' and their new US outlet (RCA) begins next week with the release of "All Or Nothing" (currently No.2 in the UK charts) in the States... The Granada TV Small Faces spectacular (filmed on August 10th - see relevant entry) may be set for October telecast around ITV network... Don Arden turned down the Bardot film... and The Faces this week began planning a move from their Pimlico home following neighbours complaints to the Police about fans gathering outside".

SATURDAY SEPTEMBER 10th
The group appears on the cover of today's 'Melody Maker', and features in an article on page 7, where reporter Chris Welch "looks for the real Small Face..........." Meanwhile, the group give two performances that evening at 'St.George's' in Hinckley.

SUNDAY SEPTEMBER 11th
The final two performances at the 'South Pier' in Blackpool.

WEDNESDAY SEPTEMBER 14th
As "All Or Nothing" reaches No.1 in the UK charts, the Small Faces are pictured in Carnaby Street, London drinking champagne.

THURSDAY SEPTEMBER 15th
With "All Or Nothing" standing at No.1 in the singles chart, tonight's "Top Of The Pops" (BBC1 between 7:30 and 8:01pm, hosted by Pete Murray) naturally featured the

ong. (The clip recorded on Thursday August 18th (see ntry) was repeated.) But due to the "Top Of The Pops" hart, and indeed the one featured on "Radio One", being ompiled from the lists of the weekly pop papers (ie. NME, elody Maker etc.), the No.1 on this particular show atured both the Small Faces and the Beatles (with their ouble A-side 'Yellow Submarine/Eleanor Rigby') tied at e 'top spot'! So in true "Blue Peter" 'cut & paste' fashion, e "Top Of The Pops" production team compiled for it's sual chart run-down, a collage of the two groups faces. (ie. ngo with Kenny, Paul with Mac, John with Steve and eorge with Ronnie.) Incidentally, the board still survives nd is in the private collection of Kenny Jones. The BBC bandoned this way of compiling their record charts in 968, when they joined 'Music Week' and the 'BPI' (The ritish Phonographic Industry) in having a weekly chart ompiled by the 'British Market Reserach Bureau'. The mall Faces give two performances at the 'Mecca Ballroom' ka 'Ashton Palais De Dance') in Ashton later that night.

RIDAY SEPTEMBER 16th

vo performances at the 'Hillside Ballroom' in Hereford. eanwhile the NME carries a news story :"A report that eve Marriott has been invited to play Oliver Twist in the film rsion of Lionel Bart's musical 'Oliver' was described as ompletely untrue" by production executive John Gilbert on ednesday (September 14th).

eanwhile, a special advert is placed in the NME today hich reads: "The Small Faces wish it to be known that eir only appearance in Peterborough this year is at the BC Theatre on October 22nd and no other arrangements ave been made to appear elsewhere in this town".

ATURDAY SEPTEMBER 17th

vo performances at the 'Floral Hall' in Southport. Following great result in the readers' poll of 'Melody Maker', the oup appear in a half-page spread on page 17 of the latest sue, with a caption which reads: "Thank You Fans For his Wonderful Tribute". Steve meanwhile appears in the ot Seat' in the latest copy of 'Disc and Music Echo'.

UNDAY SEPTEMBER 18th

vo performances at the 'Town Hall' in Newbury, Berkshire.

ONDAY SEPTEMBER 19th

e group enter the IBC studios at 35 Portland Place, ondon W1 to begin work on their next LP and single. (The ovisional release date is scheduled for November 4th.) The

session will continue until around 4am.

TUESDAY SEPTEMBER 20th

The group spend another day in session at IBC (see entry for Friday September 30th). Later the Small Faces are present in the audience at Dusty Springfield's gig at the 'Finsbury Park Astoria' in London this evening. Also in attendance were other pop celebrities such as The Walker Brothers and Otis Redding.

WEDNESDAY SEPTEMBER 21st

The group fly out from London Airport to undertake a (24 hours) lightning trip to Germany for various promotions.

THURSDAY SEPTEMBER 22nd

Following their arrival back in England this morning, the group travel to Coventry for two performances at the 'Locarno Ballroom'.

FRIDAY SEPTEMBER 23rd

Two performances at the 'Locarno Ballroom' in Basildon, Essex. Today's NME 'profile' features Ian McLagan, who is interviewed by journalist Keith Altham at the Small Faces' Pimlico House they are about to be evicted from.

SATURDAY SEPTEMBER 24th

The group perform at the 'Drill Hall' in Grantham (alongside Zoot Money & The Big Roll Band). While today's 'Disc' reports that "Steve and Ronnie have written The Nashville Teens' next recording and that the group have a new Impala Chevrolet". Also in the "Hit Talk" column, Pete Townshend from The Who, reviews 'All Or Nothing'. "Can't see why they rate it so highly", he says, adding "though it is good, maybe they think it's a progressive step, but their first record was much stronger!"

SUNDAY SEPTEMBER 25th

Performance at the 'Regal Theatre' in Gloucester, with Dave Berry. The concert only takes place after a 2,000 signature petition to perform there is presented to them earlier in the year.

MONDAY SEPTEMBER 26th

Two performances at the 'Locarno' in Bristol.

TUESDAY SEPTEMBER 27th

The Small Faces leave London Airport en route to Germany.

FRIDAY OCTOBER 14th

Don Arden announces plans for "presenting the group in their own London show this Christmas.......(Small Faces) would top a bill including several other pop attractions".

Meanwhile, the Small Faces make another appearance in Carnaby Street, London in front of Granada TV cameras for the programme "Come And Get Your Money". They appear in the 'Lord John' boutique where they fool around trying out the latest 'gear'. Although Granada shot 4 minutes 16 seconds minutes worth of black & white 16mm film, only 4 seconds made it into the finished version, when transmitted on Wednesday January 25th 1967 between 9:40 and 10:19pm across the ITV network. The programme, a look at London and its celebrities in 1966, also included Tommy Steele, Lionel Bart, record producer Mickie Most (aboard his yacht), Wee Willie Harris, Screaming Lord Sutch, Wally Whyton, Terry Dene and Herman's Hermits. But during promotions for the programme in TV listings magazines, the Small Faces' appearance in the show went uncredited, as indeed were very brief appearances by members of Manfred Mann, Jonathan King, Dave Davies, Jimmy Savile, Paul & Barry Ryan and Chris Farlowe.

The first screening of parts of the 'uncut' Carnaby Street footage occurred on Channel 4 on Tuesday November 7th 1995 between 9:31 and 9:58pm during the second series of the excellent Granada Television "Without Walls: My Generation" programmes, entitled "It's A Mod Mod Mod Mod World" which naturally focused on the Small Faces.

SATURDAY OCTOBER 15th

The Small Faces begin a tour sharing top billing with The Hollies, Paul Jones and Paul & Barry Ryan at the 'ABC Theatre' in Aldershot, alongside The Nashville Teens and Peter Paul & Mary. Problems arise on the opening night, when the Small Faces refuse to appear closing the first half of the show due to an argument over billing! Their manager Don Arden, immediately withdrew the group from performance.

A spokesman for the Small Faces told the NME that:

"When contracts were originally drawn up, the Faces and The Hollies were to share equal top billing. But on arrival at the theatre in Aldershot, this was found to be changed. The promoter apologised and agreed that, as compensation, the Faces would close the show that night instead of appearing at the end of the first half as contracted. But this proved impracticable as The Hollies were not then in the theatre to make the change. As agreement could not be reached, the group left the theatre. On Monday (17th) we were asked if The Faces would return to the tour if all subsequent printing was changed to comply with the initial agreement. We accepted this condition".

Danny Betesh, who is promoting the tour with Tito Burns, of the 'Harold Davison Organisation', said: "The Small Faces refused to close the first half of the show because they claimed that the poster billing had been altered. This was true, although it was only a matter of inches!"

SUNDAY OCTOBER 16th

The problems over billings from the previous night spill over to tonight's show at the 'ABC Theatre' in Romford, where again the Small Faces refuse to appear. The audience were not informed that the group would not appear and were being replaced by the New Vaudeville Band.

TUESDAY OCTOBER 18th

The show rolls on to the 'Odeon' in Cheltenham, where the group rejoins the tour, closing the first half of the show.

WEDNESDAY OCTOBER 19th

Two performances at the 'Capitol Theatre' in Cardiff, Wales.

THURSDAY OCTOBER 20th

Two performances at the 'Gaumont Theatre' in Taunton.

FRIDAY OCTOBER 21st

Two performances at the 'Gaumont Theatre' in Wolverhampton. The problem over billing which caused problems at the start of the tour on October 15th & 16th (see entries) continues when the NME 'Tailpiece' asks "Why no apology to audience for Small Faces' non-appearance at Romford on Sunday?". Meanwhile results of 'Readers Polls' are published in the Melody Maker, where the Small Faces come in 3rd position (behind The Beatles and The Rolling Stones) and also in the Record Mirror, where the Small Faces fare better, finishing 2nd behind The Beatles.

SATURDAY OCTOBER 22nd

Two performances at the 'ABC Theatre' in Peterborough. Meanwhile, the "Record Mirror" reports that The Hollies manager Mike Cohen hopes to have both The Hollies and the Small Faces at the Gala opening of his discotheque "Rails" next week.

SUNDAY OCTOBER 23rd

Two performances at the 'ABC Theatre' in Hull.

MONDAY OCTOBER 24th

Two performances at the 'Gaumont Theatre' in Ipswich.

TUESDAY OCTOBER 25th

The group return to the 'IBC Studios' at Portland Place for one day session.

WEDNESDAY OCTOBER 26th

Two performances at the 'ABC Theatre' in Northampton.

THURSDAY OCTOBER 27th

Two performances at the 'ABC Theatre' in Cambridge.

FRIDAY OCTOBER 28th

Two performances at the 'ABC Theatre' in Lincoln. Meanwhile, the NME publishes a near-editorial on the Small Faces billing dispute which stated flatly that the fans "paid their money to see the Small Faces....and the Small Faces they should have seen.....no matter how right the Faces feel they were in terms of contract, I reckon that morally they were wrong....in that they failed in their obligation to their fans". NME 'Tailpieces' then retorted by asking "Why should Small Faces get equal billing with Hollies?"

SATURDAY OCTOBER 29th

Two performances at the 'ABC Theatre' in Chester. While today's 'Melody Maker' reports......."Small Faces are to tour Britain again next February with a major US attraction" says their manager Don Arden, adding that "the tour will probably last 40 or 50 dates, and will take in England, Scotland, Wales and Ireland".

SUNDAY OCTOBER 30th

Two performances at the 'Coventry Theatre'.

TUESDAY NOVEMBER 1st

While the Small Faces prepare for two evening performances at the 'Gaumont Theatre' in Worcester, their manager Don Arden continues with his grandiose plans for the impending

Small Faces Christmas show, by flying to the US to line-up prestigious Pop music acts such as The Mama's & The Papa's and The Lovin' Spoonful. He now conceives the Christmas Show to have a two week run at London's 'Hammersmith Odeon'. (Negotiations with the Rank Organisation for the use of the venue are still continuing.)

WEDNESDAY NOVEMBER 2nd

Two performances at the 'ABC Theatre' in Wigan.

THURSDAY NOVEMBER 3rd

Two performances at the 'Odeon Theatre' in Manchester.

FRIDAY NOVEMBER 4th

Two performances at the 'Odeon Theatre' in Leeds. Meanwhile, the NME writes sarcastically in the 'Tailpieces' section of the latest issue : "Hope Small Faces don't change name to Big Heads".

SATURDAY NOVEMBER 5th

Two performances at the 'City Hall' in Sheffield. Meanwhile, in today's Disc & Music Echo the question "What would you burn on bonfire night?" is asked. Steve replies by saying "Graham Nash (of the Hollies). With his beard and moustache, Graham would make a perfect Guy Foulkes." In the same issue Nash replies, by saying in the 'Hot Seat' column, "we are better than the Small Faces!"

SUNDAY NOVEMBER 6th

The final gig of the Small Faces/Hollies/Paul Jones tour, takes place at the 'City Hall' in Newcastle. Following the last performance, the Small Faces along with the other acts on the bill, attend a special end of tour party in their hotel. The group naturally stay the night in Newcastle.

MONDAY NOVEMBER 7th

During the journey back to London on the A1, Steve turns on the car radio in order to listen to his old flame Adrienne Posta guesting on the lunchtime BBC Light Programme 'Monday, Monday!' (transmitted between 1pm and 2pm). At the end of the interview with Adrienne, carried out by the show's host Barry Aldis, he announces, due to Posta's previous romantic link with Steve Marriott, "By the way Adrienne, the Small Faces have a new single out this Friday, entitled 'My Mind's Eye'." Steve and Ronnie are furious when Aldis then proceeded to play the 'rough' demo version of the song that Steve had handed into Arden on September 30th. Upon returning to London, the group rush to see Arden in his Carnaby Street office to demand why the single is being released. He informs them that "It's a good song and should do well", adding "It's too late to cancel, and the release takes place on Friday." This argument was instrumental in one of the reasons why the group would leave Arden and Decca.

TUESDAY NOVEMBER 9th & WEDNESDAY NOVEMBER 9th

The Small Faces, still smarting over the Decca release, assemble at the 'IBC Studios' in Portland Place to finish work on their next album.

THURSDAY NOVEMBER 10th

With the new single about to be released, the Small Faces begrudgingly make another appearance on British Television's 'premier' pop show "Top Of The Pops". Following afternoon camera rehearsals, (between 2:30 and 6:00pm at Studio G, Lime Grove) the group mime in the live BBC1 transmission (between 7:30 and 8:00pm) the new single "My Mind's Eye" (although they were obviously far from happy about the version that Decca were to release!!) The show, hosted by Pete Murray, also featured studio appearances by Sandie Shaw and The Four Tops, who were currently in England on a short tour.

FRIDAY NOVEMBER 11th

Decca, as announced, release the 'rough' mix of "My Mind's Eye/I Can't Dance With You" (Decca F 12500). Reports at the time suggest that the A-side contains "part of a melody lifted from the Christmas Carol 'Angels From The Realms Of Glory'". Meanwhile in the latest NME, it is confirmed that "The Small Faces finish recording their album this week for early December release" and in the 'Tailpieces' section, the paper asks: "Why does manager Don Arden think NME is anti- Small Faces?". Meanwhile, the group spend the day recording at the 'IBC Studios' in Portland Place.

The group meanwhile, fly out from London Airport this morning for two days of concerts in Holland.

SATURDAY NOVEMBER 12th

The Small Faces perform two evening shows in Rotterdam.

SUNDAY NOVEMBER 13th

The short tour of Holland continues with two shows in Amsterdam.

MONDAY NOVEMBER 14th

The group fly onto Germany for a brief promotional visit (lasting eight hours). They return to London Airport that evening.

TUESDAY NOVEMBER 15th

Two days of television appearances. The first being on November 15th, when at 11:15am they appeared before the Rediffusion Television cameras at Studio One in Wembley for, what turned out to be, their last group appearance on ITV's "Ready Steady Go!". The camera rehearsals, alongside Eric Burdon and 'in-house' band The Breakaways, lasted until 12:45pm. (The group, along with all the others guests on that weeks edition, then took lunch in the canteen until 1:45pm.)

Further camera rehearsals ran from 1:45pm to 5:45pm, then, following last minute 'make-ups', from 6:15 to 7:00pm recorded live performance versions of "Have You Ever Seen Me" (which opened the show) and "My Mind's Eye" (the sixth song in the programme). The programme, as always hosted by Cathy McGowan, also featured Paul Butterfield Blues Band, an interview with Donovan (replacing Peter Quaife and Dave Davies from The Kinks who failed to show up) and from America, The Four Tops, who closed the show.

The programme was transmitted in certain ITV areas on November 18th 1966, between 6:08 and 6:34pm. Incidentally, during the afternoon rehearsals, Mac spoke to the 'Ready Steady Go!' dancer Sandy Sarjeant for the first time.

WEDNESDAY NOVEMBER 16th

The second television appearance occurred on BBC TV's "Top Of The Pops", when the group assembled this afternoon, at Studio G in Lime Grove, London. Following the regular afternoon camera rehearsals, the group (at approximately 3:30pm) 'video-tape' a first version of "My Mind's Eye". This performance will feature firstly in the edition of "Top Of The Pops" transmitted on BBC1 between 7:30 and 8:00pm on Thursday November 24th (then again on December 15th 1966, BBC1 7:30 to 7:59pm). Following the recording, the group remained at the BBC studios in order to perform another version of "My Mind's Eye", this time to be included in the edition for transmission tomorrow on BBC1 between 7:30 and 8:01pm. This 'Ampexed' (video-taped) performance was also contracted by the BBC for one future use.

THURSDAY NOVEMBER 17th

The group drive to Salisbury, for two evening performances at the 'City Hall'. This would transpire to be their ONLY ballroom date in November. Meanwhile, "My Mind's Eye" enters the British singles chart, where it stays for 11 weeks, peaking at No.4.

FRIDAY NOVEMBER 18th

The scheduled live appearance on the 1:00pm BBC light Programme "Joe Loss Show" fails to materialise when the group fails to show up at The Playhouse Theatre, near Charing Cross, for their 10:30am rehearsal. Their office cites "tiredness" and "unhappiness with their £30.00 appearance fee".

Meanwhile, the ever hopeful Don Arden offers American screen legend Jayne Mansfield a part in a Small Faces film he is planning for next year.....................

SATURDAY NOVEMBER 19th to SUNDAY NOVEMBER 27th

The Small Faces leave London Airport to begin an 8 day tour of Scandinavia, taking in Norway, Sweden and Denmark. The group's repertoire for the tour was as follows:

* "I Feel Alright " (Ronnie sings lead on his unrecorded track)
* "Whatcha Gonna Do About It?"
* "Shake"
* "Plum Nellie" (a track which features an improvised 15 minute
  Blues jam.)
* "You Really Got A Hold On Me"
* "All Or Nothing".

On Friday November 25th the Small Faces play at the 8,500 seat ice-hockey venue 'Johnanneshovs Isstadion' in Sandstuvagen in Stockholm. A low quality 'Bootleg' tape of the show still survives. While on the 26th, 'Galaxy Entertainments' (of 52/55 Carnaby Street, London) release to the music press the fact they are now the sole agents for the Small Faces. Amongst the other current pop stars on their books include The Move.
Also, the November 26th edition of 'Melody Maker' features Steve reviewing (with interference from the three other Faces) the new releases by Peter & Gordon, Sandpipers, Herbie Mann, Twice As Much, The Swinging Blue Jeans, Barron Knights, The Kinks, The Supremes, Don Covay and Herman's Hermits.

SUNDAY NOVEMBER 27th

Following their departure from Scandinavia, they immediately fly on to Brussels, to continue their overseas tour, taking in more TV appearances and concerts.

DECEMBER

Steve appears in a 'Rave' magazine article entitled 'In My Mind's Eye - The Pop Scene As Seen By Steve Marriott'. The same issue carried a suggestion for a Christmas present for the Small Faces. ".........four pairs of built up shoes"

THURSDAY DECEMBER 1st

Leave Brussels early, catching the midday flight back to London Airport, where they immediately head to the BBC studios of Television Centre, where in Studio 2, they record their fourth version of "My Mind's Eye" for "Top Of The Pops". Due to their later than normal arrival, the group could only appear in an extremely brief (4:30 to 6:00 in fact) camera rehearsal. Nevertheless, the Small Faces take their place in the line-up for the live edition of the show, transmitted between 7:30 and 8:00 on BBC1. The show, hosted by Simon Dee, also featured studio performances by Dave Dee, Dozy, Beaky, Mick & Tich, Val Doonican, Bobby Herb, Donovan and The Seekers.

SATURDAY DECEMBER 3rd

The NME 'Tailpiece' reveals that: "On new Small Faces LP, manager Don Arden takes a vocal", while in a NME news item, it is reported that "Plans for the Small Faces to star in a London Christmas Show promoted by their agent Don Arden, have been scrapped". While in the 'Melody Maker', Steve, along with other pop contemporaries, answer the question whether you are too old at 25 to be a pop star?. "I think that 25 is too old to start in pop", Steve replies, adding "but I don't think the fans realise that some of the people they idolise are as old as they are!"

SUNDAY DECEMBER 4th

The Small Faces play their last gig of 1966 at the 'ABC Theatre' in Merthyr Tydfil.

MONDAY DECEMBER 5th

Harold Davison calls a meeting with the group and Don Arden at 10:30am to discuss a change in management. The seminar lasts 43 minutes and following this the group travel to the 'Olympic Studios' at 117, Church Road in Barnes, to begin recordings for their forthcoming album and EP. The sessions would last until 2:15am on the morning of December 6th.

"Right after Don Arden sold his rights in Small Faces, along came the Move for him", and "Good Friends: Plonk Lane of the Small Faces and singer-actress Genevieve"

Meanwhile, in today's 'Disc', it is announced that: "Steve is to be on the panel of judges to find "Miss Mod Britain '67" (along with Tom Jones, Simon Dee, 'Disc' editor Ray Coleman, Annie Nightingale and 'Top Of The Pops' presenter Samantha Juste).

TUESDAY JANUARY 24th

The group return to the 'Town Hall' in High Wycombe for two more performances.

WEDNESDAY JANUARY 25th

Two performances at the 'Locarno Ballroom' in Stevenage.

THURSDAY JANUARY 26th

Two performances at the 'Skyline' in Hull.

FRIDAY JANUARY 27th

Two performances at the 'Tabernacle' in Stockport. Chris Farlowe releases the Marriott/Lane composition "My Way Of Giving" (Immediate IM 041). The single was produced by Mick Jagger and featured the playing and singing talents of both Steve and Ronnie.

SATURDAY JANUARY 28th

Two performances at the 'Gilderdrome' in Boston. The latest NME carries a photo and a story from January 24th: "The Small Faces receive their award from Jackie Trent, as winners of the latest Radio Luxembourg 'Battle Of The Giants' contest. They beat Manfred Mann in the final." While in the 'Tailpiece' section: "Last week, Rolling Stones

and the Small Faces at each other's recording sessions." and "With Chrissie Shrimpton, it seems like Steve Marriott is following in Mick Jagger's footsteps".

MONDAY JANUARY 30th - WEDNESDAY FEBRUARY 1st

Further recording at 'Olympic'.

FEBRUARY 1967

The Small Faces sign to 'Immediate' for management, Kenny Jones is the featured 'Player Of The Month' in "Beat Instrumental" and P.P. Arnold releases the single "Everything's Gonna Be Alright" (Immediate IM 040) featuring performances by the Small Faces with Steve adding backing vocals.

THURSDAY FEBRUARY 2nd

Two performances at the 'Locarno Ballroom' in Swindon.

FRIDAY FEBRUARY 3rd

Two performances at the 'Memorial Hall' in Bury.

SATURDAY FEBRUARY 4th

Two performances at the 'Rhodes Centre' in Bishop's Stortford. While the NME, in the 'Tailpiece' section, writes "Long face for Chrissie Shrimpton after splitting with Mick Jagger?... now a Small Face!"

MONDAY FEBRUARY 6th - WEDNESDAY FEBRUARY 8th

Further recordings at 'Olympic'.

THURSDAY FEBRUARY 9th

Two performances at the 'Locarno Ballroom' in Streatham, London.

FRIDAY FEBRUARY 10th

The Small Faces sign a deal with Andrew Oldham. (See next entry and the entry for February 18th).

SATURDAY FEBRUARY 11th

Two performances at the 'Winter Gardens' in Weston-Super-Mare. While the NME reports that: "The Small Faces have signed a lucrative long-term deal with Andrew Oldham and Tony Calder's 'Immediate' company, under which the group will, in future, produce all it's own records. The tapes will then be leased by 'Immediate' to the Faces' current label 'Decca'". Ronnie remembered his impressions of Andrew Oldham. "Andrew Oldham, the boss of Immediate, had a lot of influence over us because we were very impressionable. But he was a moody fucker! He'd swan around in his shades and his Limousine and he was quite amusing really. He was very camp and had this camp humour."

SUNDAY FEBRUARY 12th

The Small Faces begin a holiday, and, excluding the commitment on Wednesday February 15th (see next entry), is scheduled to last until March 2nd.

WEDNESDAY FEBRUARY 15th

The Small Faces break from their holiday to travel again to Studio G, at Lime Grove to record two 'early' Ampex (video-tape) 'inserts' for the song "I Can't Make It" for inclusion in later editions of "Top Of The Pops". But following the sessions (lasting from 2:30 to 4:30pm) the group were unhappy with the mix they had mimed to when they watched the video played back. Therefore, with the group refusing to give clearance to the two clips, the VT was never screened, and later wiped!

SATURDAY FEBRUARY 18th

With the group away on vacation, Faces' related news continue to litter the NME 'Tailpieces': "For Decca EP, Bachelors join forces with Val Doonican pianist Ronnie Aldrich and the Small Faces", and......"Will Genevieve wax version of Beatles' latest retitled 'Plonk Lane'?" and... "Latest Chris Farlowe single, a Steve Marriott composition, but produced by Mick Jagger; where does Chrissie Shrimpton fit in?"

While a report entitled "Small Faces LP Out In March" appears in today's 'Disc and Music Echo'. The report states: "Small Faces' second LP will be issued during the latter half of March under the new deal- signed last Friday- with Stones' manager Andrew Oldham. Oldham will act as their recording business manager, leasing their recording tapes to Decca."

The report concludes with the news that the: "First single under the new signing is "I Can't Get By" (of course, "I Can't Make It") a Steve Marriott-Plonk Lane composition, released on March 3rd".

Meanwhile, today's 'Disc and Music Echo' also published

the results of the "'67 Valentines Day Awards" poll taken amongst their readers.

*Small Faces : No.4 "Top Group- Britain/World"
  (behind The Walker Brothers at 3, The Beach-Boys at 2, and at No.1 The Beatles)
*Small Faces : No.6 'All Or Nothing' - "Best Single of '66"
*Small Faces : No.5 'Small Faces' - "Best Album of '66".
*Steve Marriott : No.8 "Top Boy Singer".
*Steve Marriott : No.3 "Best Dressed Boy".
*Steve Marriott : No.3 "Mr. Valentine".
*Steve Marriott : No.6 "Top Boy Singer/World".

FRIDAY FEBRUARY 24th

Steve, along with his girlfriend Chrissie Shrimpton and her flatmate Christine Myrtle Dingle, are taken to the Gerald Road police station in Belgravia, Victoria after being stopped by police late at night in a cab as it drove down Exhibition Road in Kensington, South London. This was followed by both Steve and Chrissie's flats being searched by police for drugs.

Later Chrissie, at her flat in Park Mansions, Knightsbridge, said: "They took some tablets belonging to me, but they were only tranquillisers prescribed by my psychiatrist. They also took a hypodermic syringe needle but it doesn't belong to me and it means nothing. They also found absolutely nothing on Steve. Nor did they find anything in his flat." Commenting on their activities that night, she said: "There had been about ten of us at an all-night party in my flat. During the earlier part of the evening we went to a club.

play at being policemen who pounce on Steve as he takes a leisurely stroll, was obviously heavily influenced by Steve's recent trouble with the law. (See entry for Friday February 24th.)

The short film upset many critics. In particular, the scenes where Steve kicks the Policeman's helmet as it falls to the floor during a scuffle. Steve played down the scene, describing it as a "bit of burlesque, a kind of Marx Brothers send up." Reporters asked Steve that morning, "Isn't this really a way of working off vexed feelings towards the Police?"

"No - It's not", Steve angrily replied, "I wasn't ever worried about the incident (on February 24th). But even though I

1995 between 9:31 and 9:58pm.

WEDNESDAY MARCH 15th
Two performances at the 'Ritz' in Luton, Bedfordshire.

THURSDAY MARCH 16th
Two performances at the 'Gaumont Theatre' in Southampton.

FRIDAY MARCH 17th
Marriott is stricken with gastroenteritis forcing the group to cancel their two performances at the 'Granada Theatre' in Tooting. Their replacement was Geno Washington and the Ram Jam Band, who deputised for the band within two hours notice!!

came out of it clear, other people painted me black. It was a drag. But then we had an idea to do something to make people laugh at the whole thing for what it really was. So we shot this tele film. We wouldn't try to make the police look stupid- but funny ideas come from real life, and we think there was something sufficiently funny in this to laugh at."

The film was naturally intended for screenings on "Top Of The Pops", but this, along with all the other promotional films they shot with Peter Whitehead for his "Lorimer Films" company, were never screened on the show. The first television screening of parts of the film (by which time the film had been re-edited to accompany the song "Get Yourself Together") occurred in the Granada ITV/Channel 4 "My Generation" Small Faces programme entitled "It's A Mod Mod Mod Mod World", transmitted on November 7th

SATURDAY MARCH 18th
Marriott returns to the group, enabling them to fulfil their two concert engagements at the 'Gaumont Theatre' in Wolverhampton.

SUNDAY MARCH 19th
Two performances at the 'City Hall' in Newcastle.

MONDAY MARCH 20th
Two performances at the 'ABC Theatre' in Edinburgh.

TUESDAY MARCH 21st
Two performances at the 'Odeon Theatre' in Glasgow.

WEDNESDAY MARCH 22nd
Two performances at the 'ABC Theatre' in Carlisle.

THURSDAY MARCH 23rd

Two performances at the 'Odeon Theatre' in Leeds.

FRIDAY MARCH 24th

Two performances at the 'Gaumont Theatre' in Doncaster.

SATURDAY MARCH 25th

Two performances at the 'ABC Theatre' in Lincoln, while in today's 'Disc and Music Echo', a report is published, entitled "Faces Fans Shock- London Date Dropped". The report continues: "SHOCK for London-based Small Faces fans....the Roy Orbison package show in which they appear will not now play Hammersmith Odeon on April 8. The date has been dropped by promoter Tito Burns because of "business difficulties."

was 'Itchycoo Park'.

FRIDAY MARCH 31st

Two performances at the 'Odeon Theatre' in Cheltenham, Gloucestershire.

APRIL

Jerry Shirley's group Apostolic Intervention release the single "(Tell Me) Have You Ever Seen Me/Madame Garcia" (Immediate IM 043), featuring Steve as producer. Also, this months edition of "Rave" features a cover story on Steve, and in the 'Tailpiece' section of the NME, it reads: "This time, seems Small Faces can't make it".

SATURDAY APRIL 1st

As the latest edition of "Fab 208" becomes a Small Faces

SUNDAY MARCH 26th

Two performances at the 'Coventry Theatre'.

MONDAY MARCH 27th

Two performances at the 'Odeon Theatre' in Blackpool.

WEDNESDAY MARCH 29th

Two performances at the 'Capitol' in Cardiff, Wales.

THURSDAY MARCH 30th

Two performances at the 'Colston Hall' in Bristol. Prior to the evening performances, Ronnie relaxes in their hotel room and stumbles upon a tourist magazine for the town of Bristol. The booklet mentions places of interest in the country with its 'dreaming spires' and a 'bridge of sighs'. Ronnie was greatly impressed by its descriptive elements and would use these lines in one of his songs. The song

special, the group give two performances at the 'Winter Gardens' in Bournemouth.

SUNDAY APRIL 2nd

Two performances at the 'De Montford Hall' in Leicester.

WEDNESDAY APRIL 5th

Two performances at the 'Gaumont Theatre' in Ipswich.

THURSDAY APRIL 6th

Two performances (6:40 and 8:50pm) at the 'Granada Theatre', Bath Road, Slough in Buckinghamshire.

FRIDAY APRIL 7th

Two performances at the 'ABC Theatre' in Aldershot. This night was also the final night with Paul & Barry Ryan, who

left to commence a tour of Australia.

SATURDAY APRIL 8th

As predicted by Disc & Music Echo on Saturday, March 25th, the two performances at the 'Odeon Theatre' in Hammersmith, London are cancelled by agent Tito Burns, citing 'business difficulties'.

SUNDAY APRIL 9th

The tour ends with two performances at the 'ABC Theatre' in Romford, Essex.

MONDAY APRIL 10th

The Small Faces leave London Airport to visit briefly, for the first time, Italy.

WEDNESDAY APRIL 12th

The group fly directly onto Scandinavia for a short tour.

SUNDAY APRIL 16th

The group return to Britain at London Airport, where they immediately begin a 7-day recording session at 'Olympic Studios' at 117, Church Road, Barnes in London.

TUESDAY APRIL 18th

The Small Faces travel to the studios of Associated TeleVision's (ATV) at Elstree Studio Centre, Eldon Avenue, Borehamwood in Hertfordshire to make their only guest appearance on "The Morecambe & Wise Show". Following a brief rehearsal in Studio C, which lasted between 10:30 and 1:00pm, the group (in two different sections of the programme) perform live "I Can't Make It", then return to deliver a version of "All Or Nothing".

The programme, which also featured Millicent Martin and Bobby Rydell, was first transmitted across the ITV network over six months later on Sunday October 22nd 1967 between 8:25 and 9:24pm.

WEDNESDAY APRIL 19th

Steve and Ronnie make an appearance on the programme "Pop Interview" for the BBC Russian Radio service. The session, which began at 12:00 noon, was carried out at the south-wing of the reception hall at the BBC TV Centre, Wood Lane, and was not transmitted in Russia until Tuesday July 25 at 3:45pm.

SATURDAY APRIL 29th

Two performances at the 'Winter Gardens' in Weston-Super-Mare.

SUNDAY APRIL 30th

The group leave London Airport for promotional tour of Europe, where they take in Holland until Tuesday May 2nd, and then Germany until their flight home on Saturday May 6th.

SATURDAY MAY 6th

As the group fly back into England, the latest NME 'Tailpiece' reports: "Opposite London clinic, Steve Marriott lives in same block as Cilla Black".

SUNDAY MAY 7th

For the second successive year, the Small Faces are invited to appear at the annual 'NME Poll Winners Concert' at the Empire Pool, Wembley. The concert also featured Dusty Springfield, Cliff Richard, Georgie Fame, Cream, Lulu, Jeff Beck, The Move, Geno Washington, Paul Jones, Cat Stevens, The Troggs, The Beach Boys and Stevie Winwood amongst others.

The Small Faces performance was reviewed in the NME dated May 13th: "Finally it was left to the Small Faces to

close the show in fantastic style - a pile-driving throb of sound as they gave out with some of their string of hits, and proving that the old adage of good things in small packages was never more true".

MONDAY MAY 8th TO FRIDAY MAY 12th
The Small Faces assemble at the Olympic Studios in Barnes for further recordings.

WEDNESDAY MAY 10th
P.P. Arnold's debut 'Immediate' single "The First Cut Is The Deepest", enters the NME chart at No.22.

SATURDAY MAY 13th
The NME reports: "The Faces were this week cutting tracks for a new British single. It is not expected that their new American release "Green Circles" will be issued in this country. Kinks' co-manager Robert Wace took over the Faces' management last week, although Harold Davison retains sole agency for the group". While in the NME 'Tailpiece' section, it reads: "Hard to satisfy Small Faces demands... ".

SUNDAY MAY 14th
As by way of a climax to the 1966/67 football season, the Small Faces are invited (all expenses paid) to make a personal appearance before a charity football match held at Oldhan Athletic's Boundary Park football ground. The original plan was for the group to simply walk around the perimeter of the pitch, but due to the match being a sell out organisers feared for the group's safety and scrapped the idea. Instead the group took it upon themselves to go on the pitch anyway without security in an old Vauxhall. No sooner

had the car appeared the fans came down from the stands and jumped on the car, causing it to sink deep into the soft turf. Panic set in when, due to the weight of the kids on the car, the roof started to cave in and as the vehicle started to move away it accidentally ran over a fan's legs. Stewards of the club were not told that the group were going out, and to this day, the football club have no record that the Small Faces had even turned up. The group, totally in shock, eventually left the ground telling the driver to "keep on driving" for another five miles where they got out of the car and ran crazily over the moors screaming their heads off!

TUESDAY MAY 16th
The group leave England for a tour of Europe at London Airport.

WEDNESDAY MAY 17th
The first stop is Germany, where they perform two concerts with the Beach-Boys.

FRIDAY MAY 19th
Further concerts with the Beach-Boys in Germany.

SATURDAY MAY 20th
The Small Faces make their debut on German Television's top pop-music show "Beat Club", recorded for the station NDR in the studios of 'Radio Bremen'. This show, more than any other European TV pop show, was the most valuable way for English group's to promote their records in Europe. For this month's edition (the 20th in the series since it's conception on Saturday September 25th 1965) the group mimed a version of "I Can't Make It", in a show hosted by regular hosts Uschi Nerke and from England

Dave Lee Travis. The programme (transmitted on NDR that night) also featured music by Cream, Dave Dee, Dozy, Beaky, Mick & Tich, Mr. Acker Bilk, Otis Redding, The Kinks, The Who, The Equals, The Bee Gees and Whistling Jack Smith. P.P. Arnold was scheduled to perform 'First Cut is the Deepest' on the show, but unfortunately she missed her plane at London Airport.

Meanwhile, back in England, the NME 'Tailpiece' reveals: "From his West End flat, Steve Marriott forced by landlord Sidney Brickman to move".

SUNDAY MAY 21st
The group travel to Sweden, where they perform two shows in Orebro.

MONDAY MAY 22nd to THURSDAY MAY 25th
The Small Faces fly to Copenhagen for four shows, two per day, in Denmark.

FRIDAY MAY 26th
As the tour continues with two performances in Gothenbourg, Sweden, "Patterns/E Too D" (F 12619) is released by Decca in England without the group's approval.

SATURDAY MAY 27th
The group visit Norway for two days of concerts. The first being in Oslo. Meanwhile, the latest NME includes a reports that: "Small Faces switch labels from Decca to Immediate and announce that 'Here Comes The Nice/Green Circles' is to be released on Immediate the following Friday" and… reviews the single "Patterns/E Too D", as 'chart possible', noting "this track is taken from an LP, and apparently the

Small Faces don't want to know about it. I gather they will be doing no promotion on it, which is bound to reduce it's impact… Despite the group's apathy, plenty of their fans will enjoy it". (The record never charted.)

SUNDAY MAY 28th
Two performances in Trundheim in Norway. Following the concerts, the group fly back into England at London Airport, later that night.

WEDNESDAY MAY 31st
The Small Faces again travel to Studio G at the Lime Grove Studios of BBC Television to record another appearance on 'Top Of The Pops'. Following brief rehearsals for the cameras (2:30 to 4:30pm) the group mime a version of "Here Comes The Nice" to be included in tomorrow night's edition of the show, transmitted on BBC1 between 7:30 and 8:01pm and hosted by Pete Murray.

FRIDAY JUNE 2nd
Immediate release the single "Home Comes The Nice/Talk To You" (Immediate IM 050), where it reaches No.12. On the same day, Decca release the group's second album entitled "From The Beginning". It charts at No.17.

SATURDAY JUNE 3rd
On the day the Small Faces leave London Airport for concerts in Holland, the NME reviews "Here Comes The Nice", and notes "with all the promotion they intend putting in on this one, it should see them in the top ten".

That evening, the group perform two shows in Rotterdam.

SUNDAY JUNE 4th
A further two performances in Rotterdam, Holland.

MONDAY JUNE 5th
The group return to London Airport this morning.

WEDNESDAY JUNE 7th and THURSDAY JUNE 8th
Two days of rehearsing for the upcoming set of British concerts. While on June 8th, "Here Comes The Nice" enters the British singles chart, where it stays for 10 weeks, peaking at No.12.

FRIDAY JUNE 9th
While the group prepare for two performances at 'Earlham Park' in Norwich, the latest NME carries an half-page advert, paid for by Immediate, to promote "Here Comes The Nice".

SATURDAY JUNE 10th

The group stay in the South in order for them to travel again to the Southampton studios of Southern ITV. This time, to record an appearance in show 6 of the new Mike Mansfield pop show "As You Like It". (Dubbed by ITV executives as the first new pop show since the demise of 'Ready Steady Go!', which was scrapped on December 23rd 1966- see relevant entry.) The show, a "pop request series" was introduced by Don Moss, and included the bizarre event of the singer Adam Faith, who for the first time, would take on the role as a TV interviewer. In every episode he would board a plane and fly to an unknown destination where he would gather requests for songs from people he would meet. In the first programme, (transmitted on May 9th 1968) Faith flew from Gatwick to Amsterdam in Holland. The action would then cut from Faith and back to Don Moss in the Southern ITV studios where he would introduce that group or singer who would perform that song. (Clever stuff!!) The programme was naturally billed by ITV as "The show could come from anywhere!"

At approximately 7:00pm, in front of a young, hysterical, screaming and mostly female audience, the Small Faces lip-synch, firstly, a version of "Talk To You" to open the show and then return later in the programme to perform "Here Comes The Nice", again lip-synched. The show, transmitted across the ITV network on Tuesday June 13th between 7:00 and 7:29pm, also featured The Bee Gees and an interview with the journalist David Wigg. Due to the high cost of the programme to produce, only eight shows were produced, and the series was scrapped by Southern Television on June 27th 1967. The group will go on to work with Mike Mansfield one more time in his next pop-show idea. (See entry for January 10th 1968.)

TUESDAY JUNE 13th

The Small Faces make another appearance on BBC television. Travelling up to Manchester to make their debut on "Dee Time", hosted by former Radio Caroline DJ Simon Dee. With "Top Of The Pops" now being produced in London, Dee took over the old "TOTP" studios of Dickenson Road (a disused church) for his twice-weekly show. During the forty minute show (transmitted live on BBC1 between 6:24 and 7:04pm) the group performed "Here Comes The Nice". Other attractions that night included Wayne Fontana, Marianne Montgomery, Tina Date and Mike Newman, while Dee also featured a discussion on the game of Cricket. Curiously, a close examination of the BBC contract issued to the Small Faces regarding their appearance on the show, reveals that a quarter of the payment fee was payable to one "James Winstone". (Jimmy Winston had left the group 19 months previous!!)

Incidentally, as 'Dee Time' finishes, fans of the Small Faces could then quickly turn over to ITV and see another performance of "Here Comes The Nice" by the group, this time on the programme "As You Like It" (See entry for Saturday June 10th).

WEDNESDAY JUNE 14th

"Here Comes The Nice" enters the NME charts at No.19, and rises to No.10 two weeks later.

FRIDAY JUNE 16th

Two performances at the 'Top Rank' in Cardiff, Wales.

SATURDAY JUNE 17th

Decca buys an half-page advert in the NME to promote the "From The Beginning" (Decca LK 4879) album. The copy reads "Small Faces at their best". It is worth noting that both the Decca and Immediate albums feature alternate versions of the tracks "(Tell Me) Have You Ever Seen Me" and "My Way Of Giving". The transitional period between the labels also resulted in a change of music publishing for the group. Originally with "Carlin Music", this new deal with 'Immediate' meant the groups work was now published with 'Avakak'. Meanwhile today's "Record Mirror" reports that Mel Torme's former English protege' was Steve Marriott.

THURSDAY JUNE 22nd

The group make their twentieth appearance on "Top Of The Pops" at Studio G, Lime Grove, London, where during the live transmission that evening on BBC1 (between 7:30 and 8:00pm), the group mime a version of "Here Comes The Nice". The show, hosted by Pete Murray, also featured in the studio, The Young Rascals, The Hollies and the 'Top Of The Pops' Orchestra.

FRIDAY JUNE 23rd

The Small Faces, along with P.P. Arnold and Twice As Much fly out from London Airport to Europe, where they head immediately to Bremen in Germany to begin a short tour

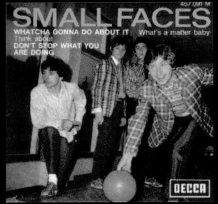

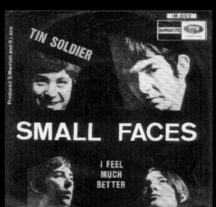

promoting 'Immediate' records artists.

SATURDAY JUNE 24th

"Small Faces" (IMLP/IMSP 008), the group's first album for Immediate is released. With the ensuing 'battle of the LP's", the NME play it safe by not reviewing either album until it's July review of the Decca LP. (Old adage: "don't bite the hand that feeds you".) To co-incide with the release of the Immediate album, the label releases a promo-only 7" single for the album (AS.1), featuring DJ Tommy Vance's announcement that "There are but four Small Faces, but only one Immediate LP." The album contains the track "Green Circles", sung by Ronnie, which features a co-songwriting credit for Mike O'Sullivan, who lived with the band at their Pimlico flat. The song was apparently inspired by a dream he had.

The Faces' meanwhile plus Arnold and Twice As Much assemble in the studios of Radio Bremen to appear on show 21 of NDR's pop show "Beat Club". The show, hosted by regulars Uschi Nerke and British DJ Dave-Lee travis was transmitted live on NDR that night. P.P. Arnold appeared to perform "First Cut Is The Deepest", Twice As Much performed "Crystal Ball" and the Small Faces performed "Here Comes The Nice". The programme also featured studio performances by Cat Stevens, Lulu, The Marquis Of Kensington, The Kinks, The Latch and The Exception.

Meanwhile, back in England where one week after the Decca advert, Immediate retaliates with an half-page advert in the NME, promoting the "Small Faces" album. Their copy reads: "…which ever way you look at it, there are only four Small Faces. But there is just one Small Faces LP. It's on Immediate".

SUNDAY JUNE 25th

The Small Faces fly out from London Airport to Europe, where they immediately head to the palace-like 'Villa Louvigny' in the Grand Duchey of Luxembourg to make a guest appearance on the Emperor Rosko French service 'Radio Luxembourg' show with P.P. Arnold and her band The Nice that evening.

MONDAY JUNE 26th

The tour of Europe continues in Brussels, where they, along with P.P. Arnold, The Nice, Chris Farlowe and Twice As Much appear as part of an 'Immediate' package on various TV & Radio programmes. Today also included a film appearance for the television station BRTN, where in the 'Drinks &

Relaxation' room at the 'Villa Louvigny' in Luxembourg, the group mime to both sides of their latest single. Firstly "Talk To You" and then "Here Comes The Nice". The setting and location for both shoots were identical.

TUESDAY JUNE 27th

The tour of 'Immediate' artists travel through Brussels for more TV & Radio appearances.

WEDNESDAY JUNE 28th

The 'Immediate' tour reaches Stockholm in Sweden.

THURSDAY JUNE 29th

Following their arrival back in England that morning, the group travel to Coventry that evening, for two performances at the 'Locarno'.

Rectory Field, Blackheath, SE London, Saturday July 1st

FRIDAY JUNE 30th

Another 'Locarno' venue, this time in Wolverhampton. (Again two performances).

JULY

"Beat Instrumental" features another part of the series 'Sounds I Like'. This month Ronnie 'Plonk' Lane is featured, alongside other bass-playing pop contemporaries such as 'Beatle' Paul McCartney, Jack Bruce (from 'The Cream') and Klaus Voorman ('Manfred Mann').

"My guitar is a Harmony" Ronnie is quoted as saying, "a special model which I bought from the St. Giles Music

wouldn't it be nice – 1968

JANUARY 1968

"(If You Think You're) Groovy", written and produced by Marriott/Lane, is released by P.P. Arnold (Immediate IM 061). The song features the Small Faces playing and adding backing vocals. Although never released by the group, a demo version of the song, featuring Steve on acoustic guitar, was presented to Arnold in late 1967. The demo still survives today, and is currently in the private collection of Kenny Jones. Also this month, Billy Nichols releases the single "Would You Believe" (Immediate IM 063) featuring an arrangement by the Small Faces with production credits for Steve and Ronnie and Traffic (featuring Steve Winwood) release their debut 'Island' album "Mr. Fantasy", featuring Steve singing backing vocals on the track "Berkshire Poppies".

WEDNESDAY JANUARY 3rd

The Small Faces accept an invitation to appear on the 'pilot' programme of 'All Systems Freeman", hosted by DJ Alan Freeman, and intended to be a replacement for "Juke Box Jury". (Axed from the BBC1 schedules on December 27th 1967 after eight years.) The programme, described by Radio One press releases as "Radio One in vision" was set in a 'mock-up' of a radio studio where groups would come in and perform, whilst intercut with various location footage of groups in performance, and interviews with pop-stars of the day and members of the public who gave their opinions on the week's new single releases.

Recordings for the Friday transmission take place on a Wednesday where surprisingly, the group again opt to take a train ride (£5 each member return - paid for at the expensive of the BBC) from London to the BBC Manchester studios in Dickenson Road, where from 10:30am in Studio A, rehearsals for the first show take place. During the evening recording (from 8:30pm) the group, along with P.P. Arnold, mime a version of "Tin Soldier". But following the completion of the 28 minute programme, a major problem occurred. The group, with the full backing of Harold Davison, decided that their usual BBC music show appearance fee of £78 15/-, considering the travelling that they had done from London, was not enough, and refused to sign their contract. With the first show due for transmission in only two days, the BBC had no option but to cancel their contract and not screen the Small Faces "Tin Soldier" clip. Instead, BBC technicians rush recorded a solo performance of 'Groovy' by P.P. Arnold for inclusion in Friday's broadcast (BBC1 between 6:40 and 7:04pm) Naturally, the Faces' performance was never screened, and was later 'junked' by the BBC in 1972.

Nevertheless, the group waited for Arnold to complete her taping, and the contingent headed back to London (with train tickets paid for by the BBC), later that night.

THURSDAY JANUARY 4th

A busy day for the group as Ian McLagan marries in secret 20 year-old former "Ready Steady Go!" dancer Sandy Sarjeant at Marylebone Registry Office in London. The event was kept so secret, that even the other members of the Small Faces' failed to show up.

Following the service, 'Mac' rushes to join the group at BBC Television Centre in London, where the others are currently rehearsing for an appearance on "Crackerjack". The rehearsals for the show begin at 1:15pm, and last until 3:30pm. The 'taping' for the broadcast runs from 5:15 to 6:15pm where the group perform a live version of "Tin Soldier". This edition of "Crackerjack", hosted by Leslie Crowther and Peter Glaze, is transmitted the following day,

that the last line of "Tin Soldier" has to be cut out of any TV or radio broadcasts because, according to a BBC spokesman, "it seemed to infer sleeping with a girl".

Steve, on hearing this news, was furious. He replied by saying: "I actually said SIT with her, not sleep! The meaning of the song is about getting into somebody's mind - not their body. It refers to a girl I used to call to all the time, and she really gave me a buzz! The single was to give her a buzz in return and maybe other people as well. I dig it! There's no great message really, and no physical scenes".

WEDNESDAY JANUARY 10th

With Mac now back with the group, the Small Faces travel again (for the third and last time) to the Southampton based studios of Southern ITV at Northam in Hampshire. This time, again working with the producer Mike Mansfield, the group record an appearance on show 3 of the new pop-show "New Release". As the title suggests, the programme takes an in-depth look at the weeks new single releases and regularly featured the top groups and singers in the studio to perform them. Recording takes place this afternoon, where the group firstly lip-synch a version of "Tin Soldier" with P.P. Arnold and then return later in the programme to perform, this time backing Arnold, on the song "(If You Think You're) Groovy". But unfortunately, only a few ITV regions would see the result, when Southern ITV transmitted the programme, for the only time, on Friday January 19th between 7:00 and 7:29pm, and Border, later that night, between 11:16 and 11:45pm. While the Westward, Channel and Anglia ITV regions would see the programme the following day, (Saturday January 20th) between 5:50 and 6:19pm.

NME journalist Keith Altham interviews the group backstage at the television studios. The article is published on January 27th 1968.

THURSDAY JANUARY 11th

Another appearance on "Top Of The Pops", where from 2:30 to 4:30 and 5:30 to 6:45pm the group, along with the others artists on the show, take part in rehearsals at Studio G, at Lime Grove for the live evening broadcast between 7:30 and 8:00pm on BBC1. The Small Faces, along with P.P. Arnold, mime a version of "Tin Soldier" in a show hosted by Pete Murray. The programme also featured music by The Tremeloes, Love Affair, The Bee Gees, Georgie Fame, The Herd and, on film, The Beatles.

on Friday January 5th between 4:55 and 5:39pm on BBC1.

The group then make a mad dash to Studio G at Lime Grove in order to make another live performance on "Top Of The Pops". With absolutely no time to rehearse, the group lip-synch a version of "Tin Soldier" with P.P. Arnold on backing vocals for the live transmission on BBC1 between 7:30 and 8:01pm. The show, hosted by Jimmy Savile, also featured Peter Tork (from 'The Monkees') as guest 'DJ', and music from The Love Affair, The Beatles, Tom Jones, Georgie Fame, Petula Clark, Engelbert Humperdinck and The Four Tops.

Incidentally, the Small Faces' BBC appearance fees had now been increased slightly. £84 exactly was paid for their "Crackerjack" appearance and £89-5 shillings for "Top Of The Pops".

FRIDAY JANUARY 5th

Mac informs the others (by phone) that he has got married to Sandy and that they are about to go on their honeymoon to Majorca in Spain.

MONDAY JANUARY 8th

Mac and Sandy return from their honeymoon, landing at London Airport early afternoon. Trouble occurs when customs men arrest Mac after finding him to be carrying, what they believe is, cannabis resin. He will appear in court on Friday January 12th. (See entry).

TUESDAY JANUARY 9th

The BBC informs the group (via a phone call to their office)

FRIDAY JANUARY 12th

Mac appears at the Uxbridge Magistrates Courts in Middlesex following his bust at London Airport on Monday January 5th. He is accused of having cannabis resin at Heathrow (London) Airport and of trying to export a dangerous drug. The Magistrates decided that his existing £1,000 bail be increased to £1,500- a third of it in his own recognisances, and the remainder in two £500 sureties. McLagan spent 15 minutes in jail waiting for someone to stand surety for him.

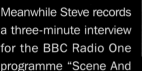

Meanwhile Steve records a three-minute interview for the BBC Radio One programme "Scene And Heard" at BBC Broadcasting House, Portland Place, in London. During the course of the interview with 'roving reporter' Miranda Ward, he discussed the impending tour of Australia. The session was transmitted the following day, Saturday January 13th, between 6:32 and 7:30pm on 'wonderful' Radio One. Incidentally, the producer for the show was Bryant Marriott (no relation!)

SATURDAY JANUARY 13th

Today's 'Melody Maker' carries an article on the rumoured unrest within the band, entitled "Is All Still Well With The Faces?" Meanwhile, pop star Simon Dupree in the 'Hit Talk' column of Disc & Music Echo revues 'Tin Soldier', describing it as the "Worst hit ever by the Small Faces!"

MONDAY JANUARY 15th

The Small Faces depart from London Airport en route to Australia, with a brief stop-over for fuel in Singapore.

TUESDAY JANUARY 16th

The Small Faces arrive in Australia to begin rehearsals for the upcoming 'controversial' tour of Australia and New Zealand with The Who and Paul Jones, suitably named "The Big Tour". (Paul Jones arrived on the 18th, with The Who joining them a day later). At one stage, penciled in for the tour was The Herd. Meanwhile, "Itchycoo Park" enters the American charts at No. 21, eventually peaking at No.16.

SATURDAY JANUARY 20th

The Small Faces/Who/Paul Jones tour begins with two performances (6:00 & 8:45pm) at the 'Festival Hall', Charlotte Street, Brisbane in Queensland. During the course of the tour, the standard running order for the 145 minute shows would be: (ie. For a 6 o'clock performance)

6:00 Introductions
6:10 group- The Questions.
6:30 Paul Jones.
7:00 Intermission.
7:30 Small Faces. (Their 30 minute repertoire included:)
     * "Sha-La-La-La-Lee
     * "All Or Nothing"
     * "Itchycoo Park"
     * "If I Were A Carpenter"
     * "Every Little Bit Hurts"
     * "Tin Soldier".
8:00 The Who (closed the show)

Meanwhile, back in England, reports are announced that the Small Faces will visit America on Friday February 5th, with a possible appearance on the February 7th edition of CBS TV's 'top-rated' Sunday night entertainment show "The Ed Sullivan Show".

MONDAY JANUARY 22nd

Two shows (6:00 & 8:45pm) at 'Sydney Stadium', Rushcutter's Bay, Sydney in New South Wales.

TUESDAY JANUARY 23rd

A further two shows (again 6:00 & 8:45pm) at 'Sydney Stadium', in New South Wales. The second concert is marred by a teenage audience who booed the group and threw coins at Steve while he sang.

THURSDAY JANUARY 25th

Two shows (6:00 & 8:45pm) at the 'Festival Hall' in Dudley Street, Victoria in Melbourne.

FRIDAY JANUARY 26th

A further two shows (6:00 & 8:45pm) at the 'Festival Hall' in Melbourne.

SATURDAY JANUARY 27th

Two shows (6:00 & 8:45pm) at the 'Centennial Hall' in Adelaide.

SUNDAY JANUARY 28th

The date of the 'infamous' aircraft incident between Adelaide and Melbourne, where the groups were accused of "insulting a passenger, drinking beer and making a hostess cry". The entourage were on they way from Adelaide to Sydney, but were taken off the plane at Melbourne and delayed for three hours. Later they were put aboard a bus in Sydney to take them to another flight for New Zealand where they were accompanied by two security guards. Paul Jones later commented on the events: "The trouble began when a hostess served other passengers, but ignored the boys. (the groups). The pilot told us to stop swilling beer. But we did not know there was a law forbidding liquor aboard the plane".

MONDAY JANUARY 29th

Two shows (6:00 & 8:30pm) at the 'Town Hall' in Queen Street, Auckland, North Island, New Zealand. The advertisements by "Aztec Services - Stadium- Miller Attractions" bill the gigs as "The Greatest Of The Big Shows Since The Beatles And The Rolling Stones".

TUESDAY JANUARY 30th

Steve celebrates his 21st birthday with The Who's drummer Keith Moon and "Wiggy" (John Walford, The Who's bald roadie) by smashing up their Wellington Hotel suite.

WEDNESDAY JANUARY 31st

The final night of the tour, with two shows (again 6:00 & 8:30pm) at the 'Town Hall' in Wellington, New Zealand.

FRIDAY FEBRUARY 2nd

The Small Faces depart from New Zealand to take a flight home. The route takes them through Hawaii, San Francisco, New York and then London Airport.

MONDAY FEBRUARY 5th - SATURDAY FEBRUARY 10th and MONDAY FEBRUARY 12th - EARLY MARCH

Extensive recording sessions at the Olympic Studios in Barnes.

SATURDAY FEBRUARY 10th

Steve issues a statement relating to the "Twisted press reports" of incidents on their recent tour of Austraila:

"Everyday seemed like a year. We never want to go back there again. Everywhere we played, the kids were great. But to the older generation, we were a team of British pop-group rowdies. They had it in for us so much, it nearly drove me round the twist".

Replying to reports that both the Small Faces and The Who were thrown off for 'swilling beer, insulting passengers and making a hostess cry', Steve said:

"When they threw us off the plane, I had been reading a book all the time! When the coffee came round they (the hostesses) served everybody except us, so Paul Jones told the Hostess: 'I think you are very rude!' She said 'Be quiet, or I'll throw it in your face'."

"None of us swore at her, and none of the Hostesses were reduced to tears. There was only one bottle of beer

belonging to an Australian group. All the reports were so twisted and warped, we just couldn't talk to the press in the end".

SATURDAY FEBRUARY 17th

Keith Altham's article "Small Faces Sink Australia" appears in the NME.

MARCH

The group undertake a tour of both Italy and Scandinavia.

SATURDAY MARCH 9th

A delayed action 'time-bomb' blows up when, following the controversial 'Small Faces/Who/Paul Jones' tour of Australia, top Aussie impresario Ken Brodziak, announces that he is "reluctant" to book further pop-groups for the time being. An article in the 'Melody Maker', on the same subject, carries a caption "Ban these scruffy urchins once and for all".

Meanwhile, Small Faces spokeman Tony Calder, contrary to popular opinions, announces "They have been invited back to Australia!"

SATURDAY MARCH 23rd

The group fly to Sweden this morning where they immediately travel to the studios of April Television to record (this time on 'video-tape') another appearance on the "Popside" TV music programme. This show, with a total running time of only 12 minutes 41 seconds, was dedicated entirely to the group where they perform, in the studio, the songs: "Tin Soldier/Itchycoo Park/My Way Of Giving/Talk To You" and "Rollin' Over". A brief interview with the group, where they were asked "Do you believe in Rock & Roll" was included between the first two tracks. Steve replied by saying "I've just trod in some."The show was transmitted the following day (Sunday March 24th) between 7:01 and 7: 14pm on Sveriges Television in Sweden. The group returned to England at London Airport following the recording of the programme.

MONDAY APRIL 1st

The Small Faces, again working with the director Peter Whitehead, shoot a colour 16mm promotional film for "Lazy Sunday" at Kenny's parents house in Havering Street, Stepney, London, E1. The clip opens up with Steve sitting on the grass in Albert Gardens (around 300 yards round the corner from Kenny's parents house) with ampilifers appearing out of thin air behind him. An old lady wearing a hairnet (Kenny's real-life neighbour, the late Peggy Dawson) knocks on number 34, where Steve opens the door carrying an LP. The two begin to argue, then the Lady grabs the album out of Steve's hands where she promptly smashes it on his head. Amongst the other events in this short clip included Steve going to the outside loo (now demolished) carrying some toilet roll. As the day continued, additional location filming was done half-a-mile away at the Thames Embankment alongside the Wapping Wall. The promo clip would be shown for the only time in England on the BBC2 music programme "Late Night Line-Up Presents : Colour Me Pop" on Friday June 21st 1968. (See entry.) Following the conclusion of shooting enough 'stock' 16mm film, the group, along with Ronnie's brother Stan, went down to the local pub to celebrate Ronnie's 22nd birthday. Incidently colour versions of the film clip seem to have been printed back to front. (Look at the door number 34 in the film.) The correct version of the film still survives in black and white.

FRIDAY APRIL 5th

Immediate release the single "Lazy Sunday/Rollin' Over" (IM 064). Although it would eventually reach No.2 in the NME charts, Steve was never happy with his "exaggerated cockney accent" featured on the record. This choice of A-side came from Steve's father William. (The original choice was the song "Song Of A Baker".)

SATURDAY APRIL 6th

The group make another live appearance on "Dee Time", hosted by Simon Dee, at Studio G, Lime Grove, London. Following 2:30 to 5:30pm afternoon rehearsals, the group mime a version of "Lazy Sunday" at the start of a live 6:25 to 7:09pm transmission on BBC1. The group shared the bill on this edition with 'Ex-Goon' comic, the late Michael Bentine, DJ Jimmy Young and fellow chart-stars Julie Driscoll & Brian Auger Trinity.

Following their performance, Steve and Ronnie (before the programme had even finished) rushed to the BBC studios of Radio One at Broadcasting House to record another appearance on "Scene And Heard". This time a live interview with Johnny Moran, (lasting only four minutes) which was transmitted at the end of the programme between 6:32 and 7:30pm. (The complete 58 minute programme was repeated in it's entirety the following day, Sunday April 7th, between 4:00 and 4:58pm, again on Radio One.)

TUESDAY APRIL 9th

The group, along with fellow 'Immediate' artiste P.P. Arnold, travel to the BBC studios of 'Piccadilly 1' to record their first (and last) session for Radio One's "Top Gear", with producer Bernie Andrews and host John Peel. The afternoon session (which included a rehearsal) lasted between 2:30 and 6:00pm and produced the following, "If I Were A Carpenter" (featuring P.P. Arnold on backing vocals), "Lazy Sunday", "Get Ready" (an instrumental version of the Tamla-Motown song The Temptations would have a hit with the following year) and "Every Little Bit Hurts" (again with P.P. Arnold).

GIANT SPECTACULAR DANCE
FOR 10,000 RAVERS
ALREADY OVER 3,000 TICKETS SOLD

U.K. & U.S.A.
INTERNATIONAL **MOJO** FESTIVAL
NO. 1

'ALL DAY' WHIT MONDAY, JUNE 3rd
Start 1 p.m. till Midnight (11 hours)

at QUEEN'S HALL, LEEDS
STARRING

THE SMALL FACES | **THE HERD**
ALAN BOWN | **BILL HALEY & the Comets**
EDWIN STARR | **THE FANTASTICS**
AMBOY DUKES BIG BAND | GOSPEL GARDEN

COMPERED BY KING MOJO HIMSELF
PETE STRINGFELLOW
& THE MOJO SOUL SHOW

TICKETS in advance 20/- or 25/- at door
TICKETS from Mojo Club, Toll Bar, Sheffield 3
(s.a.e. and P.O., or cheque, etc.)

don't want to talk about it. We're married and that's all there is to it." Meanwhile, some of the country's leading music weekly's refuse to publish the controversial 'Immediate' advert for 'Ogden's', citing it as in "bad taste". (See entry for June 1st.)

FRIDAY MAY 31st

The group fly out to Switzerland to perform alongside Jimi Hendrix, The Move, Anselmo Trend, Traffic, The Koobas, John Mayalls' Bluesbreakers, Eric Burdons' New Animals and Eire Apparent at the "Beat Monsters" Concert in Hallenstadion, in Zurich.

JUNE

Immediate release the album "Ogden's Nut Gone Flake" album (IMLP/IMSP 012). Original copies come complete in a circular sleeve. The record company, meanwhile, prepares a 'controversial' promotional advert. (See next entry.)

SATURDAY JUNE 1st

'Melody Maker' publishes the advert to promote the album "Ogden's Nut Gone Flake".

"Which were in the studios,
Hallowed be thy name,
They music come,
Thy songs be sung,

On this album as they came from your heads,
We give you this day our daily bread,
Give us thy album in a round cover,
As we give thee 37/9d,
Lead us into the record stores,
And deliver us Ogden's Nut Gone Flake,
For nice is the music, the sleeve and the story,
For ever and ever,
Immediate".

MONDAY JUNE 3rd

The group performs at the 'UK and USA International Mojo Festival', along with The Herd, Alan Bown, Edwin Starr, The Fantastics, Amboy Dukes and 'Rock n Roll' legend, Bill Haley at the 'Queen's Hall' in Leeds. The programme was compered by 'King Mojo' himself, Pete Stringfellow & the Mojo Soul Show.

SATURDAY JUNE 8th

Steve appears in a 'Melody Maker' article entitled: "I'd Like To Live In A Cave!" This evening sees the group perform at Newcastle City Hall.

SATURDAY JUNE 15th

The Small Faces switch agencies, where they are now represented by Arthur Howes. The first press release announces their plans for the end of the year. Firstly, they are scheduled to undertake a tour of Europe in September, taking in Portugal, Spain, Belgium, Holland, Germany and France. During October they will have a spell back in the recording studios whilst undertaking a 3 or 4 week tour of Britain. Then in December and January of 1969, a tour of America, Japan, Australia and New Zealand is planned.

FRIDAY JUNE 21st

The group assemble in Studio B at BBC Television Centre for the second edition of the late-night BBC2 colour music 'spin-off' show from "Line-Up", entitled "Colour Me Pop". With BBC chiefs now finally seeing the importance of popular music, (and with BBC2 now broadcasting in colour for many of it's programmes) the two elements were combined for this series, which largely just focused on one band or singer in performance, either in the studio (or occasionally in concert). The Small Faces decided to use the show as a vehicle to promote their "Ogden's" album. Rehearsals for the programme began at 10:30am and continued until 12:30pm, where, due to the BBC miming ban, the group recorded in the studio live versions of the tracks due to be used in the transmission. This was followed

Kenny Jones, drummer with the small Faces, has that star-struck expression which makes it clear that he was off in a little world of his own during the Castlereagh Park session.

by Stanley Unwin who rehearsed (and recorded) his monologue "Gobbledeegoops" 'Fairy Story' links. At 4:00pm, the Small Faces began to tape (including brief retakes) mimed performances of: "Song Of A Baker/ Happiness Stan/Rollin' Over/The Hungry Intruder/The Journey/ Mad John" and "Happydaystoytown". (The two segments were then edited to form the second side of the "Ogden's" album.)

The promotional 16mm colour film for "Lazy Sunday", directed by Peter Whitehead (filmed on Monday April 1st- see entry) was inserted into the programme after the opening song "Song Of A Baker". The 24 minute programme, was introduced by Mike Dean and transmitted (for the first and only time) on BBC2 between 11:10 and 11:34pm later that night.

The "Late Night Line-Up presents 'Colour Me Pop'" series (becoming simply "Colour Me Pop" at the start of the Saturday September 7th run) was later to become an 'Award Winning' series for both the BBC and producer Steve Turner, but this did not stop the Corporation from neglecting the series. Although two 'Best Of Colour Me Pop' compilation shows were transmitted on BBC2 on December 27th 1969 and January 3rd 1970, the archive of 49 shows were either 'wiped' (being that they were recorded on reusable 'videotape') junked, sold abroad and never returned, or taken home by BBC technicians for 'private home use'. During the early 1970's, not one "Colour Me Pop" survived in the BBC vaults. That was until the mid to late 70's, when the BBC put out requests, asking that any of their 'lost TV gems' be returned, with no questions asked. That is where the Small Faces "Colour Me Pop" show came from, returned by a technician who, according to good sources, "couldn't bear to see his favourite band be wiped". The show (that most of you reading this now most probably have a copy of), was only minutes away from being wiped forever!! (Thank you kind BBC technician!!)

Incidentally, for the programme, the Small Faces were paid £131- 5 Shillings.

SATURDAY JUNE 22nd
The complaints over the "Ogden's" advert published in the 'Melody Maker' on June 1st (see entry) continue when a letter from P.R. Davies of Kings College, Taunton in

Sommerset is published in today's 'Melody Maker':

"How dare these exponents of popular codswallop presume upon something dear and very real, to countless millions of people! I refer to the disgusting, deplorable, nauseating, sickening, base, vulgar and pretentious way in which the Small Faces have dared to interpret the 'Lord's Prayer' in advertising their latest mass wax wastage!"

MONDAY JUNE 24th
The group, along with The Marmalade and The Move, perform at 'St. Luke's College' in Exeter.

TUESDAY JUNE 25th
The group perform at 'St. Catherine's College' in Oxford. The support acts again are The Marmalade and The Move.

WEDNESDAY JUNE 26th
Another appearance in Studio G at Lime Grove for "Top Of The Pops", where the group record an 'Ampex' (video-tape) insert for "The Universal", for inclusion in tomorrow night's edition of "Top Of The Pops" (BBC1 between 7:31 and 8:00pm). The show, recorded in it's entirety today, was hosted by Alan Freeman, and also included Donovan, Gene Pitney, Dusty Springfield, The Rolling Stones, Manfred Mann, Cupid's Inspiration and John Holmes. Again, the Small Faces received an appearance fee of £100 exactly!

FRIDAY JUNE 28th
Immediate release the single "The Universal/Donkey Rides, A Penny, A Glass" (IM 069). Steve recorded the vocals to "Universal" on a small tape recorder whilst sitting in his garden playing guitar. This explains why you hear traffic going by and dogs barking!

JULY
"Man In Black" by Skip Bifferty, (a pyschedelic band managed by Don Arden), is released by RCA Victor (RCA 1720). The single is produced by Ronnie and arranged by Steve. Neither played on the session.

FRIDAY JULY 5th
The Small Faces, backed by the Sunshine & Brass Section Band, attend the 'Ards Pop Festival' in Newtownards, Northern Ireland. The festival, which also included The Soul Foundation, Cryin' Soul, Mystics, Creative Mind, The Cousins, lasted from Friday night into the early hours of Saturday morning. A brick wall collapsed under the stress of thousands of excited fans all desperate to get a better

black leather jacket and jeans. I wasn't totally surprised, as there had been much speculation in the music press about the possibility of Steve and Peter Frampton forming a 'Supergroup'. This only added fuel to the fire. Frampton took a back seat, but played some nice lead guitar and spent most of the evening on stage with the Small Faces.

I was particularly amused to see that he was wearing the same two-tone shoes as myself, newly purchased from Ravel that day. Anyway, enough of that! The band spent 90 minutes or so on stage and encored twice. By the end of the set, the fans were at fever pitch, reluctant to let them go. But finally the band left the stage, as the lights went up.

As I left the building and made my way outside into the cold winter's night, my ears were still ringing (they were still ringing for a couple of days afterwards). It had been quite a night! I sat shivering on the platform waiting for the last train back to Romford, and pondered over what had certainly been the heaviest performance that I had witnessed from the lads. It was really quite similar to what Humble Pie would be doing 2 or 3 years later.

Although I didn't realise it at the time, this was to be the last time I would see the Small Faces together. Only a couple of months afterwards, following Steve's famous New Year's Eve walkout, the band split. All the rumours in the music press regarding Steve and Peter Frampton proved to be true, with the formation of Humble Pie!"

While in today's 'Disc' (October 19th) Peter Frampton comments on his appearance with the Faces' on the 13th in Manchester: "The Small Faces and The Herd are simply good friends. I went up to Manchester to see the group and I was persuaded to sit in with them", adding "there is no likelihood of any link between the two groups on a business basis". While in the same issue, Steve Marriott is quoted as saying "Peter and I are good mates and we thought it would be a bit of a loon if he played with us that night".

FRIDAY NOVEMBER 1st

The Small Faces leave London Airport for a 3 date European Concert Tour. The first performances are in Berlin, West Germany.

SATURDAY NOVEMBER 2nd

Performances in Holland at Dordrecht.

SUNDAY NOVEMBER 3rd

Performances in Holland at Den Haag. The group fly back into England in the early hours of Monday morning.

WEDNESDAY NOVEMBER 13th

Performances at the 'Glasgow Playhouse'.

THURSDAY NOVEMBER 14th

Performances at the 'Mayfair' in Newcastle.

FRIDAY NOVEMBER 15th

The Small Faces, along with a horn-section, join the Kit Lambert/Chris Stamp organised tour featuring The Who, The Crazy World Of Arthur Brown, Joe Cocker & The Grease Band and Alan Bown. Tonights performances are at the 'All-Night' show, at the Middle Earth, Roundhouse, Chalk Farm. Their repertoire for the six date engagement was as follows:

* "Rollin' Over"
* "If I Were A Carpenter"
* "Every Little Bit Hurts"
* "The Universal"
* "All Or Nothing"
* "Tin Soldier"

SATURDAY NOVEMBER 16th

Another 'All-Night' concert at the 'Roundhouse'. Joe Cocker does not perform for the next two nights.

SUNDAY NOVEMBER 17th

Two shows (5:30 and 8:00pm) at the Birmingham Theatre.

MONDAY NOVEMBER 18th

Two shows (6:15 and 8:30pm) at the Newcastle City Hall. 'Immediate' recorded the Small Faces performance from the second show and, to date, have released officially five songs from their six track set. Three tracks ("Rollin' Over/If I Were A Carpenter" & "Every Little Bit Hurts") were featured on the Immediate album 'The Autumn Stone'. (IMAL 01/02

Released on November 14th 1969.)

While a further two tracks ("All Or Nothing" and "Tin Soldier") would feature on the 1969 German compilation album "In Memoriam". (Immediate 1C 048-90 201.) All five tracks would feature on the American 'Bootleg' EP, strangely titled "Live In '66". (Quish 001.) This means that only one live track, "The Universal" has yet to be released.

TUESDAY NOVEMBER 19th

One show (8:00pm) at the 'Paisley Ice Rink' in Glasgow.

WEDNESDAY NOVEMBER 20th

Two performances (6:15 and 8:35pm) at the 'Liverpool Empire'. During the encore, Kenny joined Keith on his drums, playing a duet on the track "Magic Bus".

TUESDAY DECEMBER 31st

At the conclusion of the 'New Years Eve' party at the 'Alexandra Palace' in London, Steve departs from the stage following a performance of "Lazy Sunday" and an introduction to Alexis Korner. Later, backstage in the dressing rooms, Steve tells the rest of the band "I am leaving!" Kenny remembers that night. "Steve went on stage that night in a bad mood and we knew something was up. He had been throwing real wobblers all week and then, half-way through the set, he just threw his guitar down and walked off, leaving us three there like lemons. We looked at each other, and it was like, "Well, see ya!" There was this almighty scream-up afterwards - Mac, he went mad, but Steve just simply said he couldn't do it anymore. He felt that we couldn't cross over from being a pop band into heavier music; he felt it was too difficult, which was wrong because we really had it all, and were going that way naturally. I'll always remember when the papers announced it, they said, 'Steve quits to play with better musicians', which broke my heart because I always thought we were alright."

wham, bam, thank you mam - 1969

FRIDAY JANUARY 3rd

The Small Faces, along with Herd guitarist Peter Frampton, travel to Paris to guest on the sessions of the latest LP by Johnny Halliday, one of France's biggest stars. The recordings would be produced by Glyn Johns, whom the Small Faces had already worked with on their two Immediate albums.

The sessions produce three tracks (all Marriott/Lane compositions, with assistance by Gilles Thibaut, who was on hand to translate the lyrics); "Reclamation (News Report)"/"Amen (Bang Bang)" and "Regarde Pour Moi (What You Will)".

The album, simply titled "Johnny Hallyday" (Phillips 844 971), would be released on April 6th 1969.

WEDNESDAY JANUARY 8th

The group return to England at London Airport.

SATURDAY JANUARY 11th

The final commitment that the Small Faces have as a band are dates that they are duty bound to do. The first is a short, five date tour of Germany and one date in Austria. This morning, the group fly out from London Airport to Munich in Germany, where they will perform one show that night. It is agreed within the band that Mac will take of all the finances from the tour. The repertoire for the short tour is as follows:

* "You Need Loving"
* "Every Little Bit Hurts"
* "Song Of A Baker"
* "Long Black Veil" (a cover of the 'Band'/Country classic)
* "Tin Soldier"
* "All Or Nothing".

SUNDAY JANUARY 12th

The group fly onto Austria for the first (and last) time this morning to perform one show in Wien. A low-quality 'Bootleg' tape of the show exists.

MONDAY JANUARY 13th

The Small Faces fly back to Germany, where, that evening, they sample the delights of German nightlife!!

TUESDAY JANUARY 14th

The group perform one show in Hamburg. Previous history books on the Small Faces report today that the group "made their US debut at New York's Filmore East". This is, of course, totally untrue!

THURSDAY JANUARY 16th

The group perform one show at the 'Galerie Links' club in Niedersachsenhalle, in Hanover.

FRIDAY JANUARY 17th

The tour ends with a concert in Berlin.

SATURDAY JANUARY 18th

The group return home to London Airport early this morning.

SATURDAY FEBRUARY 8th

Disc & Music Echo ask the question "Is Stevie Marriott quitting The Small Faces?" Tony Calder of Immediate told the paper on Monday "I have heard this rumour. I don't know whether The 'Faces are splitting yet, or not. One minute they are getting on fine. The next they are talking about going their separate ways. I do know, 'though, that the other three have been getting a bit uptight about the Peter Frampton thing." Meanwhile Steve at his Essex home told Disc himself "You're the eightieth person to ask me that! I'm looking forward to a great future. Leaving The 'Faces? I could never be out of a group, and I wouldn't want to be part of a double act either."

FRIDAY MARCH 7th

Immediate posthumously release "Afterglow (Of Your Love)/Wham Bam, Thank You Mam" (IM 077), where it enters the British singles chart on March 19th, staying for only one week and peaking at No. 36. Today, the Small Faces fly to Guernsey in the Channel Islands to perform the first of two farewell shows.

The first, scheduled at the 'Floral Hall' in St. Peter's Port, was unfortunately cancelled due to the venue suffering from fire damage.

SATURDAY MARCH 8th

The Small Faces give their final concert at the 'Springfield Theatre' Jersey in the Channel Island. A report from the concert exists:

"The pounding, ear-shattering sounds of the Small Faces will no longer echo round the ballrooms of Great Britain. And, somewhat surprisingly, they bowed out of the world of pop in the little Channel Island called Jersey at the Springfield Theatre.

Saturday, March 8th, was the date and, as the final notes of 'Tin Soldier' faded away in the distance, Steve Marriott, Ian "Mac" MacLagen, Ronnie "Plonk" Lane and Kenny Jones, the diminutive pop group, walked off stage, hearing the last applause they will ever hear as the Small Faces.

Steve is reported to be joining up with Peter Frampton, ex-Herd, but after their final performance, he refused to comment further. Mac, however, did speak. He said:

"Unless another booking comes in during the next week, and we doubt that will happen, the Small Faces are dead and buried. Steve's definitely leaving though, make no mistake about that. And we're quite excited. We can't wait for the final handshakes so that we can start again."

"And we're going to start again. There'll be a new name, a new style and a new face. But this new face won't be another Steve Marriott. We've got no intention of getting a singer as such, just a good guitarist who can sing."

"We've known the break was coming for three of four months, but we're all glad it happened. The Small Faces have done enough. Business-wise, we've been very badly handled and we haven't had a manager since we left Don Arden a couple of years ago. They've been difficult times and we've had a lot of hard luck as well as success."

"Once it was bandied around that £60,000 had gone into someone's pocket one year, but it certainly wasn't in ours. How much have we lost altogether? That I don't know, but it runs into tens of thousands of pounds. But then we never saw it, so we didn't really miss it."

"Still, we've had some good times and lived and slept well. It has taught us, however, to look upon agents and managers, etc., in a rather bad light. Perhaps that's a good thing."

"Our new group will most probably have a manager though, but he's got to be the right guy. Look at the Beatles, for example, and remember how they were before Brian Epstein died. Now look at them!"

"Regarding Steve's replacement, we're going to get a guitarist cum singer because a lot of people used to think of us as being Steve Marriott's backing group. We intend to think so as well. Since Steve announced that he was leaving, we've been writing a lot more, and there are lots of numbers that we'd like to do but haven't been able to do. Now we will be able to do them."

Mac was then asked what would be the musical policy of the new group. He replied:

"Our only policy will be to do our own stuff. There's a line to be drawn somewhere between playing for ourselves and playing what the audience wants us to play. That's the line we've got to find."

Judging by Mac's remarks, the sound of the Faces will be gone forever, but there are a number of previously unreleased tapes in existence. Don Arden holds a great many of these from the boys' old Decca days, but Immediate have also got a number of tracks.

"I suppose they'll put them out one of these days," said the pensive Mac. "But we won't be around to promote them."

small faces at the *Beeb*

The Small Faces guested on 41 television and 21 radio programmes for the BBC between August 23rd 1965 and August 22nd 1968. Here is the first complete 'check-list' of their appearances. (Only sessions that took place are listed, and not where they failed to appear.)

TV

Programme: *Gadzooks!*
Studio: *TV Theatre*
Recorded: *September 6th 1965*
Transmitted: *live*

Programme: *Top Of The Pops*
Studio: *Studio 2*
Recorded: *September 16th 1965*
Transmitted: *live*

Programme: *Top Of The Pops*
Studio: *Studio 2*
Recorded: *September 30th 1965*
Transmitted: *live*

Programme: *Top Of The Pops*
Studio: *Studio 2*
Recorded: *October 7th 1965*
Transmitted: *live*

Programme: *Crackerjack!*
Studio: *Studio 2*
Recorded: *November 10th 1965*
Transmitted: *November 12th*

Programme: *Top Of The Pops*
Studio: *Studio 2*
Recorded: *February 17th 1966*
Transmitted: *live*

Programme: *Top Of The Pops*
Studio: *Studio 2*
Recorded: *February 24th 1966*
Transmitted: *live*

Programme: *Top Of The Pops*
Studio: *Studio 2*
Recorded: *March 10th 1966*
Transmitted: *live*

Programme: *A Whole Scene Going*
Studio: *Studio 2*
Recorded: *April 6th 1966*
Transmitted: *live*

Programme: *Top Of The Pops*
Studio: *Studio 2*
Recorded: *May 26th 1966*
Transmitted: *live*

Programme: *Top Of The Pops*
Studio: *Lime Grove*
Recorded: *August 11th 1966*
Transmitted: *live*

Programme: *Top Of The Pops*
Studio: *Lime Grove*
Recorded: *August 18th 1966*
Transmitted: *later that night on V.T.*

Programme: *Top Of The Pops*
Studio: *Lime Grove*
Recorded: *September 1st 1966*
Transmitted: *live*

Programme: *Top Of The Pops*
Studio: *Lime Grove*
Recorded: *September 8th 1966*
Transmitted: *live*

Programme: *The Managers*
Studio: *IBC*

Recorded: *October 10th 1966*
Transmitted: *October 23rd 1966*

Programme: *Top Of The Pops*
Studio: *Lime Grove*
Recorded: *November 10th 1966*
Transmitted: *live*

Programme: *Top Of The Pops*
Studio: *Lime Grove*
Recorded: *November 16th 1966 (two performances)*
Transmitted: *November 17th & November 24th*

Programme: *Top Of The Pops*
Studio: *Studio 2*
Recorded: *December 1st 1966*
Transmitted: *live*

Programme: *Top Of The Pops*
Studio: *Studio 2*
Recorded: *December 13th 1966*
Transmitted: *December 26th*

Programme: *Top Of The Pops*
Studio: *Lime Grove*
Recorded: *February 15th 1967*
Transmitted: *never screened*

Programme: *Top Of The Pops*
Studio: *Lime Grove*
Recorded: *May 31st 1967*
Transmitted: *June 1st 1967*

Programme: *Dee Time*
Studio: *Dickenson Road*
Recorded: *June 13th 1967*
Transmitted: *live*

Programme: *Top Of The Pops*
Studio: *Lime Grove*
Recorded: *June 22nd 1967*
Transmitted: *live*

Programme: *Top Of The Pops*
Studio: *Lime Grove*
Recorded: *August 23rd 1967*
Transmitted: *August 24th*

Programme: *Dee Time*
Studio: *Dickenson Road*
Recorded: *September 5th 1967*
Transmitted: *live*

Programme: *Top Of The Pops*
Studio: *Lime Grove*
Recorded: *September 7th 1967*
Transmitted: *August 24th*

Programme: *Twice A Fortnight*
Studio: *Studio G*
Recorded: *December 10th 1967*
Transmitted: *December 16th*

Programme: *All Systems Freeman*
Studio: *Studio A*
Recorded: *January 3rd 1968*
Transmitted: *never screened*

Programme: *Crackerjack!*
Studio: *TV Centre*
Recorded: *January 4th 1968*
Transmitted: *January 5th 1968*

Programme: *Top Of The Pops*
Studio: *Lime Grove*
Recorded: *January 4th 1968*
Transmitted: *live*

Programme: *Top Of The Pops*
Studio: *Lime Grove*
Recorded: *January 11th 1968*
Transmitted: *live*

Programme: *Dee Time*
Studio: *Studio G*
Recorded: *April 6th 1968*
Transmitted: *live*

Programme: *Top Of The Pops*
Studio: *Studio G*
Recorded: *April 11th 1968*
Transmitted: *later that night on V.T.*

Programme: *My Generation*
Studio: *Studio 4*
Recorded: *April 11th 1968*
Transmitted: *never screened*

Programme: *Top Of The Pops*
Studio: *Studio G*
Recorded: *April 18th 1968*
Transmitted: *live*

Programme: *Top Of The Pops*
Studio: *Studio G*
Recorded: *April 25th 1968*
Transmitted: *live*

Programme: *Line-Up (Colour Me Pop)*
Studio: *Studio B*
Recorded: *June 21st 1968*
Transmitted: *Later that night on V.T.*

Programme: *Top Of The Pops*
Studio: *Studio G*
Recorded: *June 26th 1968*
Transmitted: *June 27th 1968*

Programme: *Top Of The Pops*
Studio: *Studio G*
Recorded: *July 11th 1968*
Transmitted: *live*

Programme: *Top Of The Pops*
Studio: *Studio G*
Recorded: *August 22nd 1968*
Transmitted: *live*

(This listing refers to the original transmissions and not any subsequent repeats. See text on recordings dates for that relevant information as well as broadcast times)

Note: Studios 2, 4 and B are at 'Television Centre' Wood Lane.
Studio G is at Lime Grove, in Shepherds Bush, London.
Dickenson Road is in Manchester.
Studio A was at the 'refurbished' Manchester studios in Dickenson Road.
IBC Recording Studios at 35 Portland Place, London W1.

RADIO

Programme: *Saturday Club*
Studio: *Aeolian Hall*
Recorded: *August 23rd 1965*
Transmitted: *September 4th*

Programme: *Top Of The Pops*
Studio: *Studio 1*
Recorded: *September 11th 1965*
Transmitted: *BBC TR'SC' D. (Marriott only)*

Programme: *Joe Loss Pop Show*
Studio: *Camden*
Recorded: *October 22nd 1965*
Transmitted: *live*

Programme: *Joe Loss Show*
Studio: *Playhouse*
Recorded: *January 14th 1966*
Transmitted: *live*

Programme: *Pop Inn*
Studio: *Paris*
Recorded: *March 1st 1966*
Transmitted: *live and BBC TR' SC' D.*

Programme: *Joe Loss Show*
Studio: *Playhouse*
Recorded: *March 11th 1966*
Transmitted: *live*

Programme: *Saturday Club*
Studio: *Aeolian Hall*
Recorded: *March 14th 1966*
Transmitted: *March 19th*

Programme: *Hit '66*
Studio: *Bush House*
Recorded: *March 28th 1966*
Transmitted: *live*

Programme: *Good Morning With Turrie Akerele*
Studio: *Bush House*
Recorded: *March 28th 1966*
Transmitted: *April 7th*

Programme: Saturday Club
Studio: Playhouse
Recorded: May 3rd 1966
Transmitted: May 7th

Programme: Joe Loss Show
Studio: Playhouse
Recorded: June 10th 1966
Transmitted: live

Programme: Parade Of The Pops
Studio: Playhouse
Recorded: June 22nd 1966
Transmitted: live

Programme: Pop Profile
Studio: Bush House
Recorded: July 11th 1966
Transmitted: BBC TR' SC' D.

Programme: Saturday Club
Studio: Paris
Recorded: August 30th 1966
Transmitted: September 3rd

Programme: Joe Loss Show
Studio: Playhouse
Recorded: November 18th 1966
Transmitted: live

Programme: Pop Interview
Studio: BBC Reception
Recorded: April 19th 1967
Transmitted: July 25th

Programme: Where It's At (Marriott and Lane only)
Studio: Broadcasting House
Recorded: August 4th 1967
Transmitted: August 5th

Programme: Scene And Heard (Marriott and Lane only)
Studio: Broadcasting House
Recorded: Jan. 12th 1968
Transmitted: Jan. 13th

Programme: Scene And Heard (Marriott only)
Studio: Broadcasting House
Recorded: April 4th 1968
Transmitted: live

Programme: Top Gear (Marriott and Lane only)
Studio: Piccadilly 1
Recorded: April 9th 1968
Transmitted: April 14th

Programme: Top Of The Pops (Jones only)
Studio: Studio 2
Recorded: April 26th 1968
Transmitted: BBC TR' SC' D.

Note:
Aeolian Hall was at 135/137, New Bond Street, London.
Studio 1 and 2 were at Kensington House, Richmond
Way, Shepherds Bush, London W14
Playhouse Theatre was at Northumberland Avenue.
Paris Studios were at 12, Lower Regent Street, London.
Bush House was Aldwych, London, WC2.
BBC Reception, interview in South-Wing of Tv Centre.
Piccadilly1 was at 201, Piccadilly Studios, Piccadilly.
BBC TR' SC' D stands for "BBC Transcription Disc".

in their own words

SMALL FACES TALK TO YOU: THE STORY OF THE SMALL FACES IN THEIR OWN WORDS

Small Faces were the archetypal mod band. During their short tenure as a group, they were the epitome of cool. From the beginning of their recording career, they were virtually the best-dressed, sharpest looking band in England. A brilliant band live and in the studio, Small Faces featured one of the most dynamic and electrifying singers in all of rock'n'roll, Steve Marriott. You'd be hard-pressed to find a band that displayed more sheer passion and incendiary energy. Beyond their cool image, another engaging aspect of the Small Faces was the genuine camaraderie and friendship that flourished among the members. A gang of four Jack the Lads, the group even lived together in a London home for a period of time. Like the Beatles, they were a select in-group with only four members.

Astonishingly, in only 2 1/2 years time, the songwriting team of Marriott and Ronnie Lane turned out an amazing string of twelve Top Forty Hits. Talk about prolific! Small Faces were also the first band to brazenly champion recreational drug use in such songs as "Here Come the Nice", "Itchycoo Park", and "Eddie's Dreaming". Sadly, they were also perhaps the most ripped-off and under-appreciated of all the great English bands; as of early 1996, they still receive no royalties for any of their records, and were paid a measly 20 pounds a week during their teen scream heyday.

Small Faces achieved the dubious honor of having not one but two manipulative managers -- Don Arden and Andrew Loog Oldham, and one of the most maddening and hard-to-untangle messes of released product of any major British act. The band itself released only 12 singles during its career, and three albums ("Small Faces" on Decca in early 1966, "Small Faces" on Immediate in June 1967, and "Ogden's Nut Gone Flake" on Immediate in 1968). Amazingly, there were another 4 singles released by different managers without the band's approval/and/or after leaving the label, and three more albums released without their

knowledge ("From the Beginning" on Decca, also in June 1967, "There Are But Four Small Faces" in America in early 1968- part of the British Immediate album with 5 singles/b-sides, and the posthumous "The Autumn Stone" in 1969 on Immediate). During the 1970's, there were literally dozens of albums released in various countries with odd mish-mashes and mismatches of material, and some releases under their name in which the material on the record wasn't even the band. There were also Small Faces releases credited to Rod Stewart that were in fact the Marriott-led incarnation of the band. The world of the Small Faces on compact disc gets somewhat less confusing -- even though like the vinyl era, no one paid the band or consulted with them about the releases. At least one consolation is that some of the CD's were done by fans, particularly after The Jam -- one of the two biggest bands to come out in England in the '70's -- covered a song by Small Faces and Jam leader Paul Weller listed them as their favorite group and one of their most profound influences.

In 1996, Small Faces are more popular in England than at any time since their break-up; many of the hottest acts in England -- Paul Weller, Oasis, Blur, and Supergrass to name a few -- all list them as one of their all-time favorite bands. In a recent Arena TV (British) program called "Punk and the Pistols", the Sex Pistols listed both the Small Faces and their subsequent incarnation as the Faces as being their biggest influence. Plans are currently afoot for a Small Faces all-star tribute album with such acts as Weller, Primal Scream, Squeeze, and Glen Matlock taking part. Two boxed sets of the Immediate Records material were released late last year, and a boxed set of Decca material was also issued. In November, 1995, Granada Television screened a half-hour special on the band as part of its "My Generation" series of Sixties artist retrospectives.

The four founding members of Small Faces all went on to successful careers after the original band split. Steve Marriott left the group in early 1969 to form Humble Pie. The remaining three members (Ronnie Lane, Ian McLagan, and Kenney Jones) formed The Faces with the addition of Ron Wood and Rod Stewart, and went on to become one of the top touring acts in the world in the early '70's. Lane quit the band on Easter of 1973, and formed Slim Chance, which predated the whole acoustic, "unplugged" era by nearly two decades, touring in a gypsy caravan. The Faces continued with a bassist recruited because he liked to drink champagne until 1975, at which time Ron Wood joined the Rolling Stones, and Rod Stewart left to pursue his solo career full-time.

McLagan played sessions with the likes of Bruce Springsteen, Paul Weller and the Georgia Satellites. His most noted session work was with the Rolling Stones for the "Some Girls" record and tour. Mac (as he's called by his friends) released several solo albums, and lived in L.A. for over a decade before moving to a small town outside Austin, Texas, in the Nineties. Married to Kim Kerrigan Moon, Mac has just completed an extensive world tour with Rod Stewart, and is putting the finishing touches on an autobiography. Jones joined the Who as an equal partner in 1979 after Keith Moon's death. Lane contracted multiple sclerosis (MS) during the recording sessions for "Rough Mix", a 1977 album he recorded with Pete Townshend. Subsequently he formed the A.R.M.S. organization, which was launched with a famous all-star benefit concert put on by Lane's friends, including Eric Clapton, Jeff Beck, and Jimmy Page. He moved briefly to Houston before relocating to Austin, Texas, where he performed locally with various all-star line-ups comprised of local musicians, including Alejandro Escovedo, J.D. Foster, Jon Dee Graham, and Susan Voelz. He currently lives in Trinidad, Colorado, with his wife Susan and their family. Sadly his debilitating MS prevents him from being actively involved in music; he spends most of his time confined in a wheel chair. Marriott made Humble Pie one of the most popular touring acts on the American circuit in the early Seventies, reformed Small Faces in 1976 and 1978, and toured throughout the Eighties with a succession of less well-known line-ups including Packet Of Three. He died in a fire in his house in Arkesden, Essex on April 20, 1991.

For the first-time ever, this is the true story of the Small Faces, from their formation in late 1964 until their acrimonious demise in early 1969, as told in their own words. We used an interview with Ian "Mac" McLagan conducted by frequent Goldmine contributor Ken Sharp in February, 1996, in Philadelphia while Mac was on tour with Rod Stewart, as the basic template for this piece. Small Faces expert John Hellier, who publishes the "The Darlings of Wapping Wharf Launderette E.1" fanzine in England,

contributed three unpublished interviews with Steve Marriott from the Eighties; the primary source is from an interview Hellier conducted with him in Sawbridgeworth, Hertfordshire on 24 February 1984, and additional material is from Neil Morgan on 20 July 1987 was used, along with a few quotes from the third piece. We also used a radio interview from KLBJ with Marriott conducted by Ed Mayberry that was taped when Packet of Three played Austin in the October of 1986. Ronnie Lane is featured in several interviews from Jody Denberg, currently the program director for AAA radio station KGSR in Austin; the bulk of the material was culled from a KLBJ "Critic's Choice" program from 13 April 1986, and from an interview by Kent Benjamin for Austin television taped on 5 March 1988. Kenney Jones was interviewed by Ken Sharp and Kent Benjamin at his home in England in April 1996. This piece was transcribed, compiled, and edited by Kent Benjamin in Austin in March-April, 1996; the explanatory notes in parentheses are Kent's.

CAST OF CHARACTERS:
Steve Marriott: vocals, guitar, keyboards for Small Faces
Ronnie "Plonk" Lane: vocals, bass for Small Faces
Ian "Mac" McLagan: Hammond organ, piano, occasional guitar, vocals for Small Faces
Kenney Jones: drummer for Small Faces
Jimmy Winston: original organist/rhythm guitarist, and vocals for Small Faces
Don Arden: original Small Faces manager during the Decca years
Andrew Loog Oldham: Immediate Records co-owner, 2nd manager of the Small Faces, and manager of the Rolling Stones
Tony Calder: co-owner and publicist of Immediate Records

FROM THE BEGINNING:

KEN SHARP: Not much is known about the bands you and Ronnie Lane had before the Small Faces, the Pioneers and the Outcasts. Could you give us a little background on that?

KENNEY JONES: (Laughs) It's hard to remember back that far! When I was learning to play drums -- I taught myself to play drums -- for the first three months of me learning how to play drums there was a local pub up the road from me in Stepney, East London, called The British Prince, and I used to go there when I was 13 years old. I pretended I was older, obviously, and sat there watching this band, which was a jazz band, basically. I went there every weekend for a month or so, and when the band took a break, the drummer came over to me and said "why do you keep looking at me", and I said "well, I'm learning to play the drums, and I'm watching you 'cause I'm picking up a few tips, you know". And he went "oh right", and he got to know me over the next couple of weeks, and then one weekend the band stopped playing, and the drummer said "OK, we've got a very special guest that's gonna come up and play...", and I looked around and went "oh, who's that then...". And then he called out my name! And I'd never played with anyone before in me life. I sat behind the drum and they counted me in, and I was actually sitting there kind of mesmerized because I was actually in time with everyone, and I'd never played before. After I finished playing, I went back to the table and the barman of the club came up to me and he said "my brother is playing guitar, and he's looking to start a band. Do you want me to bring him down next week?". And I said yeah. So next weekend I was there and in walks this guy, looking like one of The Beatles with a starched collar and tie, long hair -- looking great, sort of mod, you know, real early mod. And every time he turned his head, the tie and the starched collar stayed exactly the same in the front, you know -- it was quite weird. And that was Ronnie Lane. The two of us headed off and started off talking about music, and just liked each other straight away. It was just meant to be, you know! When I saw him for the first time, it was like I already knew 'im -- like I'd known him all my life.

RONNIE LANE: I'd met Kenney Jones earlier on. My brother introduced me to Kenney, who used to sneak into this public house and sit in with the band now and then, and Stanley, my brother, said: "...he's pretty good - you ought to check him out...", so I already knew Kenney.

KENNEY JONES: Ronnie was already talking to a couple of guys, and basically the outcome was we formed this band called The Outcasts.

KEN SHARP: Did you do original material or was it mostly covers in those days?

KENNEY JONES: It was mainly covers, because we were learning how to play. It was more important to learn how to play than to write songs. Although Ronnie was writing, too -- he was bravely beavering away.

KEN SHARP: Your first band was the Blue Men, and you were the singer?

IAN MCLAGAN: Yeah, no, I played the tea chest bass or the washboard, whatever, it was a skiffle group. Lonnie Donnegan was like the father of English rock in one way, you know, 'cause he started this craze...actually Chris Barber was the father of us all, he was in Chris Barber's band or was it Ken Collier's band, no, Ken Collier and him formed this group within Chris Barber's band, and they had a couple of tracks that were on Chris Barber's album and they became hits. Basically he was doing a kind of, skiffle was folk, it was kind of rockin' in a way, it was fast but it wasn't rock, it was kind of folk and blues, it was a strange mixture... you could play two chords on the guitar and you were laughing, I couldn't do that. D'ya know what a tea chest is? You'd get a chest with a broomstick and a piece of string on it and bum bum bum bum.... well everyone was into that, because it was easy. You know, a washboard and some thimbles, and away you went.

KEN SHARP: Were you playing keyboards at that time?

IAN MCLAGAN: Oh no, no, much later, I was about 11 or 12 when I was in the Blue Men, and that band didn't last very long, we was in a coupla little three-song shows, that was it really...

KEN SHARP: So you were called the Pioneers and then you were called The Outcasts? Or was it the other way around.

KENNEY JONES: It's a bit confusing. We were called the Pioneers a bit then we were called the Muleskinners for a bit.

KEN SHARP: Like Mac's band The Muleskinners?

KENNEY JONES: Yeah....but then lots of bands in them days was called The Pioneers, so then we were called The Outcasts. We only had the name The Pioneers for about five minutes. I was about 14 or 15 at the time. I lied to Ronnie and told him I was 16, and I was actually barely 14. But Ronnie says to me later "I always knew you'd lied".

IAN MCLAGAN: The Muleskinners was my first proper band, you know, that was because of "Muleskinner Blues", which was by, who was that now? I didn't play piano in the first band, I played rhythm guitar. 'Cause I had a guitar, and I never figured out how to use it, really, it went out of tune and I couldn't tune it so I dropped it again, I put it away. Eventually I met a guy at school -- Terry Monroe -- who played three chords and his mate Alan Worrell was the drummer -- he was in the Blue Men as well. He had real drums, and his mate John Eaton played two chords, and I learned one chord, so we'd do songs where I'd be on the first chord, then there'd be two other on the second chord.... Actually that wasn't the Muleskinners, that was an offshoot skiffle group, but I met four of the members that later became the Muleskinners in art school - two of them were in a band together called the Cherokees, and my mate Dave Pether played lead guitar - was real clever at that - and taught me a bit of rhythm guitar and showed me some chords, and I was his rhythm guitarist for a short while, and then Pete Brown, who was also at art school was his bass player. And then, after a bit I started to turn them on to Muddy Waters and Howlin' Wolf and Jimmy Reed and shit, 'cause I could do a basic (mimics sound of blues song), so I turned the group around basically, and changed the name and became a blues group. And...Johnny Eaton who played the two chords in that skiffle group became our singer. I was quite a finagler, y'know, I didn't realize it at the time, but you look back and you think "what a pushy little bastard...". You know, you don't know you're doing it but it's just like, going straight ahead...

I was into the blues, and I met a guy at a party. He said "oh you like the blues". I said yeah. It was a Saturday night all-nite party. He said, "oh there's a great blues band playing up in Richmond...". We were in Twickenham, about three miles away, y'see. I said: "...blues group? Oh you're kidding," "Yeah they play every Saturday", "Fuck - I wanna see 'em". So I met him later the next day and we went down to see the band -- he didn't tell me they were a white band - I figured a blues band is all black men, y'know from Chicago or from the South, and it was the Stones. I couldn't fuckin' believe it! I found my membership card last time I was in England from when I went to see them, and it was like 16th of May, 1963, 'cause it expired 16th of May 1964. They started (sings line like "I'm a Man"), and I walked down there and they're young fuckin' white guys. And I thought "...well maybe we can do it". The night I saw them I thought, well, it's possible. then I knew it was possible. I was playing and stuff, I mean we was playin' blues, but when I saw the Stones it was straight ahead from there, you know. I'd go see 'em every week, and I'd follow them around London you know. They were so great! They were rockin'!. The whole thing was a big sweaty experience, and it was a fast drinking experience for me 'cause I wanted to catch every note they played so I'd get

there early every week. Right in the back there's a dance hall in a very small room, and a bar in a corner in the back. It was the Station Hotel in Richmond, the hall called the Bull and Bush. But...you'd go in there and you'd order a pint quick, me and my mate Johnny Eaton, and force our way out -- really there'd be a crowd of people -- fuckin' push your way to get a pint, and then crowd your way to the stage and stand there. Then the band would start playing and you'd finish your pint, and on the last note you'd run past everybody else, get your pint, and then drink it down. Two pint night! And at the end of the hour you'd be so fuckin' drunk 'cause it was just so exhilarating, you know!

Well, when Johnny Eaton left the group at some point, we had Nick Tweddell, also from art school on harp, and Mick Carpenter on drums, who was Dave's old friend from the other group, from the original group The Cherokees. It was just the five of us, but then Johnny Eaton left and we auditioned a load of singers. 'Cause I was thinkin' of it-- I mean, I was kind of professional in one way, but I was still at art school. The four of us were still at art school. But I was trying to take it further, I mean basically, I was thrown out of art school because I was never there. I mean, we'd have gigs, and I'd be drinking and up late, and would miss the first half of school. As soon as I found you could miss school and all you had to do was have a note, I became a professional. And I just never went. I didn't see the point in it. I had to do the fourth year twice. I mean, the thrill wore off. As soon as I found that there was no work for me -- I mean I was OK, I wasn't great at what I did, but I enjoyed it. But as soon as I realized when I met other kids at school who had graduated and were earning small money and spendin' most of it on fares to get to the West End London office where their jobs were, and not doing anything but making tea for the real artists and designers. And these guys were great, too, so I thought what the fuck hope is there for me gettin' a job, so I thought, fuck this! So I used to just drink, and I booked the band. I booked the Stones for the art school, and I booked Rod (Stewart) with the Brian Auger Trinity. So I eventually got thrown out, and I fought, did the artwork in the summer holidays, got accepted back into art school, got the grant, and then fucked off and became a professional musician. I got to town every day, and haunted the Stones office for more work every day from their agent, Eric Easton. And I got the band opening for the Stones on a short tour around England. And at that point, I was singin'! It wasn't very good (laughing). I was even doing ridiculous things like Mick! Embarrassing!

So then we got a real singer in, Terry Brennan. And this is all happening in about 6-9 months and a year --

'63-64 -- and we got him in and he was a real soulful singer, he had a lot of great records and stuff. After a bit, I thought I figured this out on guitar, let me see if I can figure it out on piano. I got a Hohner pianet at home -- no, it was a Cymbalet, which was even worse. You would hit the keys no matter how soft or loud and it was all the same volume, so you can't play gentle with it. If you hit it, it don't make it any louder. So, I played it for a bit and.....it's all in the book, folks. As soon as I heard "Green Onions" by Booker T and the MG's, I said what the fuck is that? I want that! That was the first time I heard a Hammond organ -- that's when I first realized that was a Hammond organ.

I picked it up pretty quick. I saw an ad for a Hammond organ, free two weeks on approval to go home. So I had some balls, I said yeah, I'll have that Hammond organ for two weeks, and they brought it down. I wasn't at college, my parents didn't know I wasn't at college. They brought it down and I had to explain it to my dad later that day. After two weeks, the guys had to sign the forms, and I bought one.

See on the piano, you got to be clever, and on the Hammond you can hit a chord and hold it -- you don't have to do too much with it. Of course, the trick is to do something with that. So I started playing it, and soon after that I was offered a job playing with another band -- we used to play at the Marquee a lot. That was the Boz People, and they saw me play there -- their manager did; they asked me if I would join this band, and Muleskinners were doing OK, but this was serious. I was with them about five months and realized they were a bunch of losers -- I mean, they didn't care. And then I got a phone call to join the Small Faces.

FOUR SMALL FACES:

KENNEY JONES: Ronnie was playing a Gretsch guitar, and he was playing rhythm, a bit of lead. Very early in the band he said to me "I don't want to play lead guitar". He was very quick to notice he had limitations on it, and he would prefer to play bass. So I said "alright, let's go up to the shop where I bought my drum kit, called the J60 in the East End". And we went up there, it was a Saturday morning, and this guy was in there, real cocky little guy, and it was like instantly "I know you -- I've known you all my life" sort of feeling.

RONNIE LANE: The Small Faces got together originally in 1964. (Ed. 1965) In London at the time, nobody wanted to play the bass. The bass was not an attractive instrument,

actually. I thought though, I don't know why everyone's so shy of the bass -- it had to be an ego trip, right? They had to be the lead guitarist or the singer, no one wanted to be the bass guitarist. I had a guitar, had just about learned to play it, but I knew if I had a bass, I'd always be able to find work. I spoke to me father, who'd bought me this guitar for a lot of money, I said there's a bass down the road, it's not much money, and I said "...If I get this bass, I can pay for my guitar, I know I can...". So he said "well alright son", and we went down to this shop to buy this Harmony bass I'd seen for 40 pounds, and I went into the shop and this guy came up and said: "Can I help you sir?", and I said I'd like to have a look at that Harmony bass over there. He said "oh, that's the best bass in the shop...". I got on well with this guy, and he had some great records of Stax and Motown. It turned out to be Steve Marriott. So I said why don't you take my guitar, and I'll take this bass and we'll start a group. So he said okay! It's funny, that bass guitar - making the decision to play the bass, started the Small Faces.

KENNEY JONES: And Steve got a load of basses out for Ronnie to try, and I got behind a drum kit, and we were playing right there in the shop. Annoying everyone, basically. We invited him to our gig in the evening, a pub in Bermondsey.

STEVE MARRIOTT: When Kenney met me he said he'd had a dream or something, and he got in the van and I was sitting there as a friend of Ronnie's, and he sort of backed off, and I said "What's the matter" to him, and he said "You ain't gonna believe this. I've never seen you before, but I had this dream and your face was in it". It's weird, innit? He said he dreamed that they were playing somewhere huge with me, and he said "You were there!" And it was Ronnie and him and me. He couldn't see anyone else. Strange -- that's something we've never been able to explain. It sounds ridiculous, but Kenney's too straight to make up anything like that. And he told me about it straight out on the way to their gig in Bermondsey. Small Faces were a fated group!

KENNEY JONES: We got in the van, got there and set the equipment up, and we got him up on stage on the piano, and he broke the keys all off the piano, he got really carried away. The rest of the band members looked at Ronnie and I in absolute disgust, like "God, what've you done here -- we're gonna all get thrown out". And sure enough, we lost the gig, he threw us all out. We'd brought the house down, it was a great gig, but we'd broken his piano. In the end the band all sort of went off, they didn't like it, and there was the three of us. I had my drum kit, Ronnie had his new bass and amplifier, and we're sitting outside on the curb, everyone else had gone home. So me Ronnie and Steve looked at each other and thought "Right! We'll form our own band". And that was the start of the band. Steve took over the payments on Ronnie's Gretsch guitar.

STEVE MARRIOTT: The Outcasts were Ronnie's group when I first met him. We got paralytic when Ronnie had me first play with them. I don't know if it was nerves or what or friendship or both. We got paralytic and went on stage. I can't remember much of it, but I think I smashed the piano up or something -- Jerry Lee Marriott impressions. I was banging the shit out of it, jumping on top of it. They lost out on the residency gig that they had at this pub in Bermondsey -- I know it was in Bermondsey. George was the singer, but I can't remember much about him. He was there, and he sang a bit and that was about it. He looked more like a plumber or something. Ronnie and Kenney left the Outcasts, I think. So we said, "let's form a band of our own". Either that or they semi-left and semi-got booted because of the way that pub gig turned out with them losing the residency. And Ronnie lost his job about the same time at Selmer's because he was trying to get me a free P.A. It was for The Moments, the band I was with. So I'd go down there and he'd be testing P.A.s and going, like "...free P.A. for Marriott", and they sacked him for it.

I remember the next job he had was running errands for the War Office or something like that, or the Home Office. So we were sitting in the Giaconda looking at maps of Polaris submarine bases. We opened the tube, and it had brown sauce all over it by the time we'd rolled it back up again. I think Ronnie had to deliver it somewhere -- it was on its way from "A" to "B". And it just sort of got diverted -- we couldn't believe it. I'm not sure we planned to meet there that day. He knew I used to hang out there and I think he may have just popped in, 'cos he was just around the corner, to see if I was there. I'd hang out there because it was like Tin Pan Alley. If people wanted demos made, they'd say "Can anybody play drums?" and someone would say "Yes, I can" and we'd put our hand up immediately for anything. It was at least a few quid in your pocket. That's why a lot of us used to hang out there. I'd do anything: drums, vocals, harmonicas, backing vocals, guitar, bass, anything. I don't really remember any of the things I worked on - most of it was foul! There were some good writers around, and they, like, favoured me for singing their demos.

They were, I think, publisher's demos, not recordings as such.

Did Ronnie tell you of the job we had washing up at Lyon's Corner House? I was only there a couple of days, four I think, and I didn't drop anything, much less dishes. I got pissed off with it and the staff there were mad. My hands went all brown and the skin started falling off because of the bleach they used to wash their shit up with. And I used to have to wash them and Ronnie'd rack them and push them though a shower. It was a nightmare -- just a conveyor belt of eggs and bacon and shit. It's horrible. I think we got 8 quid a week, and Ronnie stayed on to get his full week's wages, but I pissed off. I couldn't handle it. There used to be this mad Scotsman who used to go around with a knife all the time when he was working in there. And this other mad woman used to turn on all the gas taps and giggle. It was crazy! And the Scotsman would pick up a carving knife and yell "I'll fucking kill the bitch" and go after the one who turned on the taps. It was fucking mad!

I found Jimmy Winston. He used to come to the J60 the same way as Ronnie, but he was more of a regular. I think his parents were tenants at the Ruskin Arms, I'm not sure; it was a great pub. I went around the pub once and he was mucking about on guitar. He was proficient on guitar, more so than me I think at the time. His family were much more well-off than mine, so he had some decent equipment. I didn't even have a guitar until I took over Ronnie's payments. I played a little bit of piano at the time. He had an organ too, you see, and a van -- which was the big thing. He used to fight a lot. I remember he always got into fights, over chicks probably, I have no idea, but he was always scuffling. Jimmy played with me in The Moments.

Basically Small Faces formed for bar mitzvahs and weddings as a generalism. Any chance to play -- not trying to make it. Just to have a laugh. I think we might have done one wedding or something. I thing we did one at Loughton -- we played at a chick's wedding, and she jumped over the balcony. This was before we went North, but it wasn't a gig. This was where we were living and they had a party at the house, and we just had the equipment there so we played. I was living there with Mick O'Sullivan and his friends from acting school, and Ronnie'd sleep there sometimes, and when Kenney'd come over we'd have a little play. Mick got a writing credit on one of our songs, he was living with us later at Pimlico. (I got) a Marshall -- either a 50-Watt or an 100-Watt - the old ones with the big cooker knobs on it, black and white. It was massive for those days. We were loud, notoriously loud! If you can't play, play loud!

I don't know where Terry the Egg came from, I suppose he must have been an acquaintance of mine, not a friend, and he ended up doing some roadie work for us and driving us about. We had done about four gigs in London before we went North, including the wedding and some working men's clubs. In Manchester we did the Twisted Wheel, a r'n'b club -- that was the first gig on the trip. I don't think they'd ever seen Mods before. There were a few on the border, but not quite as into it as we were at the time. We were all dressing Mod at the time -- it didn't have anything to do with the money, it had everything to do with how you wore what you had, you know. We were totally into it. During the gig, some bastard lent our black van out for an hour, and came back with a fucking load of leather coats in the back -- done a job when we were playing. Me and Ronnie and Kenney all got a leather coat out of it!

In Sheffield they kicked us out after the first couple of songs. While we were playing all these old members shouted out. I remember this one old girl. I said "I'd like to do a number by James Brown" and this old woman - to me she seemed old, she must have been around forty - started screaming. She loved it! She was hip, so we kind of played to her, the only one in the audience who know what we were doing. And the guy just slung us off after about three numbers. Paid us off and told us to piss off. We also played at the Esquire club, a trendy blues club. We played the next night at the Mojo -- the biggest club we'd played -- 'cos they put us up for the night. It was a great club, it really was. A very appreciative crowd. Very much a Mod club. I think we only did the one gig there until we had a hit record, then it was all over. It wasn't very long after, just a matter of months, that we hit. We were their band -- it was like they discovered us, so they went crazy when we went back. They used to go fucking berserk whenever we played there -- we used to play two sets a night for a couple of nights. It was a special place for us, because of the crowd and because they did give us a break when no one else was willing to do so.

RONNIE LANE: We had a guy called Terry the Egg, he was our agent, and he got us a residency at the Cavern Club in Leicester Square -- which wasn't the Cavern Club in Liverpool, though it was obviously taken from that -- it was beneath a church, I think it was. Anyway, we played there for three or four weeks, and even though we was kinda busking, we got very popular, you know! We pulled in more of a crowd each week, and in the end a guy called Don Arden turned up, and he signed us up as a manager. We

was all kind of excited, you know, 'cause he'd had Gene Vincent. He'd had him. He had us, as well, but we didn't know that then. He got us a contract, and put us in a studio and we made our first record, "Whatcha Gonna Do About It?", which Ian Samwell penned. Don Arden introduced us to Ian Samwell as well; he was a good guy, Ian Samwell. Then that was it....

STEVE MARRIOTT: We played the first Cavern Club gig that weekend after we got back to London, or the next weekend. I think we went down there and blagged the guy for the gig -- went and chatted to see if we could play there once. The manager, an Irishman, kept saying "Can you do two more" and we'd have to repeat. We only knew about five numbers. He saw the crowd reaction and said we'd be playing there the following week as well, and then the following week. We had about five gigs, a little residency going -- I think it was on Saturdays -- before we were sort of snatched out of there. During that time we got a lot of notoriety amongst club managers and organizations. I think it was our energy, we had a lot of energy -- a lot of push-- and a little bit of flair, which was missing on the scene. I think that's what it was. We were little Mods, and by that time devout. Arm-flingers, feedback players. And I think it had a lot of charisma just to look at. The size of us, and the kind of music we were doing coming out of these little people.

We had that place packed every time after the first time we played there. Kit Lambert came down to see one gig and got a lot of flak from The Who because he was going to take us on at one point. And then Maurice King, and then last of all -- I think they all came down at different times -- and last of all was Don Arden. He was the one who actually got ahold of us. A chick from Arden's office spotted us, his secretary. She just happened to be around. I'd seen her before at the Starlight Club that Maurice King used to own off of Oxford Street. And that chick had seen me down there, too. We had done some rehearsals down there. Like Maurice King was interested in me at the time, so I asked him if we could use his place to rehearse. Kenney's playing at that time wasn't too clever at all. Up until that time, I was used to sort of playing with older people. Small Faces were all sort of the same age, and the other bands I'd been in were sort of older, more experienced musicians. He was OK but I didn't realize that it was the material that he was playing. He set his drums up, and we were just farting around and he just went berserk! For about a half hour he made Ronnie and me just kill ourselves laughing! And we were giving him the encouragement "go on, my son!". And he really opened up. It was like a different drummer -- he just got better and better and better. As he is today, one of the best drummers around. It really was an eye-opener, and there was no looking back. Every song we did swung like Hanratty. I don't know what it was, it was like a revelation. It was to Ronnie and me, I'm sure, because we just couldn't believe it!

KENNEY JONES: When I first started playing drums, I remember never learning anything. When we formed the Small Faces, I wasn't surpressed. As soon as I got behind a kit, it all came out. I was given absolute freedom of expression. Nobody told me ever, not once, what to play. And it was almost as if I knew what was going to come next, sheer natural telepathy....

STEVE MARRIOTT: So Don Arden's secretary asked for my number, where I was staying in Loughton. I don't think we were on the phone, 'cos I remember going to call boxes to make calls. They got hold of my mother. I'd make a call to my mother once a week to be sure she didn't worry about me too much -- living on my own was still frightening to her, I think. So she said this office has been trying to get ahold of you, Don Arden, whoever he is. I knew about him, had seen his name on blues posters, because he used to bring over Jimmy Reed and John Lee Hooker, people like that. So I was very impressed with that. Told Ronnie about it, called them, and they came down to see us at the Cavern Club -- Pat Meehan came down.

And Ronnie and I had just taken a terrible beating. We were a bit exhausted and it was freezing, and we got off the bus, and there was this van following us with six or seven chaps who must have been about twenty or something, which was old to us then. They were like skinheads, and we were Mods. So they jumped out of this van and beat the shit out of us. They beat the shit out of me with a bottle -- we found out later what caused it, but at the time we had no idea. They did Ronnie with this bit of wood that had a nail in it, so he had a hole in his forehead, and I've still got this scar on my forehead from the bottle which I used to use as a parting -- I got into using it as a parting for my hair when I had bangs on the front. We were covered in blood, really badly beaten -- kicked to bits, heads bleeding. We found out later that a couple of boys from Loughton had gone down to Tottenham and smashed up a few cafes and stuff, so this was a return visit. We were just bystanders. I was floored, on the ground, and Ronnie's got this hole in his head, and we've got blood spouting everywhere and in the shock of it we couldn't stop laughing

about it to each other. We were blowing bubbles with the blood, and laughing. We went to the Woodford Hospital, and we were still laughing from the shock. This nurse came out, and I'll never forget the line, said: "Be quiet! This is a hospital" which hurt us that much more because we couldn't stop laughing again. So they wouldn't do anything. They threw us out saying it was a maternity hospital anyway and we didn't have any right to be in there! And the next day we had an audition when we were playing the Cavern Club for Don Arden. It was fucking hilarious! Every time Ronnie hit a high note singing, his fucking stitches would open up and the blood would be running down. My face looked like a gargoyle, two black eyes, very fat lips, stitched up head. They liked us, apparently! I think this was the last time we played the Cavern, although there could have been one more.

KEN SHARP: What do you remember about the film Dateline Diamonds? It was great seeing the band with Jimmy Winston. (Small Faces appear in the 1965 film performing "I Got Mine" with Jimmy Winston on guitar.)

KENNEY JONES: Well, I haven't seen it actually.... I'll never forget doing the film because it was the launch of the great group wagon - the van, you know. A transit van. They launched it in that film, they kept it under wraps, under a sheet. We saw it and said we want one, so we went straight home and bought one. It was a bandwagon, you know, where you put all the gear in, the amps, the drums, and you all get in and go to the gig and have a laugh.

RONNIE LANE: Our original organist, Jimmy Winston, wasn't working out. He couldn't play -- I mean, none of us could play, but we was keen. Jimmy Winston couldn't play, and on top of it he had an ego as if he could play the piano, so he had to go! We chucked him out of the Small Faces. Very exciting times, the Sixties, there'll never be another time like it, I'm sure.

STEVE MARRIOTT: We had to sack him (Jimmy Winston), really. We told Jimmy the same day that we met with Mac, or Don Arden did. I don't think I did. I know he came to the radio show at the Lyceum where we had to mime in front of a live audience. I can't remember the name of the show but it was an evening show. And he came down there and was asking why and he got very upset about it. I think Don Arden would have told him. And I said, "Sorry mate, but it's just not working out between us all, and we've got a new kid and everything". I tried to be as honest about it as possible. The guy on the train who talked with Mac didn't know that there was a vacancy in the group. He said to Mac "You should join the Small Faces" he said jokingly "'cos you look like one". That was the story and the next day he got a call from Don Arden on the Monday to come to the office. Don met him first for a bit, and then we met him later on in the afternoon, shook hands, kitted him out with some gear, got his barnet cut. Might have gotten cut the next day when we had that show, got him a Telecaster. got the clothes down in Carnaby Street, it was still good down in Carnaby Street then. I think it was over the weekend that we stayed in the hotel to keep out of Jimmy's way, 'cos we knew then that we were looking for somebody to replace him. It had got a bit much. We weren't even speaking, so it was silly to continue. He got very moody. He actually used to call himself James Moody before he started using the Winston. But James Moody gives you a picture of the guy: collar up, coat on, shades. We were too busy being lunatics to take things as seriously as he was.

RONNIE LANE: Ian McLagan we saw in a magazine, [Ed. Beat Instrumental] and I said he looks like one of us. And we asked our manager Don Arden to call (McLagan), and sure enough, he wasn't really doing anything so he started to play with the Small Faces.

IAN MCLAGAN: Don Arden called me. I'd seen the Small Faces on Ready Steady Go! I thought they were great. My dad called me down because Ready Steady Go! came on about 5:30-6pm, and I was upstairs getting ready to go out and he says "Here Ian, come 'ere and check this band out -- this bloke looks just like you". And within about 4-5 months, I was in the band. There was a photograph of Boz which they used -- he was a handsome guy, and he was singing bad jazz at that time, and there was a photograph of him in a review of the Boz People that raved about me, and they thought it was me because my name was under the picture. So, when the Small Faces were looking to get rid of Jimmy Winston, so they thought, "Oh, let's check this bloke out -- he's good lookin' and he plays great Hammond...." They wanted the Hammond in the band, you know, and Jimmy Winston really couldn't play. They got me into the office, they were checking me out, one at a time around the door, and I didn't know which band it was for, or if it was for a session or what. (Arden) had the Animals, the Nashville Teens, the Clayton Squares, the Small Faces, I thought: "...ain't gonna be the Animals 'cause Dave Robey just joined, don't know about the Clayton Squares, Nashville Teens got a piano player, ain't gonna

be the Small Faces. And it was! So later that day I joined the band. Steve and Ronnie Lane just picked me up and hugged me, and we just laughed 'cause we were all the same size.

KEN SHARP: So you hit it off pretty quickly?

IAN MCLAGAN: Yeah, immediately. I can't explain to you....it's like being picked up, pulled out of your life...I'd always dreamed that some day I'd become famous.

KEN SHARP: It's like it was fated - everyone loved each other and it was like a gang -- usually people are friendly or whatever, but a band's like a business arrangement....

IAN MCLAGAN: Yeah, it's been disappointing ever since -- I mean, the Faces were like that too, we were very close, at least while Ronnie Lane was still in the band. The only band I know that with no regard for the audience, I mean, like fuck them if they don't like it, we're here to have fun...never rehearsing. We used to have the expression: "fuck the gig...here's a pub let's have a drink, then two drinks later it was all downhill, and we'd go home. It's horrible, really, but...."

KEN SHARP: Your first gig with Small Faces was with Radio Luxembourg and you had to mime?

IAN MCLAGAN: "Ready Steady Radio", and I had to mime the guitar part to "I Got Mine" (Ed. note: the song originally featured Jimmy Winston on guitar with Steve), and Jimmy Winston showed up. It was kinda sad...he was fine with me, but I think he's still bitching about it (getting fired). I think he should fuckin' get a life....

KEN SHARP: What's the story about you getting paid more than the rest of the band?

IAN MCLAGAN: I know if you've heard this from Paolo Hewitt....he tells some stories that are just totally untrue. I know the stories Paolo is trying to tell but he's heard them from someone else and he always gets the stories completely wrong. Don Arden said to me: "...how much are you earning at the moment..." and I was getting five pound a week. We weren't actually...I mean the Boz People.... My dad was earning a good wage for the time at 20 pound a week -- I think doctors were making about 50 pound a week -- my dad was a works manager at an auto shop, and he made 20 pound a week. A good wage, a fair wage...so when Arden asked me I lied through my teeth and told 'im: "Twenty pound a week" with a straight face. So he said "ya start at thirty". Now if I'd said thirty he wouldn't have believed me, he'd have given me twenty or fifteen. He thought he was a gangster, he used to be a singer, but he liked to believe he was an American gangster - like James Cagney. He was a thief, he was a thief to us, and he is a thief to this day. But before, on stage, he used to do impressions, and he used to do James Cagney. So when he'd go into his little spiel he'd become a James Cagney kind of thing, but he believed it. James Cagney was acting, you know, but he'd believe it...so he said: "...ya start at thirty, and you're on probation for a month, and if everything goes alright, ya get an even split with the band". So a couple of months went by, and at this point I'm living with Ronnie and Steve (see: Party Central), and eventually I said to Ronnie like, "well...not going to happen, right?". And he said: "what choo talking about?". So I said "I'm on probation right?" And Ronnie said, "aaahhh, that's bullshit! Fuckin' probation! Let's go up to Don's office...". So we go in, Ronnie points at me, and says: "...Here Don, he's on the same money as us, alright!? He's in the band". And from that point onwards I got 20 pound a week 'cause that's what they were earning. And I never said anything either, never said anything until the Faces days when I broke it to Ronnie, and he laughed....

KEN SHARP: So you were getting paid 20 pounds a week? Did you have like expense accounts like at clothing stores?

IAN MCLAGAN: Yeah, we had expense accounts. We had to, we were doing television shows every week - you couldn't wear the same clothes. We were doing like two shows a night sometimes, and a television show; you couldn't go on in the same clothes. That wasn't where our money went - that's what someone suggested. That's bullshit! We were earning millions! We've estimated --our accountants have estimated -- that we've lost somewhere in the amount of 12-15 million pounds! When I saw it was lost, it was stolen from us, so I mean, you buy twenty shirts -- that ain't gonna do it....

GLORY DAYS:

KEN SHARP: In 1966 when the Small Faces were really starting to tour and happen, the Beatles and the Stones were pretty much not touring in England, or off overseas, and the Small Faces were kept constantly busy by Decca touring, doing radio, doing television, recording...does it surprise you that you were able to sustain it? to survive it? I know Ronnie and Steve both collapsed at one point....

IAN MCLAGAN: See...all the bands I was in up until there, I could never get enough work, and to play in front of a crowd...The Muleskinners we had to work hard, humping the gear and all, and now, I didn't have to hump gear, all I had to do was play. Hello! And could play every day and we did play every day. And when we occasionally had a day off, we'd get more wrecked. We were taking alot of pills to keep going, and smoking dope to relax, and you can't do that for....I did it from 1963-64 until 1985....but when you finally got a chance to work, no one in that band said no. It was like: "Yes!!!" We were going faster than anyone could possibly handle. We'd take as much work as we could possibly get.

KEN SHARP: What were gigs like that back then? Could you actually hear? What was the audience breakdown -- more guys than girls?

IAN MCLAGAN: More girls. And sometimes you'd have guys there kinda gettin' the needle too, because their girlfriend was lookin' at you, but we did have guys who were there for the music, and girls who were there for the look. More girls than guys, though.

RONNIE LANE: We was teenyboppers! We was in our late teens, it was weird, really weird, not like anything I've experience before or since, to have thousands of chicks screaming, and if they got ahold of you they'd tear you to pieces man.

JODY DENBERG: So did that mean you had to be careful who you approached?

RONNIE LANE: Well.....not that careful!

KEN SHARP: How long would you guys play?

IAN MCLAGAN: It got shorter and shorter the bigger you became. It's like the more famous you are, the less you have to pay for equipment. That doesn't make any sense. Equipment -- like, we didn't have to buy equipment, I mean I bought my guitar that time, but... we used to play about an hour, at the most, but then it became forty minutes, then two twenty minute slots. We'd play a few minutes then someone would break through the barrier and it would get out of control and we'd have to quit.

KEN SHARP: Could you hear yourselves?

IAN MCLAGAN: You couldn't hear much, it was all screaming. We would go on and play. Now, you go on and do the hits, but they wouldn't even listen, they were screaming, you know, it was a funny old scene -- it was like they were watching television. You know, I got to straighten this out -- Paolo told this story that girls would pee themselves -- now what the fuck is that, that's bullshit. The truth of the matter is -- we saw this a lot -- girls down in front row would be fiddling themselves. And it's like a kid with television -- it's like they're watching something, no connection with it at all -- I still see this today, it's like they're not seeing Rod so much as they're completely separate to it, until he's within their grasp and then they grab for 'im. And they don't even seem to grasp that you can see them -- I mean they're in the front row! And it was overwhelming, it wasn't the smell of pee, it was overwhelming. It's like strippers -- now I know how they feel when there's guys out in front touching themselves as if they can't be seen. It was ugly. It was horrible. We were sex objects.

KENNEY JONES: You couldn't hear yourselves. Girls would sit in front and diddle themselves. It never went away. Well, it went away briefly because we sort of buried ourselves in the studio a lot, and we were always playing abroad and what not. But it haunted us. Although we had to like it, because it was a way of showing appreciation. You couldn't knock it on the one hand, but it became irritating on the other. Because all we wanted to do was play to 'em, and say "listen to the music, you know, and then scream at the end...". But it never happened that way.

STEVE MARRIOTT: It was mad. It was a bunch of noise, a bunch of screaming little girls. It wasn't like today where people actually listen. It was just a screaming row. The P.A.'s were sort of archaic, you could never hear. Monitors to me were people who brought the milk round at school! You used to stick your finger in your ear to hear yourself properly.

KEN SHARP: How about now? Does the same thing still happen? Would you welcome it?

IAN MCLAGAN: Naahh! We never welcomed it then, it

wasn't pleasant. I mean, they were watching something that wasn't happening -- they were watching a screen.

KEN SHARP: Did the rest of the band feel that way? Did they want to be treated more like musicians?

IAN MCLAGAN: These were pubescent girls. They were 11-12-14 years old. It was unpleasant, it was overwhelming. You'd go on, you'd say, well fuck this, they're screaming, they're fiddling themselves, we're gonna play what we want to play. So we'd play anything we wanna play, we'd just jam. Jam on one chord, organ solo for ten days. Kenney and Ronnie doing this Cuban/Latin bump thing....

KEN SHARP: What British bands really forged a relationship with the Small Faces? Were the Beatles friends? Obviously the Who had to be....

IAN MCLAGAN: The Who were, but you see, the Beatles were already rock gods and we didn't bump into them....

KEN SHARP: You played with them at the NME Pollwinner's Concert in 1966...

IAN MCLAGAN: Did we? I didn't know that.... I used to hang around with the Stones, but I didn't know them. I mean, I knew Brian a bit, and Mick, they were the two friendliest. I didn't know Keith in the Muleskinners days.

KENNEY JONES: Ronnie and Steve used to bump into McCartney quite a lot in the Hippy Trippy sort of days.

KEN SHARP: Did they dig the band? Did they tell you?

IAN MCLAGAN: No. I almost met John Lennon, in the studio when the Stones were doing "We Love You" and he and Paul were doing background vocals. I was in the studio next door laying down piano tracks, and John stuck his head around the door, and I looked down at the piano, looked back up and he was gone.

KENNEY JONES: McCartney was a big, big fan. In fact, all the Beatles were big fans. I only saw John Lennon walk through Olympic studios once, sort of said hello and walked out. After the fact, I'm good friends with Ringo and Paul, and see George here and there and say hello, whatever. I've had the opportunity to play with Paul, did the Rockestra with Paul and John Bonham, one of the last things he did before he died. The Beatles were great fans, they thought they knock on the door, and then they go through, and they go out to the sort of outside loo, in back of the yard. The woman that played in it, and was holding her fist up, was my next door neighbor.

JODY DENBERG: The Small Faces did a package tour of Australia with The Who. What did you do to bring the wrath of the Australian government down on you?

STEVE MARRIOTT: Well, it was a bad rap. We did a press conference, and I put out my cigarette the only place you could, which was on the floor, so they'd pick on that. But there was no ashtrays! They called us Dirty Old Englishmen. I was seen to scratch behind my ears, but I'd caught mange off my dogs; I didn't know....so there was all this sort of bad rap. By the time we got to New Zealand, we'd just about had it with the lot of them.

RONNIE LANE: Well in actual fact, we didn't do anything that bad. The Australians back in the Sixties didn't like the English, and the press decided we were good-for-nothing type people, and they really slagged us off and said alot of things we'd done that we really didn't do. In the end, we decided we might as well do some of the things we'd been blamed for. We never did get around to some of....well, a couple of televisions did get thrown in the swimming pool, but what's that between nationalities. We obviously can't blame Keith Moon because he's deceased, and can't answer back.

STEVE MARRIOTT: The Australian trip was a total disaster. It was fun -- midgets on manoeuvres. It was fun and we had a lot of laughs on it, but we came away owing money -- smashing up rooms and stuff like that. In Wellington it was my 21st birthday, and they gave me the only suite in the hotel, which was really nice of them. Me and Keith Moon and Wiggy (John Walford, The Who's road manager, called Wiggy because he was completely bald and wore a wig) destroyed the place. I'll tell you how it started. EMI had given me a little portable record player as a birthday present, so I'd gone and bought a bunch of great records that you can get over there, because they're so far behind you could still get stuff you couldn't get in England. I started playing it and it fed back into itself and made a terrible humming sound that you couldn't get rid of, so I threw it over the balcony. And Wiggy went down and got it and I threw it over again, and before you knew it, there were chairs, TV's, settees, everything was over the balcony and through the windows -- mirrors, everything, the whole

fucking deal. There was quite an audience watching it all come down. It was ridiculous, I was hurting with laughter, it was so funny at the time -- pissed as newts. We'd be lying on the floor gasping for breath, and someone would see something that wasn't broken, and then break it and sling it over the balcony and it would start again.

Anyway, we were sort of lying there wondering what to do. When we came to, we could see what we had done -- all the French doors were gone, every window, there's nothing in the room 'cos it's all on the pavement. I think Ronnie and Pete (Townshend) were there to begin with, and Pete said to Ronnie: "This ends in the nick", and they split and left the three of us to do it -- me Moony and Wiggy. We were the culprits, I'm afraid. So I had a great idea -- "Let's say someone's broken into our room and complain about it". So that's what we did, and the police were there interviewing us and all that. So Keith Moon rings up the reception and says: "Look, what kind of security do you have? Our room's been broken into and vandalized, and we paid good money for these..." The police came and like, Wiggy was seen carrying an armchair and throwing it over. He's got a bald head, and there's this wig hanging by the bed, and they're talking to him: "Do you know a bald man?" and he'd say "No". It was simple as that, and we got out of it. I thought "great", the next night would be cool. They spent all day refurnishing this place, putting in new French windows and everything. Come the evening, Keith comes up and says "They done a great job" and immediately put an ashtray through the French windows. And off it goes again, furniture over the balcony again, see. We didn't get away with it again, not a chance. The second time it was like "Oh, God, we can't get away with it", so instead, Keith put on his bravado, which was always funny to watch. We were drinking champagne, still celebrating twenty-one, and the manager came up in his dressing gown. It was late, about three in the morning, and he said: "I know it was you this time. Who has done this?" And Keith put the manager's tie in his drink and said "I did it". Like, whatcha gonna do about it? "Moon's the name". So I think he took most of the rap for that, which he should have done really.

The party got the army round. They sent the police in first day, and we got them drunk in the room listening to Booker T. We were wearing their helmets and still smashing the place up. So they brought the Army in, and we had a man outside each door with a rifle! And if we opened the door, it was like "Get back in your room". And that was the story!

RONNIE LANE: We got on the airplane early one

morning, we'd been up raving the night before and I fell asleep on the plane. But an Australian support band was also on the plane, and they'd brought aboard a couple of cans of beer. Or, as they call them in Australia, "a couple of tubes of beer, sport..." They started drinking them, and in those days it was illegal to drink on planes. So, a couple of stewardesses took a very dim view of this, knowing it was "...that confounded English tour that was going on..." and what she'd read in the papers, so she refused to serve us any coffee. I woke up with Paul Jones (ex-Manfred Mann singer/solo artist) who was a very proper schoolboy -- not one of us geezers from the East End -- very loudly demanding his coffee. The stewardess burst into tears, and went up to the pilot and reported this whole incident. The pilot had also read the papers about what a lot of scalywags we were, and the pilot made an unscheduled landing at an airport. When we landed, there were all these police and television cameras there, and we were carted off. The television cameras was on the plane, so I said to everyone "...go out with your hands on your head, and it'll look like the plane was hijacked -- it'll look really good on TV...", so we did!

STEVE MARRIOTT: I think Paul Jones was our spokesman 'cos he spoke the better, correct English. "It didn't really have anything to do with us" he was saying, and we were making raspberries behind him. Terrible slags we were -- terrible liars. I think they let us do one more show, then we were deported. The police saw us out of their country! New Zealand was enjoyable. We got to the airport and Pete Townshend immediately smashed one press guy's camera -- throws it. Oh, here we go again! But they kind of understood, because I don't think they're too keen on Australians, either.

JODY DENBERG: So that's where you met Pete Townshend on that tour. Quite an auspicious beginning!

RONNIE LANE: Yeah, and it was a religious thing, too. I was reading a couple of Sufi books, and he was reading this book about this guy called Meher Baba, that had this thing called Sufism Reoriented. So I started to learn about Baba, and he seemed like an alright guy, and Pete and I had fun. So the song "The Stone" (a.k.a. "Evolution") came directly from Meher Baba's teachings.

STUDIO CATS

KEN SHARP: Can you talk about how the band changed so much from Decca to Immediate? Did you guys enjoy the innovation and experimentation that more studio time allowed?

IAN MCLAGAN: Well, as Ronnie Lane said in that Kent Benjamin piece, "...we could have as much studio as you wanted...", as if studio were something you could hand around "...here's some studio...". But we were given a free reign with Andrew. He at least, I mean he stole from us, but he let us get our head in the studio. Arden was like, in and out, fuck it -- we were given like three days to finish an album.

KEN SHARP: Did you guys prefer being in a studio to playing live?

IAN MCLAGAN: No, but it was opened, it was another side of us that we hadn't been able to explore, so now we could check it out a bit, and that was alot of fun. But of course, see Arden had pushed us and pushed us and pushed us like a good old fashioned manager. Whereas Oldham was more, here was a guy wearing a caftan and smoking a joint, you know, he though he was one of the Mamas and Papas in San Francisco which didn't interest me in the slightest. But it was cool in that way that he gave us room. But he didn't force us out on the road so we played less and became less of a band, and became more of a studio band which was a shame, you know?

KEN SHARP: What did Andrew provide as a producer?

IAN MCLAGAN: Dope. That's about it. We never allowed him in the studio. None of 'em, fuck no, it was the four of us. It was total bullshit; he had nothin' to do with it! The Andrew Oldham Orchestra, did you ever hear of that? He was there with a caftan and a joint. He didn't provide no arrangement, he wouldn't know how to produce a fucking paper bag.

STEVE MARRIOTT: I liked Andrew's flair -- we all did, thought it was great. He had a lot of style. They wanted us involved with all their artists -- wanted us to produce for artists, write for artists, the whole thing, you know. So, like at least we were involved with it (Immediate). We came in very handy, but I can't slag Andrew. He was a very nice man, really. He had his moments, we all did. I think Tony Calder ran that company, him and the massed bands of Tasmanian accountants. Too many accounts. And Tony Calder was basically running it -- I don't think Andrew knew what was going on, he knew up to a point, but only up to a point. Don't think he really wanted to know. Sort of hid from it. Then everybody did a runner - zoom! Men overboard.

Immediate folded. Andrew told me about it about a month before, which was nice of him. He said, "Get out now. It's going to go down. I release you of your contract". I didn't believe it at the time, but it folded about a month later. Andrew was sick of it all. Once all the accountants had moved in, his idea of running a little bastard record company, as he liked to call it, disintegrated. It was getting to be quite a major. Then it was out of his hands. All of a sudden it was a company, and he hadn't got the strength to run one like Chris Blackwell had.

THE SONGS:

STEVE MARRIOTT: To be honest with you, me and Ronnie didn't write an awful lot together. We wrote apart, just like McCartney and Lennon, Jagger and Richards, they didn't write together, they just heaped it together. "Rene (the Docker's Delight)" is probably the one me and Ronnie laughed at the most, and a thing called "HappyDaysToysTown" on "Ogden's Nut Gone Flake", we wrote that together, oh and "Itchycoo Park". We actually wrote those together. Well nigh on all the rest were written apart. I wrote "Tin Soldier", "Lazy Sunday", "All or Nothing", stuff like that. Ronnie wrote the more obscure stuff -- really great songs, good songs. I tended to write the hits as it were.

RONNIE LANE: Our first single in 1965 was "Whatcha Gonna Do About It?", which was a bit of a rip-off of "Everybody Needs Somebody to Love". We didn't have much integrity, did we?

KENNY JONES: One of the bands (on the tribute album) have covered the song "I Got Mine" and have done it just absolutely amazing. They've basically copied us, It's really Who, and I love it. I reckon if it goes on the air, it'll be a hit, and I'd love it to be a hit because it was a flop then. "I Got Mine" is a great song.

KEN SHARP: I was going to ask you about "You Need Lovin'" (from the first Decca album). Supposedly Robert Plant was a huge fan and would come to all the shows, did you remember him from those days?

IAN MCLAGAN: Oh yeah, he was a little kid, used to go out and get us cigarettes and drinks. Steve was doing Muddy Waters, we were doing "You Need Lovin'", Zeppelin got it from us.

KEN SHARP: When you hear "You Need Lovin'", Steve did his own innovations vocally on that, all the vocals Plant copied lock, stock, and barrel. How did you feel about that, were you flattered, because I don't think it ever bothered Steve too much that Zeppelin copied it?

IAN MCLAGAN: I think it's great, I think it's fine with me, it's not like they owe the Small Faces any money, if anything they should pay Muddy Waters, so should've we, you know.

STEVE MARRIOTT: Willie Dixon wrote it, called it "Woman, You Need Love" or something like that. It was fantastic, I used to love it! Muddy Waters recorded it, but I couldn't sing like Muddy Waters, so it wasn't that much of a nick. Whereas Robert Plant could sing like me. That's basically where it's at. I had to make up a lot of my own phrasing -- I couldn't sing like Muddy Waters, Long John Baldry had that down. I was a high range and Muddy was a low range, so I had to figure out how to sing it. So I did, and that was our opening number for all the years we were together, unless we had a short set. That's where Jimmy Page heard it. He asked about it, and Robert Plant used to follow us around at the time -- he was like a fan, a very nice chap. That was one of his favourites. Page, when he was playing bass with the Yardbirds at a gig in Paris, and Jeff Beck was with them -- they wanted to form a group and they asked me to come with them. I was very tempted but said "Nah that's bullshit" and didn't. But I thought they were great musicians. When I heard "Whole Lotta Love" I couldn't believe it. I was astounded, quite astounded. The phrasing was exact. I thought "Go on my son, get on with it". I couldn't believe it, but I was glad someone took it and did something with it. It was always a good song, but the phrasing was direct. As I said, he could sing like me -- he could sing a lot higher than me but he got a bit screechy -- but he took that note for note, word for word. It's terrible, innit? It's funny -- you gotta laugh.

STEVE MARRIOTT: I don't like "Sha-La-La-La-Lee", I think that's fuckin' awful. I don't like "My Mind's Eye", I think that's fuckin' awful. "Hey Girl", bordering....

IAN MCLAGAN: I think "Sha-La-La-La-Lee" sucks, I hate the organ bit in the bridge, the middle. Kenny Lynch was friend from the Boz People, and we liked him - used to back him occasionally. He was a bit of a pushy character, he was a Jack the Lad, and he had this song he'd written, and he decided he wanted to sing background on it -- I don't know why -- and he was louder than any of us -- we were all crowded around one mike doing background vocals. He's the real high (KEN SHARP: annoying...) voice on it. You know what I really like is "I Got Mine", "It's Too Late", "All or Nothing" (which I played on), "Whatcha Gonna Do About It?" I think is a fucking great record. I play that with my current band, and I always play that "Beat Beat Beat" (German TV) performance for my current so they can learn it, because a lot of 'em have heard of the Small Faces, but never really heard 'em, so I say when you're doing "Whatcha Gonna Do About It?" it's gotta have this feel, because it's fuckin' drivin' as hell.

KEN SHARP: Everyone in the band hates "Sha-La-La-La-Lee". Are you gonna be the only one who doesn't hate it?

KENNEY JONES: (Chuckles) I understand what they mean. When we were recording it, I think the reason we don't look upon it so well -- I don't think we hate it, we hate what it stands for. We had "Whatcha Gonna Do About It", the first one, it was written by Ian Samwell, and that was a hit. So we said we're gonna write the next one, and it was called "I Got Mine". It was great, and it was a flop. So Don Arden said "I'm not gonna risk you guys having a flop again..." so he brought in Kenny Lynch and Mort Shuman, two hot songwriters, and they wrote this song. And Kenny Lynch, he's a dear friend of mine now, and I always remind him what he said to me. We were recording "Sha-La-La-La-Lee", and Kenny Lynch came out, and it's the only time anyone's ever told me what to play. He came out and said "Don't play anything you can't mime to...". And I went "awww, fuck that". But I always remember that and I always remind him of it.

I like the cowbells on that track. It sounds like strings. Funny enough, I was out in the fields the other day, with my horses and stuff, and I was singing "Sha-La-La-La-Lee", and all of a sudden I was singing it with another phrasing, and I thought "I could hear Elton John singin' it..." and I thought "right, when I get back I'll have to call somebody and get a message to Elton...". He'll probably think I'm nuts, but with a longer different arrangement, I can actually hear him singing that.

KEN SHARP: The song "Hey Girl" was written by Steve

and Ronnie forged their writing partnership, occasionally with you. Do you feel that was a real turning point for the band or was it later with "All or Nothing"?

IAN MCLAGAN: Well, see, it was only because "I Got Mine" which wasn't that big a hit, and so our manager Don Arden came to us said we've got to get outside writers, because "Whatcha Gonna Do About It?" was Ian Samwell. So, as I came in, we had to have Kenny Lynch for one ("Sha-La-La-La-Lee"), then "Hey Girl", then "All or Nothing" was a huge hit and after that we could write all our own material.

KEN SHARP: When you guys recorded "All or Nothing", did you sense then that there was a magic to the song?

IAN MCLAGAN: It was very easy on the ear, very direct, like you'd heard it before. I hate the middle part though, the (sings) -- silly part. I do it with my band though.

RONNIE LANE: "All or Nothing"...I remember Steve wrote it, we went in the studio and recorded it, and it sounded really good. It came out and it was Number One, yes it was!

STEVE MARRIOTT: Arden is an excellent manager -- excellent! After he was talking with our parents, our relationship was bad and it never really recovered. The release of "My Mind's Eye" was after the drug thing. We presented a bunch of demos -- left them in Arden's office -- and then we were on the road, and the next thing we knew it was out as a single. We hadn't really been asked about it. I think he took it straight from the tape of the demo. But we hadn't finished with it, and even if we had, we wouldn't have wanted it as a single. Our reaction to him when that happened begins with a "C" and ends with a "T".

KEN SHARP: What do you remember about the first Small Faces album on Decca?

KENNEY JONES: I remember doing it in IBC Studios, Portland Place, and Glyn Johns was an engineer there, and the desk he was using had great big knobs, faders, on it. Great desk, big old valve desk. We recorded it in no time at all, we just played. Do one or two takes, and we were gone. "All or Nothing" was also recorded there.

IAN MCLAGAN: We were on acid for it.

KEN SHARP: (laughing) That early?

IAN MCLAGAN: Yeah. In 1966. Yeah. I mean, Kenney wasn't, but the three of us were. I can remember -- it's all a little vague, but we did it in three or four days, because it's only on four track.

KEN SHARP: There's a real excitement that pervades that record, though, I mean the songs aren't that complicated but....

IAN MCLAGAN: They're not that worked out, really, because we didn't rehearse.

KEN SHARP: Would you do live vocals?

IAN MCLAGAN: No, we'd do the instrumental backing on one track, lead vocal on another track, any organ or guitar solos on the third track, and backing vocals on the final track.

STEVE MARRIOTT: The Cavern was one of the nicest places we played. I don't think it had a bar in those days. I remember when we were down there we thought we'd invented words like "spliff" and stuff like that -- off the Jamaicans we used to score the shit off of. We had a song called "Pass the Spliff", and all these guys in the audience would just crack up. We thought it was our word -- our in-word, just between each other, something to laugh at. We'd do the number "Pass the Spliff" -- then it was very taboo. The song "E Too D" was just that, E to D -- the two chords in it. A two-chord song. It was not meant to have "too", just "to".

RONNIE LANE: "Itchycoo Park" was my idea basically, but Steve helped me to finish it off.

STEVE MARRIOTT: I used to take the piss as much as I could. "Itchycoo Park" is a piss take, 'cos we were never too Hippy Trippy and all that. We used to take the piss out of ourselves and everything. We had a good sense of humor.

IAN MCLAGAN: "Itchycoo Park" has always annoyed me. It's a lovely song though -- I like the song, it's the chorus that I don't like. See, if you picture it as a Ronnie Lane song, which it was almost entirely, if Ronnie Lane had sung it....see I don't like Steve's voice when he sings like that -- I can't bear it when he sings with the pretty little voice like that -- I want to smack him! (Imitates Steve singing

chorus) It's just too sweet. But see when Ronnie Lane sung it... He asked me to tour with him in 1990, and I said yeah, I'd love it, but on one condition -- I don't wanna do "Itchycoo Park". Now I look back on it, it was pretty rotten of me, but I really didn't want to do it. We did the tour and we rehearsed it, but we didn't do it.

KEN SHARP: Mac said he didn't like it when Steve sang in that sweet, pretty voice. How'd you feel about it?

KENNEY JONES: No, I didn't mind it, I liked it. The thing was, it showed a different side of Steve, of his talent, and the great thing was, you knew when he sang like that, he wasn't for long, you know, before he really hammered it down. I think Steve had a great voice in the songs without the power behind it as well.

STEVE MARRIOTT: It was basically a nick from an old hymn called "God Be in My Head", it was an old melody that stuck in Ronnie's mind, I think. I mean, Ronnie came to me and he had the melody of the first part, and the chorus, and I thought of the sort of mad middle eight bit. It's one of the few combined writing efforts that me and Ronnie did, 'cos usually we wrote separately, and then presented them to each other, and maybe suggested little bits. I remember when I thought of the middle eight for it we were in two cars coming back from a gig and he was in the car behind me. We had braked and I'd gone running out -- it was at night -- and I sung it to him and said "Whaddaya think that is", and a police car pulled up opposite, and about 10 policemen leapt out and ran towards the car. And I thought "Christ, we're going to get busted", you know we were doing what you do (laughs). And I was leaning in the window talking to Ronnie, and they run right past us. It was one of those freaky things I've never forgotten. It was a burglary going on in the shop that we'd pulled up outside of. My heart stopped for a minute because it was very illegal then to do anything naughty, you know.

IAN MCLAGAN: Yeah, it was pretty difficult (to play "Itchycoo Park live). We weren't a good band then. That Australian tour -- The Who slaughtered us, really. It was a shame really, but they were so great. They'd been touring non-stop and were still making their albums in 4 or 5 days really, and we'd had almost a year all off. We had only the occasional gig; we spent the whole year in the studio.

KEN SHARP: Where was Itchycoo Park? Didn't it have

another name?

IAN MCLAGAN: I don't know the name, but it was in the East End. That was the nickname for it because there were stinging nettles there. They should have fucking renamed it, don't you think. You know, the Beatles got Penny Lane.... (Note: Paolo Hewitt identifies the real Itchycoo Park as being Manor Park).

KENNEY JONES: "Itchycoo Park" is basically a statement. Although, there was a place in Ilford -- but there was a place everywhere, even in the East End. Although I grew up on bomb ruins -- Hitler's bombs fell on our street, right -- so my playground was the bomb ruins, right. I just played on all this stuff, I never questioned it, just had a wonderful time playing on all this rubble. And there was a lot of stinging nettles that grew there, and you'd have on short trousers, and they'd sting your legs and you'd get all itchycoo, right. And everyplace had its own "Itchycoo Park", really.

KEN SHARP: Where was that photo taken - the cover of the American "There are But Four Small Faces"? Was that Itchycoo Park?

IAN MCLAGAN: No. I'm not sure I remember, but it might have been Hempstead.

KEN SHARP: How about your song "Up the Wooden Hills to Bedfordshire"?

IAN MCLAGAN: Do you know what that means? Up the stairs to bed. Wooden hills. It was an expression that Ronnie Lane's father used to use when he was about to go to bed "....well, it's up the wooden hills to Bedfordshire...". I thought it was a lovely line. It's a drug song I suppose. I used to be stoned all the time....you know, when you "sleep"...trying to explain how you felt. "When you're slipping into sleep..." isn't falling asleep, it's gettin' stoned.

KEN SHARP: What about "Here Come the Nice"? Were you guys surprised that no one caught on to what you were really saying?

IAN MCLAGAN: We figured everyone was fucking stupid. You know, we used to roll joints and try to be neat and perfect. We used to have competitions: Top Ten spot and all.

KEN SHARP: Who was the best?

IAN MCLAGAN: I was, usually.

KEN SHARP: Who was the worst?

IAN MCLAGAN: Ronnie Lane. He was often second or third. But...I'd get a good neat one, and I remember one time we were driving north somewhere and we were in the back of the car, and as we were turning round a corner there was a policeman at the corner, and I lit it -- I'm just like so cocky I'm thinking "...yeah go on, what're ya gonna do..." and he didn't notice. The whole thing was our little game: we're stoned and you don't know it, and we're laughing and you don't know why we're laughing. Just a silly thing. And like, "Here Come the Nice" was really pushin' it. Steve was really pushin' it to the extremes. "Itchycoo Park", too, for that matter.

KEN SHARP: "Nice" was like speed? A speed dealer?

IAN MCLAGAN: Yeah, "Here Come the Nice" was from the Lord Buckley track, "Here Come the Nazz". The Nazz meant Jesus, it was like a rap, a real rap. It was Steve's way of using it, it was like here come the nazz, the nice, a dealer, basically. He meant here comes the man who gets you high. A friend. It wasn't like a dealer nowadays, the dealer was your friend in those days when you were buyin' dope.

KEN SHARP: How about "Green Circles"? Was that inspired by somebody who used to live with you guys, like a dream he had?

IAN MCLAGAN: Yeah, I suppose an acid trip, I dunno....yeah, Mick O'Sullivan, he lived with us at about that time. He even gets songwriting credit, I don't suppose he gets any money, though, either (laughs).

KEN SHARP: One of my favorites is "Talk to You"; do you like that one? It's like a little blues riff...

KENNEY JONES: Yeah, "Talk to You" is a great song, they're all great songs. All those songs are great. When you've got great material, you can really play great, really do something to it. When you've got songs that are just ordinary, you've got to really search yourself to find something to do with it. It should be natural.

IAN MCLAGAN: I can't recall that one, haven't heard it for such a long time. You know, Paul Weller always loved was in the booth with Glyn Johns, and Steve was trying to show him how to play it, and I went on the mike and said "here, if you'll just do it like....well, I'll just come down and show you...". So I got on the kit, and showed him, and remember, I'd never played the song before. And he learned it, and then they came to another point where it just wasn't right, so I showed him another part. And in the end he said "...come on, you just play it..." and I said "no, that's not right, you play it...". And everybody else chimed in, so in the end I just played it. It wound up being the whole Small Faces on that cut.

KEN SHARP: Do you remember any other songs you played on with P.P.? Were you on her big hit "The First Cut is the Deepest"?

KENNEY JONES: I can't remember, really. We did a lot -- I did quite a lot of sessions for a lot of different people in those days. The great thing about it then was it was like being a gigantic band. All the bands played together.

KEN SHARP: Were you involved in any of the tracks by the Andrew Loog Oldham Orchestra?

KENNEY JONES: More'n'likely, 'cos I did a lot of sessions.

KEN SHARP: Is seems like regardless of the things that went down later with the money and all, all the artists wanted to help each other out....

KENNEY JONES: Oh yeah, without a doubt.

KEN SHARP: Let me ask you about some specific tracks that have been listed as existing Small Faces outtakes. How about "Be My Baby"?

IAN MCLAGAN: No, I don't remember it. Could have.

KENNEY JONES: Yeah, we did that one, yeah. It exists somewhere.

KEN SHARP: The Supremes ' "Love is Here and Now You're Gone"?

IAN MCLAGAN: Sounds like too many chords for us to have handled... Don't remember it.

KENNEY JONES: I can't visualize that, but we must have done it.

KEN SHARP: How about "Mind the Doors Please", a send up of the London Underground with chanted vocals by Ronnie Lane?

IAN MCLAGAN: I do remember we used to go (funny voice) "...mind the door!...". As a song I don't remember it.

KENNEY JONES: Oh yeah, that was funny. We did that at Olympic, and it was just me fucking around, basically. 'Cos all it was, was I was just fucking around on the tom tom's. I used to just constantly play, you know, just searching for different ways of playing fillings, different sounds. And they used to just let me do it, just leave me alone -- they knew I was searching for different ways of doing things -- that was one of the great things about the band. Even though the tom toms were kind of annoying, and I got this nickname "Shut Up Kenney", you know. So I was on the tom toms, and I had this particular sound, and I played the drums as if I were on a train (makes sounds). And it gets faster, and Ronnie heard what I was doing, and instant telepathy again, played this fast descending bassline as a rundown, if it was a train, and we all joined in. And that was it, really.

KEN SHARP: How about "Shimmer"? These could be working titles you know....

IAN MCLAGAN: No.

KENNEY JONES: No.

KEN SHARP: How about "Uncle Charlie's Fruitgum"?

KENNEY JONES: No.

IAN MCLAGAN: Now that sounds like Andrew Oldham. (heatedly) These sound like bullshit titles! We had "Donkey Rides, Penny a Glass" and it sounds like Andrew was trying hard to come up with titles that sounded like us.

KEN SHARP: How about "Wallop McKenzie"?

IAN MCLAGAN: Now that was quite likely a title, because Wallop McKenzie was what our driver Bill Corbett used to say: "...now you go down here, and you go down there, and Wallop McKenzie there you are...". It's like gibberish.

KENNEY JONES: Yeah, that exists. I don't remember it, though. And I'll tell you where they are, all those songs exist on the multi-tracks, and I've got to get the multi-tracks, whoever's got them. I want to protect them. All the real outtakes.

KEN SHARP: "Shake" was originally sung live on stage by Ronnie (ed. note: see the BBC live sessions on various bootlegs).

IAN MCLAGAN: That's right it was always sung by Ronnie. Ronnie had a Wilson Pickett song he always sung, too.

KEN SHARP: Why were the Small Faces doing covers at the end of your career of songs like "If I Were a Carpenter", "Every Little Bit Hurts", and "Red Balloon"?

IAN MCLAGAN: We just loved 'em. They were great songs. We did a Lonnie Mack song called "Why", we used to listen to it along, can't remember if we ever recorded it. There might be a few tracks lying about, like "Be My Baby". I don't know. We used to do alot of stuff live we never recorded.

KEN SHARP: Were there ever any songs the band wrote and never recorded?

IAN MCLAGAN: No, we pretty much recorded everything we ever wrote. We did record about 20 tracks and only put out 9 though, you know.

KEN SHARP: So there's really not much unreleased?

IAN MCLAGAN: I don't think so, no. I listened to some of those things on the Charly box set, but I don't know. I'm not sure all that's even us. There's an album available on cassette called "Rod Stewart and the Small Faces" but there's no connection between those. That lineup never existed. Immediate is the connection, we were on Immediate, Rod had an album on Immediate, so you get one side of Small Faces and one side of Rod Stewart on the album. And it's all those phony remixed tracks, no vocals, and so on.

KEN SHARP: How about the backing tracks that don't have vocals that came out? What's that stuff?

IAN MCLAGAN: (heatedly) I've no idea, I'd like to see the boxes. I don't even know if some of it is us!

OGDEN'S NUT GONE FLAKE

JODY DENBERG: The Small Faces album "Ogden's Nut Gone Flake" was described by Rolling Stone magazine as "...a strange combination of programmed music, fairy tales, and soul-based rock, and it's fairly wonderful, one of the least pretentious and most successful spin-offs of the "Sgt. Pepper's..." era...". Were the Small Faces at the time psychedelically influenced by the music (i.e., "...Pepper's...") or by the psychedelics?

RONNIE LANE: Naahhh! It was the drugs! It (the album's title) came from us just thinking if it (marijuana) was legal, what would it be called....

KEN SHARP: Who came up with the idea for the cover of "Ogden's..."?

IAN MCLAGAN: See, it wasn't gonna be a round cover. The idea was it was gonna be a tobacco tin. Andrew got us delivered the actual Ogden's archives, scrapbooks -- Ogden's is a real tobacco company, see, very kind of them really -- all of their very thick scrapbooks from the 1800's of all of their labels, the actual labels, and we had the real things in the Immediate offices, really. And we found "Ogden's Nut Brown Flake", and Steve went "oh!", and it was a rectangular cover tin, you see, most of them are. And it opens up inside just like the album. We had an artist come in, we didn't change it, see -- all of the pictures, slogans, all of it was exactly the same, it's just that instead of "Nut Brown" we changed it to "Nut Gone", and it was a beautiful thing! And the pound box on the back I found in the book. And then Nick Tweddell and Pete Brown, who were in the Muleskinners, did the inside sleeve. Although the photograph Gered took -- that's my banjo, my cat on my shoulder. Steve was George the cleaner with the mop in the background. (Pointing to pictures) that was in the Immediate office, that was Ronnie's flat....

KEN SHARP: Tell me about the "Ogden's..." album. Were you guys writing that to be a concept album, or did you just put it together that way?

IAN MCLAGAN: We had the idea. We took a boat out. This was before we lived out in Marlow together; I remember it different from Ken, I don't remember him being there, but I suppose he was. But anyway, we took boats out on the Thames, and we'd stop and have a smoke, have a drink, and play - work on songs. I still have a tape of that, it's very bad quality -- I daren't play it for anyone -- but we worked on songs like "The Fly", "The Journey", "Happiness

Greyhound bus tour with six other bands in a bus, 4th on the bill, very little money. I mean, what were we gonna say? No!!! It worked, 'cause he didn't want us to go, see.

STEVE MARRIOTT: I think it's a case of English managers didn't like you going to America in those days; put it this way -- they didn't like you to go because they didn't have any control over you. It would have meant that the English management would have had to farm you out to American management. The same applies now to American managers, having had a few American managers, they don't like you coming over here (to England) because they're out of control, they want complete control, and when they can't have it they get the horrors, so obviously the English would rather keep you in Europe and the Americans would rather keep you in American territories. That's the way they work 'cos the minute they have to farm you out to other businessmen, then they get the horrors that they're gonna get shafted like they're shafting you.

KEN SHARP: Did it mean anything to the band to capture America?

IAN MCLAGAN: No. Well, we wanted to go, but it was too late. If we had gone in 1966 when we were still up-and-comers, it would've been great. I mean, we were headliners in England. The Who were very clever, they opened for Herman's Hermits. Jimi Hendrix opened for The Monkees. I mean, they were awful bills, but it made the Who, it made Jimi Hendrix. We never got a good offer, a realistic offer.

PARTY CENTRAL:

KEN SHARP: Tell us about the house in Pimlico at 22 Westmoreland Terrace, that sounds like it was the greatest place...

IAN MCLAGAN: It was Party Central!

KEN SHARP: How long did you guys live there?

IAN MCLAGAN: A year.

KENNEY JONES: I mean, we was all cocky little guys, but it was one of those where you wake up in the morning and you couldn't wait to be with each other. Even though we had times when it was quite tense, and I mean it like, when

we was in the studio, and before I could do a track I'd have to wait until bleedin' 2 o'clock in the morning. And I was always an early to bed and early to rise person. That was the big difference to me, but I couldn't wait to be with everybody. I mean, in the studio was a pleasure, being around everybody was a pleasure. But that's why I didn't live in the house in Pimlico, because I would get no rest. But I was quite happy you see, because I'd live with my parents, and I could drive there in five minutes flat from the East End to Pimlico, which is Chelsea.

KEN SHARP: Kenney didn't live there did he?

IAN MCLAGAN: Well, he was living at home, he had a happy home live, and we were Jack the Lads and we wanted to get fucked up and get stoned. You could take a pill and no one would know you'd taken a pill, but you couldn't smoke dope around the house without your parents knowing, y'know. It was a terraced house with four stories. We had a youngish maid called Liesel who was a character, she was just a bit older than us -- I haven't seen her since I left England in '78, but she was our housekeeper on and off through the years. She was later Woody's housekeeper, she may still be. We were in the house from Christmas night 1965 until Christmas 1966. We'd all split up with our girlfriends that day. I was living with Ronnie at his house, you know, his parents house, or Kenney's house -- we were on the road. And Steve had gotten this house and wanted me to move in that day. Pimlico is behind Victoria Station.

KEN SHARP: So lots of people came by, I heard Brian Epstein came by one night....

IAN MCLAGAN: He came by. The guy he brought spiked us with acid for the first time. It was fabulous.

KEN SHARP: Did the neighbors bother you?

IAN MCLAGAN: Never once. We ignored 'em.

KEN SHARP: What was a typical day like?

IAN MCLAGAN: There wasn't a typical day. We'd get up late, Liesle would cook us breakfast -- we told her we didn't want no weinerschnitzel when we first get up. The party would begin as soon as we got up. Roll a joint and keep going. Downstairs in the dining room we had a piano. In the sitting room we had our guitars and stuff. All of our songs from 1966 were written there. The photographer from the photo session for the first album had chalked this wall with kids' faces on them. And Steve had started drawing joints in the mouths. On different covers you can see them. When I'm signing covers, I always outline the joint now.

KEN SHARP: Did a lot of fans come around the house?

IAN MCLAGAN: Oh yeah. There's a great shot in Paolo's book - I don't know where he got it - kids would keep their distance respectfully behind the wall at the end of the road, and when we'd come out they'd come running up the road. I think the neighbors shooed them away as well. We had a year's lease, so it had run out by the end of 1966. We'd fired Arden, and he paid the lease, so it had run out. By that time we'd had enough. That's a long time for three people to be in and out of each others' pockets so we split up at that point and got separate places.

But we actually did live together again later, with our girlfriends! That was out in the country in Marlow. We didn't have any money and we figured that would be cheaper! It was actually very much fun and we got to play more than we did at the other house. The girls got along alright, but they were excluded in a way because we were playing music all day and all night, but it was fun.

I'm always making notes for my book, and this morning at breakfast I suddenly had a flash -- my memory is incredibly vivid, you know, which is amazing for someone who used to smoke dope morning to night -- I don't do that anymore, you know. Anyway, I suddenly had a flash of being back in the car with Ronnie, Steve, and Kenney. We had one of those little record players in the car. We had Freddie King's "Hideaway", and the b-side was at 33 1/3 rpm, and you couldn't play it on those things! But Fontella Bass' "Rescue Me" was Steve's favorite for awhile, and he used to play it over and over, and I used to hate the trombones on that record. I heard it the other day and I went: "...damn trombones! Damn Steve!...". We used to put a blanket up in the two windows in the back, because Steve, Ronnie and me'd be in the back smoking, and Kenney would be in front with our driver Bill Corbett. Kenney would always be in the front turning the heater up, and we'd be in the back going "...turn the fucking heater down" 'cause we were stoned, you know. Kenney was a pill popper like us, but he was living at home, and he didn't smoke dope like us. I mean, he was in the car, he'd be smokin' it (passive smoke) -- you couldn't avoid it. Our driver was stoned the whole time and he used to complain because he used to drive the Beatles, and he'd say: "...you little

bastards, drug addicts, not like the Beatles..." as if they were from another planet or something, and we'd all say "aw fuck off Bill. What do you think fab gear means?". And he'd say it meant "good clothes" and we'd say "...bollocks, it means good hash. 'Fab Gear' means 'good hash' ya idiot". It was like a code. We used to have this expression "It's nice to be nice" which meant its good to be stoned.

WE ARE THE MODS

KEN SHARP: You know, The Who always tried to present themselves from 1964-65 as mods, but the Small Faces were real mods....

IAN MCLAGAN: (Interrupting) (Roger) Daltrey was a real mod. Pete (Townshend) was at art school so he couldn't afford it - you had to have a job to afford the clothes. (John) Entwistle of course wasn't....Daltrey was a mod...Daltrey was quite a heavy little...a tough little bastard! But I wasn't a mod when I joined 'em. I was at art school, I didn't have money for clothes, it was like brown corduroy jacket and Levi's. I wasn't interested in mods....there was a couple of guys at art school who had the parkas and the scooters. I mean, I liked the jackets, the clothes, but the parkas I thought were stupid.

STEVE MARRIOTT: I was a mod, I had me anorak (a parka). I think to establish yourself, in the very early stages, clothes can really set an image for you, really work for you, or, it can make you a laughing stock. It was a good thing while it lasted, but it's over now. Kids are always searching for something new, and I think music has taken over from alot of things... (from BBC radio, July 1966).

KEN SHARP: Were the rest of the guys in the Small Faces mods? Even Kenney?

IAN MCLAGAN: Oh yeah, oh yeah. They were from the East End. I was from the other side of London, west of Oxford, Heathrow airport, Hounslow.

KENNEY JONES: We was all mods before we were in the Small Faces. Funnily enough, when we met up we were all already mods. We had all identified individually with what we wanted to be before we had actually met. It was absolutely amazing that when we all bumped into each other we had absolutely similar fashion senses, absolutely similar tastes, similar outlook. The reason is because we were the first young generation after the war, and I remember growing up as a kid in black and white. And really, everybody did wear black and white, and we were the people to wear colour, and it was amazing. We started to wear all these bright things, and it was alright to dye your hair then. A lot of mods actually dyed their hair blonde. It wasn't called dyed, it was called bleaching your hair then. Because it was the bleach, that was all we had to do it with.

STEVE MARRIOTT: I just was one (a mod). There weren't a lot of mods to begin with, there was only a few, and I just loved the clothes. I used to save up all my dough and go down Carnaby Street. The funny thing about the street was that it was only a couple of dingy little shops, and they used to import all their stuff from France, and a mate of mine, who I used to hang around with at the Square Ring coffee bar in Manor Park, turned up wearing all this gear, and he told me where to get it. It was expensive, so I had to save up for it.

But really, we used to get laughed at. Me, Ronnie and a couple of the others -- Mac and Kenney weren't really mods -- used to get wolf whistles from geezers on building sites, and me old man didn't like it at all. I mean, it took a lot of courage in those days. But to be honest with you, I think there's a lot more mods now than there was then, to begin with anyway. Now, every gig I play I see mods; in those days it was a very select crowd. If you went up North, there were no mods up there at all, to begin with, but in the end they really took it up, I mean Manchester and Sheffield became totally mod.

It was nice to be different, well, that's the way I felt about it anyway. It's all to do with mates as well. I mean, you look around and there's got to be one geezer that looks different, you have a look, ask him where he got the gear (clothes) from, he tells you, and you become a mod without really thinking. That's the way it went.

KENNEY JONES: I had my mini then, and I'd get home, park outside -- I was obsessed with this mini then, all I did was clean it and polish it and put clocks on it and stuff. It was the extension of the scooter, if you know what I mean.

KEN SHARP: Did you enjoy the mod image? The clothes?

IAN MCLAGAN: Yeah! We could go down to Carnaby Street and fill a taxi with shirts and hats and stuff...

KEN SHARP: Do you ever look at pictures and wish you still had some of those clothes?

IAN MCLAGAN: Oh yeah, yeah, I mean that green suede jacket with the black leather collar that's on the cover of...actually Kenney wore it on one album then he gave it me and I wore it.... And some of the shoes, the suits....yeah!

KENNEY JONES: I do that all the time. My mother had a load of stuff, and I think some of it was given away or auctioned off for charity, but there's not much now.

JOHN HELLIER: During the Sixties, clothes played a major part in the mod culture, did the Small Faces ever try to impress an image, or was that just the way you were?

STEVE MARRIOTT: No, it's just the way we were, mate. I think the difference between us and groups like The Who, was that the Who actually had a manager, who saw Mod, and dressed them that way. We were just of the street. The Small Faces were what they were before anyone discovered them. We were just a little moddy band, whereas The Who actually got things bought for them. I thought (The Who) were great. It's only in retrospect that you can look back and see that Pete Meadon (The Who's first manager) -- a great mate of mine -- the way that him and Kit Lambert kitted them out. But then, you had the legitimate (Mod) bands like The Action, they were the same age as the Small Faces, they were just of the streets, they weren't groomed. There were a lot of bands like Grapefruit, John's Children, and the Gods that were groomed that way. They were sent to go and get all these clothes from this particular shop. There was a lot of rotten horrible bands that had a lot of money spent on them and amounted to fuck all, really. So out of that quagmire of bands, The Small Faces came to the top because they were legitimate, and I think it showed.

KEN SHARP: Because with the Small Faces it wasn't just the music, it was the clothes, the image, everything intertwined.....

IAN MCLAGAN: The big part of it to me -- I mean the clothes were alot of fun -- it was great to be able to have a lot of great clothes and shoes and always have a choice of what to wear. I don't have that choice these days, I wish I did, if I see clothes I won't buy 'em. I mean, Rod, he goes out and spends $7000 on clothes just like it was nothing.... But the music was really the focus of the Small Faces. The core of it was Muddy Waters, Marvin Gaye, Booker T. & the MG's, Otis....that's what the Small Faces were. There's all kinds of inferences around, but that's what we were, it wasn't clothes.

STEVE MARRIOTT: Mod meant money. A way of life gone wrong. It went up its own ass, see. As soon as too much money gets involved, the people who are in it can't get into it any more -- as soon as it starts to cost money. Mod never really did cost money at first. You'd buy the cheapest things, but in the style you wanted. And then they'd start producing it because they realized there's a demand for it, and upped the price. The whole thing was to be individual, and as soon as they started mass-marketing the stuff and up-pricing the hell out of it, then the thing of being an individual is lost. Mod was individual at the time. It's like saying that you wanted to be an individual but within a group. That's a contradiction, but it's a good one. You want to be an individual, just a little bit, but not too much -- just that little niche. It is down to the individual what they want to wear within some set rules. There were some set rules, no doubt about it, like the length of trousers, colour of socks, length and style of hair, that kind of thing. But the rest is up to you. Always with the hair, the trouser length, and the shoes -- you had to have that. That was a code that said you were. The rest of what you covered your body with didn't matter so much. But then it got out of hand, and like anything, as soon as it got out of hand it was lost.

KEN SHARP: Do you still follow the mod movement a little bit?

KENNEY JONES: Oh yeah, the great thing about the mod movement is that it'll never die, even if it goes out of fashion, there'll always be that spark movement, and that'll always keep it alight. And every time it comes back, it'll get stronger. Because it's the sentiment behind the movement of the mods, not just fashions, but the mod statement, which was we are here, take notice of us, we're just people in a group and we're having fun. And it's all right to have fun! Nothing wrong with it. And if we get a little bit outrageous we don't mean it to upset anyone. Stay cool....

KEN SHARP: And you guys are like the Godfathers of Mod right now...

KENNEY JONES: I think it's great that we're finally seen as being...while this was going on everybody was sort of hyping The Beatles and The Stones, and there we were. And now everybody's realized all these years later that the biggest fashion...the biggest statement made in the Sixties was by the Small Faces. We were ahead of our time, no doubt.

STEVE MARRIOTT: The media gave us the name and called us Mods. We didn't know what the fuck it was, y'know, we just liked button downs, and when I look back it was fucking great! But I couldn't do it myself now. I'd be like a cartoon of myself, a parody. No, I'll leave it up to others to carry that flag. If I did it now I'd look stupid. I'd be like an old man dressed up in young clothes. It would be stupid.

INFLUENCES

STEVE MARRIOTT: Buddy Holly has gotta be the biggest influence of my youth. I used to run about the room wearing a pair of thick glasses -- no glass in 'em, just the rims -- and I had a tennis racket I used to mime with. And I made a record once called "Give Her My Regards" copying him -- it was dire! It was a rotten record! (as guest DJ on BBC radio, May 23rd 1987)

IAN MCLAGAN: Stax, Motown, and Muddy Waters. We used to do songs on stage live that would just be jams, really. "E Too D" or "Come On Children" evolved from just jams basically. Steve would sing -- James Brown was another big influence too -- he would sing some James Brown lines and throw in a few Muddy Waters licks -- that's where Zeppelin got "Whole Lotta Love" was from us....

STEVE MARRIOTT: My main influences (during the mod years) were Booker T and the MG's, then people like Otis Redding. I mean, if it wasn't black, then I didn't listen to it!

IAN MCLAGAN: I was on this airplane a few years ago, and I was walking down the aisle, and I heard this voice singing "...in places/Small Faces abound...." and I looked and it was David Crosby. He said "hey man, we wrote that line about you, you know.....". And we never did know it then!

KEN SHARP: Did you get to see any of your idols back then, Otis, Booker T?

IAN MCLAGAN: I saw Otis, Booker T., Arthur Conley,

Sam'n'Dave, and Eddie Floyd all in one night. The four of us went to see our favourite band at the Hammersmith Odeon. The curtains opened, "Green Onions". It could've ended right then, and I coulda gone home happy. It was fantastic! Otis did "Try A Little Tenderness". But Sam'n'Dave stole the show.

KEN SHARP: Have you ever met any of them?

IAN MCLAGAN: Not then, later yeah. I meet Booker T every time and it's the first time he's met me every time.

KEN SHARP: Like with Chuck Berry meeting Keith?

IAN MCLAGAN: Yeah. The last time he played in Austin I went him and his organ was fucking up. I went to see him afterwards -- 'cause Steve Cropper remembers me, Duck Dunn remembers me -- they're all very much gentlemen, but every time with Booker T it's like (nice as can be) "...nice to meet you...", and I said anytime you come to Austin please call me, and I'll bring my own Hammond and Leslie, it's beautiful and sweet B3 and you'll like it...so maybe he will.

Q: Have you ever seen or heard any of the current mod bands, and what do you think of them?

STEVE MARRIOTT: Yeah. It's very difficult, how shall I say it, 'cos they are doing something that I've done. Even the tones on the guitars they use. To me it's a compliment. But to be honest with you, I think they've got their influences a bit mixed up. They are more influenced by the Small Faces or whoever, whereas we were influenced by the black r'n'b/soul artists. They're really not taking it to the roots. What worries me is that the sort of music that we had when we was nippers is no longer available. Alright, you can get compilation albums, but they're not the same thing. We had the more obscure stuff like The Contours and groups like that. It's hard to get ahold of that stuff, and it's a shame....

KENNEY JONES: I can see a lot of bands, a lot of drummers, playing like me, which is really strange. I'm incredibly flattered, and I can see similarities in Ronnie, Steve, and Mac in the look of the bands now. Even in Oasis, the lot. They're the first ones to say so, as well, but it's quite weird. Of all the bands in the Sixties, the biggest hyped bands were the Stones and the Beatles, basically, but we were right there, and we were quite big at the time.

But because we had "poppy" records -- the record company kept releasing these poppy records --but it was our fault, we wrote them. So nobody would listen to the album tracks, and the album tracks were bloody great. We were a lot heavier band than people sort of gave us credit for, but we could never lose that pop image, if you like. Which funnily enough I'm actually quite proud of now, because there is strength in the pop side of music. I think it's actually been abundantly clear now, people have actually realized it's not just pop, it's just a commercial record. "Pop" is just a term and you can actually still be heavy under that label.

IAN MCLAGAN: I've worked with alot of younger bands, when I lived in L.A. I got more work with younger bands who were familiar with those records...you know it's like a wave, or a cycle. Now people are familiar with the band again, but in five years I'll have to be telling people who they are again. When I moved to Malibu in 1978 after the Faces split up in 1975, and in 1975, we couldn't walk anywhere in the States. My hair is pretty much the same, a bit greyer, and I went to the market in Malibu, and this kid started laughing at my hair -- he didn't think I could hear 'im, talking to his mum "...look at 'is hair...", and I'm thinking "..wait a minute!". And then about two years later, kids have got hair like mine again, and I'm thinking, wait a second, you're probably the same kid who was laughing. It all starts again now. I had someone come up to me yesterday and say: "...are you Rod Stewart?". Give me a break....

SMALL FACES AS MUSICIANS

KEN SHARP: Were the shows pretty similar throughout the three years you guys toured? Did you play a lot of different styles and material?

KENNEY JONES: We played pretty much the same, consistently, all the way through. We played slightly differently because there was a natural style progression change. When we signed with Immediate, the music was very similar, but it was actually more dynamic approach to it. My drumming, I'll never forget, I thought I'm gonna think like a classical drummer, and I'm gonna think "powerful". And that's all I did say to myself, and I played some amazing fillings. Incredibly simple but...(Ken: very effective)...the timing of them...I think it's stunning now.

KEN SHARP: I loved your drum sound on the

Immediate stuff onwards.

KENNEY JONES: What I had there is I knew exactly what I wanted by then, and we all had the good fortune of working with Glyn Johns as an engineer. And he progressed with sound -- new tape machines and things like that -- more toys. One of the greatest sounds I've ever had, I think, is in the early Olympic studios, because downstairs they had an echo chamber room, a natural echo which is set up with one mike and a speaker. Glyn and I used to love it, we used to go down there and reposition it, and come back up and feed it though the deck and you'd get this lovely ambient sound. And I love ambient sounds. I love big sounds, I don't like to dampen the drums in any way. I like the sounds of the drum to be exactly what it is, 'cos that's what it is.

KEN SHARP: Did you have a lot to do with that drum phasing on "Itchycoo Park"?

KENNEY JONES: Yeah, we looped two machines together and went 'round the back of over a chair so it just continually went (makes swooshing noise). It was great.

KEN SHARP: It's a sound that Glyn Johns says he consciously never used again with anything.

KENNEY JONES: Yeah, that's right. I did. What I do sometimes is I love to put a little bit, just a little hint -- it's like a spice as I call it -- of phasing onto a drum sound, which is lovely. It gives you the edge -- it gives you that floating feeling. And sometimes when we play live I love to feed the mixer out front and put phasing through it. It's great. Just ever so slightly so you don't hardly know it's there.

KEN SHARP: What keyboards did you use in the Small Faces?

IAN MCLAGAN: A Flattop Wurlitzer piano, and an M100 Hammond.

KEN SHARP: Do you still have those instruments?

IAN MCLAGAN: I don't have that very one, I have two, one's a real old one that gives the Ray Charles sound, you know like "What'd I Say". It's a flattop with a wire music stand, and there's a later one with a wooden music stand that isn't. And then the Wurlitzer, the A200 with the rolling

top, like the one I played on stage last night, they don't sound half as good. The other ones just don't travel well, don't stay in tune, but I love the sound of 'em. I've got four or five of 'em.

KEN SHARP: How did you first hear a song? Did Steve and Ronnie come in and run it down on acoustic guitar?

KENNEY JONES: Well I hated hanging about in the studio, so I'd be downstairs working on my mini outside the studio nine times out of ten, because I hated waiting about. And a roadie would come down and say "Right, okay, Steve's got it down now, you can come up and do the drums now" and half the time I never even knew the song. I never even heard the song, we'd just run through it once or twice and we'd get it. That's the best way -- it's almost like I knew what was coming next.

KEN SHARP: It's amazing that the band improved tremendously in a short period of time. I mean, Steve, and Ronnie really became inventive on the bass....

IAN MCLAGAN: Oh yeah, Steve always underrated himself. So did Ronnie. He was one of the classiest bass players because he had no aspirations of being a bass player, he was playing for the song. Always! And you can't ask for more than that. And Steve was a fantastic rhythm player. You know, he was Keith Richard's first choice for the Stones, but Mick couldn't compete with that voice. Mick wasn't going to have that voice in the band, because he knew Steve couldn't stay quiet. I love Mick's voice, he's got more voices than Steve. Steve had that scream. Steve would overuse that -- eventually I got to hate it; I love his early stuff.

KEN SHARP: Hate the Humble Pie stuff?

IAN MCLAGAN: Well, I never listened to that really.

KENNEY JONES: I didn't like it, no, and I'll tell you why. It was trying to be too heavy. It was a band that was trying to hard. It was overarranged, I thought. It was oversung. It was overkill, basically. And it was over there in America where you are. We all ended up heavier anyway. We formed the Faces, and got over to the States and were quite successful anyway.

KEN SHARP: Why did Steve say that he wasn't a good guitar player? You hear him on a song like "Song of a Baker" and he was a.....

IAN MCLAGAN: (interrupting) He was full of shit in that way. He was a great guitar player.

KEN SHARP: Why was he insecure about his guitar playing?

IAN MCLAGAN: Because he was modest, but to the extreme of saying he was a crappy guitarist. But it was false modesty. He was a fucking great guitarist.

KEN SHARP: Do you think he knew he was a great singer?

IAN MCLAGAN: Yeah! Shit yeah! He was confident in his singing and his guitar playing, it was only when he would talk about his guitar playing, it was secondary to his singing, so he figured he'd say that he was...I never believed that for a minute, you know. Keith Richard wanted him for the Rolling Stones, you know.

KEN SHARP: Do you ever listen back to those tracks critically?

KENNEY JONES: I'm a big fan of the Small Faces stuff now, it's been so many years. Even now I listen and go "how'd I do that" and I can't quite remember.

IAN MCLAGAN: Actually I'm constantly amazed that it sounds okay. I mean, I don't listen to it alot. I just got all the stuff that's been put out in the last couple of years by Charly and Castle, and it's like, right, put it on top of the counter, and well, I've got it but I'm not gonna listen to it. It's hard to go back to it. I just get impatient, I listen to it and it's like, yeah, heard that, been there, did it right! I'd rather listen to music that's fresh, that doesn't have all those overtones of emotion for me -- sometimes happy, sometimes sad.

STEVE MARRIOTT: As far as a philosophy of production goes, I think Ronnie and I felt that if we got a good drum sound and a good bass sound, the rest is cream on the top. That the rest would produce itself if the bass and drums are sounding punchy and clear. That's what we went for every time. Everything else was easy once you got that down. I can't understand people who try to get a guitar sound before they go for the kit. Everything should be behind the bass, not in front of it. The "Wall of Sound"

thing didn't really affect us -- I didn't want to be the Ronettes. We were looking for a Tamla sound, which was bass and drums, basically. Same as Booker T -- that's why we opted for that line-up.

KEN SHARP: The sad part about the Small Faces' gigs is that very few if any gigs were ever recorded properly, except the Newcastle gig which always turns up on albums. You'd open up with "You Need Lovin'" and really stretch out...

KENNEY JONES: I know. Towards the end there we had quite a good band -- we had Speedy Aquaye on the congas, and we had Eddie -- who we wrote that song with, "Eddie's Dreaming", with the Georgie Fame brass section, and we went out on the road with it and all of a sudden we were fucking great. That sound, I would've liked to continue with that. We would definitely have gone into....I don't know, I wish we would have never broke up....

D.I.V.O.R.C.E

STEVE MARRIOTT: Immediate wanted us to re-sign, and we wouldn't at the time. We were saying "No, we want this much dough to re-sign", and they, for some reason, decided not to pay us what they owed us, let alone what we were asking to re-sign. And for about two months we didn't have anything. The original contract must have been for three years (JOHN HELLIER:: 10 June 1965 until 9 June 1968), it must have been. "The Universal" was released right around that time (June 28th 1968). We left Immediate then, anyway. We had totally lost confidence in them. We knew that Tony Calder was even taking Andrew for a ride. I'll probably get sued for that, but it was true. We tried to warn Andrew and said "Look, if we're getting took, don't you think that you are? You're a bigger lunatic than all of us?" And he did -- he got took. But they done us good.

I'll tell you how sick they were at the end of this. I'd fallen out badly with Andrew by then, although I didn't really know it. I asked him to lend me £1200 so that I could finish off the completion of buying this house, and he said "Yeah, if you'll get the rest of the band to sign for two more years. And I can keep your publishing". I said: "Goddamit Andrew, I can't do that". And this nice agent -- Arthur Howes -- lent it to me, and I was very glad to give it back in cash a year later. We left Immediate before the breakup, and went with a thing called Shillingford Lamm -- they owned a place in Marlow where we were staying -- they were an advertising firm who made TV commercials, and they said "we'll manage you". We didn't know what to do -- we were kind of lost. So we went from one to another like that. The last thing to come out was "Wham Bam Thank You Mam" with "Afterglow" on the A-side. We had to force them (Immediate) to put it out, and since they didn't like it, they didn't do anything about it. We'd already left their management before that -- we had to, they weren't managing anything.

It suited Andrew's purposes to keep us in the studio. And so the road thing really suffered. By the time we came out of the hole, after being in the studio for a year, the road sounded terrible to me. That's when I thought "it's got to be over". See, since Andrew had a record company, he didn't have to work hard as a manager, did he? We were on his label and under his management. So it suited his purpose to have us turning out records he just has to market rather than manage us on the road and worry about all that kind of shit. We loved the opportunity to use all the facilities of the studio, but we just didn't sound that good when we came out of the studio, not for awhile.

RONNIE LANE: In actual fact when the Small Faces got calmed down a little bit, and then we heard ourselves...that's why Steve Marriott left the band.

STEVE MARRIOTT: I think when the screaming stopped and you actually heard what you were playing we went: "Jesus Christ! It's a bit bad, innit?" We grew out of screaming, and also they started to label everything: if you got screamed at, you were teenybopper. Even the crowds became conscious of that, so they wouldn't scream. We didn't want to be a teenybopper band anyway. There weren't any labels when we started doing what we were doing and getting screamed at -- it was just called "excitement", that was the label. So the louder you got screamed at, the better you supposedly were in successful vibes -- The Who got screamed at, The Stones got screamed at, Spencer Davis got screamed at -- that was how you gauged how popular you were. There was no other way.

KEN SHARP: Could you sense any dissatisfaction from Steve at that time?

KENNEY JONES: Oh, yeah. After "Ogden's...", we'd all reached kind of a plateau, and it was like "where do we go from here?". "Ogden's..." frightened us a bit -- how do we top this one (ed. note: it was a huge #1 hit album). We were all proud of it, but I think Steve was thinking it was a good time to depart. Everybody was deathly sick of

the whole teenypop image. It was like we were the Monkees, but we weren't, and we knew it. I think Steve wanted to get a bit heavier, playing around with Frampton and all that.

IAN MCLAGAN: I didn't sense any dissatisfaction from Steve. He was becoming more and more sort of self-centered. This was while we were living together. We did "Lazy Sunday", and he did "The Universal" which he cut on a tape machine in the woods behind that house, and then we overdubbed it. He told me years later that when "Lazy Sunday" came out and it was a big hit, he was pissed off. We all were really. Then when "The Universal" came out -- and it was all him, basically, and it was an even bigger hit, he felt like he was dragging the group down. I personally think he was full of shit. I don't think he thought that at all. What does that change? I love Steve, bless his heart, but he was a pain in the neck to be around. He was very, very intense, the most hyper guy I've ever met. He didn't need any leapers. He was always like that. A very intense guy. I mean, you'd go to bed and it was like whew! (sigh of relief).

STEVE MARRIOTT: Then I suggested that maybe Pete (Frampton had just left mega-popular teenybopper group The Herd, and had just been called "The Face of 1968" in England) should join, because I just wasn't satisfied with my live playing. I'd lost something in the studio -- got very "studio" about playing guitar, and had forgotten how to do it right. I didn't have the confidence anymore -- expand the band a bit so we could do more, so I wouldn't have to play or worry about playing too much -- I could sing more. Pete was a fan of the band's.

IAN MCLAGAN: Peter Frampton sat in with the band a couple of times. I don't know, who knew what Steve wanted. Steve was like twenty miles ahead of you. We didn't need him (Frampton). Fuck no! We never needed him. It was Steve's way of saying he was a better guitarist. Frampton was nowhere near as good as Steve, he had no fire. Steve was feisty, you know! He wanted to give the guitar role to someone else and concentrate on singin'. But Frampton was never gonna join the Small Faces! (said as an ultimatum.)

STEVE MARRIOTT: The reaction to that idea was terrible -- wish I'd never said it. It just didn't go down too well. Ronnie didn't want it, no one wanted it. So that's when I first thought, "Well, Christ, I want to play live, but not the way I feel about it now". I'd just lost a lot of confidence.

KEN SHARP: How was the gig with Frampton? Did it add something to the band?

IAN MCLAGAN: Z'alright. It didn't "add". We didn't need him.

KENNEY JONES: No, it worked, it was great, no problem. I don't think Frampton was ever asked to join. Marriott and Frampton started playing together and then they formed Humble Pie.

STEVE MARRIOTT: I don't know why they didn't want Frampton in the band. Maybe they thought he was wimpy or something. The kid had come around the cottage a lot and stuff and played some real good guitar, and I knew he was capable of playing some really tasty stuff. He'd never heard of Booker T & the MG's or any of these things I had. Once again, it was like opening up a flower -- they heard this music and go crazy 'cos they've never heard it before. So, he wanted to play that kind of stuff, and I thought, "Well, the time's right". That's my role in life -- turning people on to r'n'b. That's what I've done all the time. That's how you form groups, 'cos you play them things and they freak out and love it so much that you decide to play together. That's exactly what happens every time.

I told Andrew what I was going to do, and asked him what he thought of me and Peter playing together 'cos I was broke. We were all broke -- desperately broke -- and I couldn't get out of that contract. Not unless he wanted to give it away, and I'm certain he wasn't about to do that. The accounts that were still outstanding came about because of Don Arden. See, Don Arden didn't pay us any money because he said he was paying off money, and apparently he didn't pay them. So at the end of the day we were left with bills that we thought were paid years ago. Immediate bought our contract off Harold Davidson for £20,000 and it was our thing to pay them back. And we were paying and paying -- that's where our money was going, to pay them back. And I though that if we paid them back, the contact became ours, surely. Ronnie and I investigated and said, "Well, have we paid it back?" And I remember Tony Calder's reply was "What? Paid what?" We said "The £20,000 that we've been paying back the last year and a half". And he said "What £20,000?" 'Cos we didn't have anything on paper -- it was just an understanding. According to Calder, there never was a 20,000. We lost that plus -- you're talking about hundred of thousands probably by then, a year and a half later.

KEN SHARP: What do you remember about the album when you guys backed up Johnny Hallyday?

IAN MCLAGAN: I have a CD of that now. It's unbearable to listen to. It's pretty rotten. That was with Frampton. Mick Jones of Journey (KEN SHARP:: you mean of Foreigner) was writing and producing with Johnny Hallyday, and Glyn Johns was engineering...(everybody laughing) I never know who's who in those bands -- they're like the Beatles and the Stones of blandness! Industry rock; I always say the wrong band. But anyway, Mick Jones was writing and producing, and we were basically fucked, we didn't have any money and didn't have any idea what was going on...we were looking for.... maybe Steve was already leaving....I think Glyn Johns was trying to get Steve and Pete together. That was when they got together. Mick Jones told me that Glyn Johns definately broke up the Small Faces. I wrote a chapter in the book about it, but I don't know if it's true! (laughing) I gotta speak to Glyn about this -- I don't know if I should hate him (laughing). I don't know why we did the album, we were short of money, I think. I can't listen to it. It wasn't a great time in my life, I was pretty pissed off. I don't know which came first: Glyn Johns or Peter Frampton or Steve.

STEVE MARRIOTT: The best we sounded (at the end of the group) was when we did some sessions for Johnny Hallyday, and I took Peter Frampton with me to the sessions in Paris. This is where I thought "Oh he'd be good in the band itself". When we did these sessions, we were officially still on Immediate, but unofficially not. We were still under contract to Immediate, kind of, because they pulled an option on us -- that was what the dispute was over. They just let it ride and didn't tell us they had an option. Something like that went down. Glyn Johns asked us to come to Paris 'cos Johnny Hallyday had always been a fan of ours, and wanted the Smooth Faces -- as he used to call us -- to come over and back him. So it was great, we unloaded some songs on him, too. Songs from way back like "That Man" and stuff like that. And some new ones that I'd just began to write which appeared on the first Humble Pie album: "What You Will" and "Buttermilk Boy". I'm still getting money for that and it's terrific -- thank you, Johnny!

KENNEY JONES: I remember playing great. I actually enjoyed playing with Peter Frampton because his guitar playing at the time was great, he really impressed me.

RONNIE LANE: You remember all the Supergroups that

started around that time, Cream and the like? Steve Marriott decided he wanted to be taken seriously, and so he went off with Pete Frampton and left me, Ian, and Kenney in the lurch!

IAN MCLAGAN: The gig at the Alexandra Palace (31 Dec. 1968) wasn't the last gig. We did a tour of Germany after that. Read the book! That was the gig where Steve told us he was leaving. In fact, he got Alexis Korner to come on-stage and jam with us -- that's how I know we did "Lazy Sunday" live 'cos we ended with it, and where it goes to the end and it fades, he said Alexis is gonna come on-stage, and then he left us. Just walked offstage. The fucker! And left us just jamming on one note with Alexis, so we walked off after awhile. He told us he was leaving there in the dressing room, I think Frampton was there, and said he was forming a group with Pete. Well, fuck off! We had a tour of Germany booked, and as we'd been ripped off, I took over finances on that and made sure we got paid.

STEVE MARRIOTT: I couldn't hear nothing. It was just a waste of time, and the worst thing was that it was my idea to get Alexis Korner on the stage and Nick South. That was the night we'd come back from Paris. The sound was appalling anyway, but when the other two came on it was just like everyone was sort of heads down. I couldn't make heads or tails of what was going on, so I just put my guitar down and split. I couldn't hear a damned thing -- it was just a big mash of sound. I didn't even know what we were supposed to be playing, you know. It wasn't really stoned that night, but it was a big echoey hall. Everyone was turned on full and there was no contact with the audience. You lose that eye contact, which is important on stage, when you do alot of studio work. You've got big cans to use, and you lose eye contact. I couldn't get anyone's eyes to know where the fuck we were. It just sounded a total shambles and I couldn't fit in. So I said, "Bollocks, I've had it with this". It was very unprofessional of me, I know, but I couldn't handle it. In the dressing room I had a row and said I was out. There were still some gigs to go in Germany, so we went to Germany and finished them off. We had some heart to hearts about it -- me and Mac did at least, I don't think Ronnie was talking to me. But it had to be done. I think it was the best thing to do right then 'cos we were digging a big hole for ourselves, really. It allowed them...you know, me, to have a good start. What they didn't realize was that it allowed them to have a fresh start. That's the drag of having a front man -- when the front man falls, the band falls. And I had fallen. I wasn't a good front man on stage at all after that -

- after making "Ogden's...". Lack of confidence.

KENNEY JONES: I have no recollection of that last tour at all. No memory of it. I remember Steve walking off stage at the Alexandra Palace, and Steve walking off stage and that was it. I can't remember the other thing at all.

IAN MCLAGAN: The last tour was alright actually. Yeah, the pressure was off, and we just had fun. It was okay, I don't have any bad feelings about it. I've got bad feelings about how the money got sorted out at the end, but you'll have to read the book for that.

STEVE MARRIOTT: I told Andrew what I was doing, that I couldn't handle this anymore. I had a lot of pressure not to do it because it was not good in a business way, but I said that had nothing to do with it. I just don't feel comfortable anymore, and if you don't feel comfortable and actually feel uncomfortable, there's no point. I didn't talk to him before the Alexandra Palace. I'd been feeling that way for awhile but hadn't said anything -- maybe I should have done, should have gotten it off my chest. But I really hadn't, so I just blew up. Which is good 'cos that sort of thing just has to come out. And he (Andrew) took me on, but really wasn't interested in the rest of the band. That's the fate of a front man. It's always like that. See, it's a very short-sighted view, and I was quite amazed that he didn't see the talent in Kenney, Ronnie, and Mac. I think they are very extremely talented people. I don't think Ronnie really wanted to be more to the front. What we were playing on stage I don't think was Ronnie's cup of tea anyway. He wanted to sound like him, but the songs we were doing on stage were sort of derivative from me. He sang "Shake", I think, but even that was derivative. And he wanted to sound like Ronnie Lane which is fair enough. And at least the breakup gave him a chance to. I was quite an overwhelming kind of person, both in the studio and out of it. If I didn't like the way someone was playing something, I'd go and play it myself. So that was the vibe. They'd say, "Well, you fucking play it" and I would.

KEN SHARP: If the band had stayed together and Steve hadn't left, what direction musically do you think you would have gone in?

KENNEY JONES: I think we would have been messing around with the same music we played between us all. As a new instrument came out, we would have been using it to our advantage. Who knows? I think we would have done wonderful stuff! I think the Britpop movement now are doing it for us. They're taking the best elements of Small Faces, and they're making a new flavor of ice cream.

IAN MCLAGAN: Oh, I would have left, I mean, I already left when we were doing those other sessions, "Wham Bam Thank You Mam" and "Collibosher" in the studio, he was being too pushy and I said "...oh, fuck you, I'm leaving!" and got a cab home. And the motherfucker got Nicky Hopkins in. He phoned him immediately, and he played on "Wham Bam Thank You Mam". There's two versions, I'm on one of them. I know Nicky played a great piano on it, God rest his soul! (Hopkins passed away not too long ago.)

STEVE MARRIOTT: I think I left at the right time. I think that if I'd hung about then maybe it would still be the Small Faces and maybe they wouldn't be the legends they are now in your mind. We could have stuck it out and maybe gone all shitty, but I think we split at a fucking good point -- on a high note, so to speak. I mean, at the time Ronnie couldn't understand it, Mac couldn't understand it, it was like "...what the fuck are you doing?", and I said, well, If I leave now it gives us a new lease on life. Individually you can do such and such, and I can do this, with all this under our belts. With a bit of self respect. I did the same with Humble Pie, too, I left when it was peaking. But that's what you've got to do, as soon as it becomes money, and not the music, ya gotta go.

KEN SHARP: "The Autumn Stone" was issued after the band broke up. I know you didn't have any involvement with that, but what do you think of that album in retrospect?

IAN MCLAGAN: I don't listen to it. It's got kind of a bad taste when I listen to it.

STEVE MARRIOTT: There was a time when we didn't have anything at all, just a couple of new songs that Andrew didn't want, and then later on he put them out on "The Autumn Stone". He didn't like (the song) "The Autumn Stone", and then he had the cheek to call that Immediate album "The Autumn Stone", and we thought "Oh, you bastard". It was like me telling him I wanted to call the Apostolic Intervention (Jerry Shirley's band, who released a Small Faces cover "(Tell Me) Have You Ever Seen Me" produced by Marriott and Lane) The Nice. He said "You're not calling them that. That's a stupid name". And then he went and called (P.P.Arnold's backing band with Keith Emerson) The Nice. And I said again, "You bastard". He

was a thief, an idea thief-- that Andrew.

RONNIE LANE: We didn't know what to do for a while. The old man always told me to stick together, and I encouraged the boys to stick together. One day we were gonna stick together, by night time we weren't, the next day we were gonna stick together, then we weren't, and so on. This went on for about nine months. In the end, Ron Wood (originally in mod groups the Birds and The Creation, then just leaving a position as bassist for the Jeff Beck Group) phoned me up to ask if I'd join his new band he was getting together. So I went down to the Rolling Stones' rehearsal studio in Bermondsey, which was run by Ian Stewart -- he's no longer with us, you know, bless him! So I tried it out, you know, and I didn't like it very much, so I said why don't you come and join me and the boys, what's left of the Small Faces -- me, Mac and Kenney. I saw Stu, Ian Stewart, and said "...can the boys have some space down here..." and he said "...sure, The Stones would like to help you out...". So anyway, we went down there, and Ron Wood came down and he brought his friend Rod Stewart, who he'd played with in the Jeff Beck Group. Rod started to come to the rehearsals, and he's hang around upstairs. So one day Kenney said "...why don't you come down and sing with us...". Rod started to sod about -- I quite liked Rod's sense of humor, he's a very comical guy, as is Ronnie Wood. We started to play together and our whole thing was rather than do it like a Supergroup where you really take yourself seriously, y'know like Serious Blues, we'd just come on stage and we'd get pissed (drunk) and sort of have a good time.

JODY DENBERG: Now you were artists!

RONNIE LANE: Well, no, we were drunks! It went down good, and the record company, Warner Brothers, said you've gotta keep the name Small Faces because the group was so popular, and we said: "...we're not that Small anymore..." -- Rod and Ronnie anyway, so that's how we became The Faces.

JODY DENBERG: Ron Wood was asked to join the group, but Rod Stewart just kind of hung out and sang a bit, and finally someone asked him to join the group?

RONNIE LANE: Kenney Jones did, silly sod!

JODY DENBERG: The rock industry has developed to where there are managers who maybe won't rip you off, good sound systems, booking agencies, and stuff. In essence, the Small Faces and their peer groups were like guinea pigs for modern bands.

RONNIE LANE: (Wistfully) Yes, they was. It hurt, too.

STEVE MARRIOTT: Growing up together as we did, of course there would be hard feelings. I don't think Ronnie believed me -- as close as we were -- he thought I was just pulling a moody, I think. When he realized that I definitely did want out, he didn't talk to me for a long time. I think we're over that now, I hope so. We must be.

IAN MCLAGAN: (Don Arden) has to sleep at night, I don't know how he does. We'll have our day in court, I'll tell you that. Him, Andrew Oldham, Tony Calder, Charly, Repertoire, and all these other labels. Sony have come around. Decca is next. Decca never paid us a penny until after Steve died, now they're coming around. That's why all these labels are putting out the box sets now, because of the renewed interest. But we're after them, they should be all be a little worried because we were all under 21. We don't have a contract with Decca anyway, never did. We had a contract with Arden and he leased them the material. But they'll all get theirs, one of these days. I really want us to put out -- not a box set, it won't need to be a box set. We'll have a Decca set and an Immediate set, it'll have the date they were recorded, and in a chronological order, every b-side and everything. And no fucking "alternate takes" because we never kept any of that shit -- Andrew just went in and remixed them in the interests of making up extra product. All those alternate takes are just Andrews remixes just to make more money for himself. There's only one take of "Itchycoo Park", "Tin Soldier", the rest we dumped.

REUNIONs:

KENNEY JONES: There have been moments, even in the reformation of the Small Faces, which should never have happened, where we played great -- the jamming we did and all that stuff. The songs weren't that good because they weren't there, because we were trying too hard, basically. The chemistry still existed, but we should have stopped it the second time...

KEN SHARP: What prompted the band to get back together in 1978, and why did Ronnie opt out? That video with Ronnie still in the band....

IAN MCLAGAN: Andrew and fucking Tony Calder....it's a long tangled tale over the rights to those songs. It was really sort of a shuffle from one hand to another. In 1976 or so they were with a company that was gonna release "Itchycoo Park" again, and it was going up the charts, and they contacted Kenney or Ronnie or someone, and asked us if we'd get back together for a video for the song, and promised us some figure - $10,000 each or something, if we'd do it. And do one live show and they could film it and record it and release it. 'Cause we weren't too keen to get together. So we got together to do the video and he never fucking paid us, and it hit the charts again. So we were pissed off with him double! But we did get back together again, and then the first day of that, Ronnie got stroppy and said "fuck this!" and so he was booted out of the group.

KEN SHARP: Why do you think he didn't want to do it? Old wounds?

IAN MCLAGAN: Yeah, probably....And then I started writing with Steve, and we got Rick Wills in on bass, and we had nothin' else to do at the time, and it wasn't.....

RONNIE LANE: They tried to get me! I dunno, I find Steve Marriott kinda hard to take in my old age, my boring old fart age! I really wouldn't go out of my way to talk to him. I don't know what's going on in his mind -- I really don't....

STEVE MARRIOTT: I think Ronnie tried to explain to me once that he didn't get involved in Small Faces Mk. II because he didn't like the idea of it at the time, and also, he'd just found out he had MS or something, and was still trying to come to terms with it. 'Cos in the studio, Ronnie kept falling over, and I couldn't work it out and got angry with him. I thought he was drunk, but I don't think he was, thinking about it. He was trying to sing, and he'd sway and fall. But he did have a bottle of brandy, too. If he'd told me then I would have been alot more sympathetic towards why, instead of being annoyed.

KEN SHARP: What do you think of the albums, "Playmates" and "78 in the Shade"?

IAN MCLAGAN: There's a couple of my songs that got ruined. "Darling This Just Song's for You" is a little country song I wrote for Kim (ed. note: Kim Moon, ex-wife of Keith Moon, now McLagan's wife of about twenty years) -- we weren't living together then. It was a little country song and

Steve just fucked with it -- fucked with the words. Good album covers, but I've never listened to them.

STEVE MARRIOTT: "Lonely No More" is with Ronnie playing bass on it, just that one track with the four of us. Ronnie had left. I stayed up all night to edit it, to make it twice the length it was because it was only a minute and a half, so I edited the back track together so it went on for about three minutes, and then we worked on it. It's really good, and we wanted to put it out as a single -- that's how good we thought it was.

KEN SHARP: What was the tour like?

IAN MCLAGAN: Steve was into his post-punk spitting at the audience phase, which was kind of tragic. And here we were doing "Itchycoo Park" again....(sings) "It's all too beautiful...", and I hated it. After the Faces it was like going backwards. We did "All or Nothing", "Tin Soldier". Even if Ronnie had stayed, you couldn't have saved that project. It was a train wreck. It was awful. It was a rotten idea.

JODY DENBERG: There was one more project that never did get off the ground, something of a Small Faces reunion with Steve Marriott and Ronnie Lane in 1981; what happened?

RONNIE LANE: Oh yeah, Magic Midgets! That was just a kick-around. I still had my mobile studio, and Steve wanted to do something. I had nothing to do, I'd just had this attack (ed. note: Ronnie was stricken with MS -- Multiple Sclerosis -- in about 1977), and in my mind I was crawling up the wall, so it gave me something to do. I was a no-go as far as the record industry was concerned because of my MS, and they didn't want Steve either, so it never came out. The punk attitude was that everything that came out before was rubbish, so I did a song to kind of say "...who are you to disrespect your elders? What have you done?...". We recorded a bunch of songs, but nothing ever came of it.

STEVE MARRIOTT: We had another stab at it in 1981 when me and Ronnie did another album, but it wasn't released. Ronnie's mind is over active, but physically he's knackered -- but he can still write. The way he writes is to tell you something, you know, do this, do that, play that chord with these words. He can still do it. (The Magic Midgets album) was done in Loughton at the Corbett Theatre in 1981. We hired the theatre and took Ronnie's mobile studio down there. It was alright. Ronnie was singing,

I was singing, played some keyboards and guitar, wrote some songs. Jimmy Leverton was on it, Dave Hines was the drummer. We done some good stuff, but I don't think Ronnie really wants it released. Took it to everybody nigh on. But they couldn't see what we could do. Took it to Arista, CBS, Virgin, A&M, Atco. We thought Keith Richards was going to buy it, but at the last minute he said no as well. Don Arden might have taken it on Jet, but I don't think any of us wanted to go that route. I've got copy tapes, but I haven't got the master tapes. Ronnie's got them. It was alright. We're pleased with it, but not a lot of people know we did it.

IAN MCLAGAN: We're gonna reform the Faces this year! That relates because I'm hoping that will be really good. Me and Kenney have been working on it for some time. Rod's up for it! Woody's definitely up for it!

KEN SHARP: Who's gonna be on bass? Tetsu?

IAN MCLAGAN: No way! No way! I don't know. I want Carmine Rojas, Rod's bass player. He's a very good bass player, he plays Ronnie Lane lines, he'll help Kenney alot, and he'll give confidence to Rod. I know Rod has a feeling he wants somebody famous in, knowing it will help.

KEN SHARP: Does Ronnie give his blessing to it?

IAN MCLAGAN: Oh yeah, I haven't spoken to him since Christmas...but he'll be there, we'll fly him in for it. He's gotta be there, the Faces ain't complete without -- can't do it without him! But I don't know, I want Carmine. I know Rod's keen on Bill Wyman. I like Bill alot; Bill would probably do it, he played with us once before when we did it. But anyone who plays with the Faces had better play Ronnie Lane. Bill could do it but I want him to play Ronnie Lane. What we'd like to do is an 8-week tour this summer, and maybe 3-4 gigs in England. We did a "secret Faces reunion" in Dublin in December at the end of one of Rod's gigs, all of us, and it was good really. We're movin' ahead, I really want to do it. The way I look at it, everyone's a millionaire except me and Ronnie, and it wouldn't make us millionaires, but it would be a good chunk of change for both of us. I don't expect to get the whole 15 million, but a couple of million apiece would be good, you know!

STEVE MARRIOTT: Frankly, records never earnt me any money anyway, they were just a giggle, and let's face it, you've got to live. So that's why I'm playing live as much as I can. Records had never been me living, so I don't worry about it. Someone got the fucking money, but I didn't. So who cares?!!

AFTERGLOW:

KENNEY JONES: It's sad because he (Marriott) still had a lot in him. He was getting himself together. He was off the booze. He was in great shape. He was in L.A. working with Frampton on Humble Pie. I was looking forward to hearing it because he wouldn't have entered into an arrangement like that unless he had songs to back it up.

KEN SHARP: Had you been in contact with Steve before he died, and how did you hear the news?

IAN MCLAGAN: No. I had nothing to say...I'd pretty much avoid him. When Steve came to your house, he'd pretty much stay until there was nothing left to drink, you know -- 3-4 days. Back in those days we was still doing coke, and after a couple of days, Kim, my missus, would have just had enough. Just dread it. So I avoided him. And it turned out he was in L.A. recording with Peter Frampton, and I was doing a gig at the Coconut, and a geezer popped a bit of paper in my hands in between songs, and said Steve's in town and wants you to call him -- here's his number. It was a Thursday or Friday night. And I thought, oh great, file that under I Won't Use This Number, and I never called him. He flew back the next day or something, and then died the day after that. Fucking tragedy. I don't have regrets though, 'cause I would still not get in touch with him, you know. Glyn Johns said when I spoke to him some time after that said when I asked about Steve "...yeah, he's a fucking cunt. I fucking hated him..." and that's a bit sharp. I didn't hate him at all, he was just too much. God bless him! If he was in this town today, I'd change my name three times at this hotel, I'd still be avoiding him.

KEN SHARP: What do you think he'd be doing now? Would you guys have gotten back together?

IAN MCLAGAN: Hopefully he would have been in the studio and had a band with a name you could tell your parents, unlike Packet of Three or something... No, no, fuck no we wouldn't have done anything. I mean, it's a blessing really that we can't. The Faces is a different thing. Steve would never just be cool -- he would try and do "Itchycoo Park" in a spitting frenzy on stage! It was fucked!

KENNEY JONES: I would have loved for the band to have gone off and played "Ogden's..." on stage in its entirety, with Stanley Unwin narrating it on-stage. One of the great things that's pushing me to do the animated version, because I thought "am I tampering in a sacred area here?" And I thought, no one's stopping me, and Steve's sort of up there pushing me to do it, in weird sense that he wants me to do it. 'Cos one of the things I've thought is that if the Small Faces was still together as a band, we would absolutely have reworked "Ogden's...". And I know that for a fact -- very much like The Who have reworked "Tommy". "Tommy" wouldn't have come about if it hadn't been for "Ogden's...", you know.

KEN SHARP: First, what I did want to ask you about is everyone from Blur to Paul Weller to Oasis, Supergrass - many different people -- there's such a resurgence of interest in the Small Faces, in fact the band is probably more popular now than in 1996 than they ever were, what's that like for you -- is that a good feeling?

IAN MCLAGAN: It's a very good feeling. We were just in London in November and December last year, and just...there were so many articles that I was cursing..."dammit, why aren't we gettin' paid...". There was some act that had "Itchycoo Park", it was the third time "Itchycoo Park" had been a Top Ten hit in England... M People. I dunno, you'd hear this crappy version of "Itchycoo Park", frankly, and it just pissed me off thinkin' there's Ronnie sittin' at home in Colorado, y'know, and all that money never goes to him, y'see. There was an idea that alot of bands were gonna put out a Small Faces tribute album out, but I, um, hope they don't do it, in fact I've suggested they don't because we don't get any money out of it, Ronnie doesn't get anything out of it. It's a nice idea, but let's see if we can get our publishing back first, cause that money is just going to the same thieves who've thieved from us all the time, y'know. Andrew Oldham, Tony Calder, and Pat Meehan, and the record companies that we're still negotiating with to do a settlement.

KENNEY JONES: Most of the Britpop bands in the young movement -- some great bands comin' up now -- they wanted to help Ronnie Lane so they're doing a tribute album to Ronnie -- a tribute to the Small Faces. It's coming out on our record label, because I don't trust the record companies after all we've been ripped off. So, what we've done is to form our own label, Nice Records, and it's coming out on that. And when you read the book, 'cos I was reading this and I chuckled, I'd forgotten all about it -- we rewrote the Lord's Prayer. When you find it in the book it's amazing. And that's gonna be our motto: "For Nice is the music, forever and ever, amen....". Ronnie will get all the proceeds. With a bit of luck, if the record sells we'll achieve about £400,000 for him. He deserves it. It'll be great. Because his medical bills are incredibly high. I know we all send money over -- all of us, and I'm tracking down royalties. Whenever I find it, I send it over. And Rod and Woody send a few bob over there to keep him sort of going, but it's not enough -- you can't hide behind that. It's very commendable what they're doing, but it's not enough, you know. The tribute record will help, but even that is not enough. Ronnie's like a paraplegic, you know, it might as well be the same thing as Christopher Reeves -- he can't move. He can talk, and move his arm a bit. He can hardly talk. So what he needs is a house that's like specially built. You ask, I mean Christopher Reeves is going virtually broke because of his medical bills. It costs millions! And that's the idea of going out and reforming the Faces, and earn millions, and give it to Ronnie....

KEN SHARP: What I wanted to ask you was he (Kenney) looks at the band real tearfully like it's...I guess he doesn't see the positive aspects, because you know he looks at it like: Steve's dead, Ronnie's got MS, I mean, you're doing OK, he's doing OK, but it's kind of like it was a gang of four kids who were great pals, it broke up....how do you feel? Do you have a different angle?

IAN MCLAGAN: I think I must do. We were like a bunch of four little characters who were in each others' pockets for like four or five years. We were four very good friends but we would've drifted apart anyway. That's what happens. Read my book -- you'll know what it was like behind the curtains and between the sheets youknowwhaImean - but I was there!!! But he (Paolo) has no idea what it was really like, you know. No one else was there but us four, he does have a different angle, he's looking at it totally from the outside, and he wasn't into the Small Faces at the time.... I've been told he wasn't into the Small Faces, all I know is that he's a good mate of Paul Weller's, and I love Paul, and that Paul turned him onto the Small Faces. So he's come into it late and looks back and sees it quite differently, you know...

KEN SHARP: But Kenney has the view -- I think when they met up either to look at the book or they even talk about it in the book -- where Kenny says I can't look at this anymore, like they left, the meeting was very short because Kenney got really sad about it, the fact that four mates that four of them can't even get together anymore, one of them's already gone, you live in the States, Ronnie lives in the States, there's a fragmentation, but you still view the experience with a much more positive light.....

IAN MCLAGAN: We were four very lucky, very happy guys. I mean, we were stoned out of our heads so much of the time. I mean, we were listening to the best music, we were trying to play the best music we could you know. We had nothing to do but have fun, youknowwhaImean, I mean, what the fuck else do you want? We had girls everywhere you look -- just, everything was perfect! Couldn't be better! I don't look back at it at all sad. I'm sad that Steve's dead, obviously, and that Ronnie's ill, but....and that we never got paid, you know, but that wasn't why we did it - we didn't do it for the money in the first place. So when we do finally get our money from these thieves, it'll be FANTASTIC!

KEN SHARP: It'll be great, you'll have a big party...

IAN MCLAGAN: Small party, yeah...

KEN SHARP: Let's set the record straight on royalties since 1970....

IAN MCLAGAN: No royalties ever from Small Faces records! Ever! Penny One we have not received. Steve died without getting one penny ever from publishing or recording. 12 - 15 million pounds is what we've conservatively estimated we're owed. The legal fight hasn't even been really started. We're negotiating with the record companies, Decca, Charly, Repertoire, Castle Communications. Fuck Immediate! We can't get to Andrew Oldham, Tony Calder, or Pat Meehan. Sony have taken our stuff off the shelves. They're the only ones who've really been fair. They've said, okay, we realize you've been conned, we're not gonna deal with your stuff anymore. That's the solution temporarily...all of a sudden there was no Small Faces stuff on the shelves, until we can deal with this. It's kind of sad that with this whole re-interest that's happening, and they're all banging out box sets -- get that fucking shit out to just scrape money off the shelves and then run off with it. Well, Decca, Castle, Charly, Repertoire, Sony, all these people, we're gonna settle with 'em, whether they like it or not. We don't even think they have the rights. We have the feeling that all these people have been leasing stuff from people who don't even have the rights in the first place. We're gettin' to the bottom of it. If we can find out they don't have the rights, then we can get the rights for ourselves. That would be the ideal situation -- that we can get the rights for ourselves. Then we could put it out on Small Faces records, and we could present it in the best possible way -- real good vinyl, real good CD's, real good quality cassettes, real good quality books. And put out the Decca stuff exactly as it should have been. You know, when we left Decca they put out that "From the Beginning" album, b-sides and outtakes.

KENNEY JONES: We are hopefully in healthy discussions with Decca. We are in litigation at the moment. We feel good about things, that's all I can say right now. Our lawyers are talking to the people at the top. We've sold hundreds of millions of records, and not received a penny for it until now. If we'd had the money, none of us would have been suffering, even now. Because none of us is that well off, really. I'm as confident as I can be that things are gonna work out. We've got a good investigator on it, and everything that goes out comes to me now, and I put my legal people onto them, and we'll eventually get around to them. They'll never escape!

I can assure you that once we get all the rights, we'll make the catalogue far more interesting than it's ever been. I can assure all the new fans, all the old fans, that once we get all the rights, and can control the quality of the stuff the way it should be, that everything will be done right and will be available.

KEN SHARP: Do you think Steve was proud of the Small Faces? I think it was his best work.

IAN MCLAGAN: Shit yeah, he was proud of it. I think so too, y'know. See there was an innocence about it. When you try to get heavy, you're just kicking yourself. You're pissing in the wind, it doesn't work. You know, it was some of the best stuff I've ever played, really, I look back and think - that ain't bad! I can play it better now here and there, but it was good. It was representative of what I was capable of then, and it was done quick and fresh. It's good and it's got a twenty-year old attitude. I can't play like that now, I'm fifty now.

KEN SHARP: Are you fifty? You look great!

IAN MCLAGAN: Thanks, I feel alright most days! Grey is okay, you know!

KEN SHARP: Who was the tallest person in the Small Faces?
IAN MCLAGAN: I dunno, Ronnie Lane? Me? We're all within a half inch. I mean, I was 5 foot 5 and a half, but my license says 5' 6" because you're not allowed to have a half inch. So I said can I be 5'5" or 5'6" and they said yeah, so I said alright! I'll be 5'6", so when I moved to the States I gained a half inch I don't really have!

For more information, we recommend a fabulous Small Faces fanzine contact John Hellier at "The Darlings of Wapping Wharf Launderette E1", 7 Waterdene Mews, Canvey Island, Essex SS8 9YP, England.

words of winston

JIMMY WINSTON

JH: "How did you come to join the Small Faces?"
JW: "I was over in the 'Ruskin Arms' pub one night singing, and Steve came in with Ronnie Lane. Steve wanted to get up and play a bit of Harmonica. He played a bit and then we got chatting and taking about some ideas over a few beers and really that night was the launch. I hadn't met Kenny then because he wasn't there. Later, we sat around and got fairly plastered on ideas and all the possabilities. But it's really weird because of that whole period of drama school and I was all geared up to go on from there and at that moment I was about to throw it away playing in a band.

JH: "Why did you change from guitar to keyboards?"
JW: "To be honest, I was an out and out guitarist, but when we met that night, Steve had already said that he wanted to play guitar. He had already geared himself up for that, and obviously Ronnie Lane only played bass and Kenny was on drums. In a way, what they needed was a keyboards player. I'd never played keyboards so really it just occured. So when people unjustly say 'He wasn't a very good keyboards player', well, I actually wasn't a keyboards player, so you can nearly agree, but it was a case of finding what you needed for those initial songs. It wasn't elaborate, it was a bit like playing guitar on keyboards. So originally I used to play guitar and keyboard in the band and on certain tracks I used to play guitar anyway. Especially some of the ones I used to sing, so it was really more of a necessity.

JH: "How much rehearsal time was allocated before the band began playing live?"
JW: "About 24 hours! (laughing) I mean it wasn't a lot of time. From that particular night, we all sat there in the early hours, having a jar, talking about your dreams and ideas, playing a bit of of music, bit of blues, and sharing your enthusiasm. The great thing about these moments is that you merge instantly. I suppose within the next couple of days we'd set up a rehearsal. I think what was good about getting together at that time was that you get together and do a lot acoustically, just sitting around and playing guitar. You didn't have to set up with 2000 watts of power. I would

imagine that within a couple of weeks we were doing a raw set."

JH: "Can you tell me about the very first gig?"
JW: "The first gig was at the Kensington Youth Centre up the road in East Ham, and they didn't know what to expect anyway, and it was kind of a lot of bluff, there was only about 5 songs of sorts, and different variations. You'd play it back to front and then play it again differently. We just set up and played. It went kinda well."

JH: "What numbers were in the set at the time?"
JW: "It was kind of things like 'E Too D', 'You Need Lovin', it was all the raw ones. If you look at the early Decca stuff, half a dozen of them were virtually the ones anyway. They've all got a certain kind of feel about them. They are like a jam that has become a song."

JH: "How did you come to meet Don Arden?"
JW: "Well I think it was really after a couple of months of rehearsing, going out on the road and playing at the 'Cavern'. It was so quick! During that four week period, his assistant Pat Meehan came down and had a nose at the band. He was obviously quite interested. He didn't say a lot, but he went back and then eventually came forward and got the band to go and meet Don Arden in Carnaby Street."

JH: "Is it true that Don Arden was once an 'Opera Singer'?"
JW: "Yes, he even did a record. I heard it once, "My Yiddisha Momma" or something like that! But certain people had that kind of nature but in the real world it's been and gone, thank god! I think it's not where it's at, at all. They're not really participating going along with the bands and the music. Somewhere along the line, it's all gonna go wrong, isn't it? They're just working for themselves really!"

JH: "Who was your closest friend in the band?"
JW: "I don't know if that can be answered. The interesting thing is, we've got to remember on that interesting night in the 'Ruskin Arms' when we met for the first time, we had no pre-history. Steve and Ronnie had met but they hadn't

know each other for a long time. A few things I've read, makes out that they had played together in bands, but it wasn't really quite the case. They'd had a little bit of time together, but there was no pre-history, but it wasn't like they'd been together at school. It was all absolutely fresh, it's kind of got it's good and it's bad. The good is you just take off on a crest of a wave, there's no history and everythings kinda new. My energy was with Steve really because he was similar to me in a way. He had a lot of drive, lot's of attitude and a lot of things he wanted to do. With great respect to Ronnie and Kenny, they were slower and just coming out of their thing, they hadn't kinda been out there doing so much. Me and Steve had both been at it for a few years to find something to carve into a career, and our energies were higher. So in a way we kind of fascinated one another, but it was all unknown territory. It was kinda good in respect that you could bounce off one another and get a lot going quickly."

JH: "Can you describe the musical talents of each individual member?"
JW: "At this particular time, Steve was also learning the guitar. He wasn't a good guitarist. Ronnie had been playing bass in a few bands and Kenny the same. Everyone was slightly raw to be honest."

JH: "Did you play on the whole of the first album?"
JW: "No. I recorded 'X' amount of tracks that ended up on those early Decca releases and I think they put on extra bits and pieces afterwards."

JH: "How did you feel about being left off the cover of the first album?"
JW: "Well unfortunately it was to be expected. When the split came, knowing Don Arden and the way he works, he would basically change it as raidly as possible and carry on undisturbed, so I think that was fairly predictable. Oh yeah, it did peeve me a little bit."

JH: "Do you quit the Small Faces, or were you fired?"
JW: "It was a combination of a few things, but I think one of the main things was that at the time we were all enthusiastic and it was all going well and we all wanted to do it. No one had a buck, we didn't have any transport to get anywhere. There's this notorious story of my brother who loved the band and he was also keen. He was like everyone else. He didn't have very much either, but the few hundred pounds he did have, he said 'I'll buy a van and set up to do the roadieing for you'. we agreed to pay him 10 per cent for the transport. He was going to buy the van, maintain it, insure it, tax it and all the things you do and drive you there. Sheffield and back, and all that. We all agreed and I thought it was all fine. I'd go in and get the money for the gig and i'd take his 10 per cent out and pay him and the rest of the band got grumpy about it. I don't want to say they were mean or anything, but I think we were all young and full of attitudes and egos. I started to to get into conflicts with them about it. It's one of those incidents where I was stuck in the middle. Things were going quite well, and all of a sudden you've got a problem Don Arden saw this 10 per cent as 10 per cent of his money. All of a sudden, you're finding yourself having a few rows and he's got me thinking about it. Me and Steve for one thing, was starting to have moans and groans about

all this. He said 'This is just not going to work, get yourself another band and we'll record you'. He gave me an alternative really. I'd have been better to have gone off with somebody else, it would have been fresh and a lot better scope. At the same time, we were starting not to get on and problems got in there. It was a drag. The Who were always rowing as far as I knew, but they had been together longer and it was a part of the bands concept to have a row with one another and they had kind of grown with it. But I think with the Small Faces, that wasn't really there."

JH: "What was your opinion of the Small Faces after you had left?"
JW: "I suppose in a way, I was disappointed and a bit angry from the point of view of of things being handled behind closed doors, behind your back. I was definately disappointed and let down."

JH: "Did you ever see them live after you left?"
JW: "No. I mean literally as soon as this occurred, I was a bit uptight with them, the whole kind of sneak of it all with one thing and another, I got another band together, it was the only thing to do."

JH: "What were your first bands like to work with?"
JW: "The first 'Reflections' were a good band. Musically, it was a really good band to work with and we got straight ahead and got straight out playing very quickly and we did all the things you do. We played around parts of Europe, we went to Paris for a while and played out there. We did the big venue out there and we did a gig with Johnny Hallyday, which I believe the Small Faces did. We did the big Jack Barclay show over there where this year particular year they had an English theme. They had the red buses and the English police and all that. "

JH: "Have you ever met Mac, and what are your feelings towards him?"
JW: "Never met Mac. To be honest with you it's not his fault. I have nothing against him and in the same respect, he can have nothing against me. It wasn't his fault what occurred. He just ended up in a good gig, but with resect to the guy, he ended up in something that was already going."

JH: "Have you ever seen Paolo Hewitt's book?"
JW: "Read it. Didn't like it! Because, to be honest with you, I'm a free spirit and into your own sort of things. I've played and I've been a part of a lot of things, I'm still in the industry and I'm playing and I like what I'm doing. But I've got a

sensitivity to that time and I really don't take to the bull too much. I made myself sit down and read it, from front to back. I thought I know what's gonna come in here, you'll get to certain clips about the time of the break up and the same old bullshit coming out. There was that and there were inaccuracies all over the place! Even though it angered and pissed me off a bit, I read it because I thought I'd get up to date with what they're doing. The only thing I regret is he (Paolo Hewitt) didn't get in touch with me to do something in it. At the time I declined, but after reading it, I thought I should have got involved and tried to put a few of these things to right. What does come out is that as everyone gets a bit older, people get a bit blasé and things that were once just little conflicts have now been blown out of all proportion."

JH: "People I've spoken to, all thought that the title "A Young Mods Forgotten Story" was a tad pretentious, almost totally at odds with the entire Small Faces ethics. What do you think?"
JW: "I totally agree, sounds like 'Play For Today'."

JH: "What have you been doing since you left the Small Faces?"
JW: "During 67, 68 while I was still with The Reflections, I still had the yearning to act again. I did one show before going into 'Hair'. We were playing in the band and things were going quite well, you've had enough opportunity as anybody else, it may or may not happen. I went down to the 'Theatre Royal' in Stratford one night and had one of these quantum leaps. My life has had a lot of these quantum leaps. I was watching the show and I actually fell in love with it. I said to myself 'I wanted to be in something like this'. One thing lead to another, (involving me pouring my heart out to Lady Joan, the owner of the Theatre), and I found myself in the show the following Monday. I later appeared in 'Rablai' at the Roundhouse, a four week episode of 'Dr.Who', and various other bit-part work. I alo did a couple of things for Decca again, namely "The Princes Ball". I got another band together for that. "

JH: "Do you still play now Jimmy? Do you still do gigs?"
JW: "Yeah, I play mainly acoustically. People like what I do. I've recorded throughout this period as well as recording other people for the fun of it."

JH: "What are your thoughts on the amazing resurgence of interest in the Small Faces?"
JW: "Yeah, I think it's good."

selected discography

Release Date: *June 24th 1967*
Title: *"Small Faces"*
Catalogue number: *Immediate IMLP/IMSP 008*
UK chart position: *12*

Release Date: *May 31st 1968*
Title: *"Ogden's Nut Gone Flake"*
Catalogue number: *Immediate IMLP/IMSP 012*
UK chart position: *1*

Release Date: *Nov 14th 1969*
Title: *"The Autumn Stone"*
Catalogue number: *Immediate IMLP/IMSP 01/02*
UK chart position:

II. IMPORTANT CD RELEASES:

Note: As you've read in the accompanying chapter, the Small Faces don't at present get paid for anything you might buy on CD or vinyl -- they're working on correcting that problem. Still, bearing that in mind, these CDs are good value for the money despite not being the carefully thought out package the band deserves. We wholeheartedly recommend you AVOID ALL OTHER SMALL FACES CDs LIKE THE PLAGUE! Wait for the band-approved real thing if you can; otherwise these will give you all the material that's available in affordable packages at least done by fans.

1. "Small Faces: The Decca Anthology, 1965 - 1967"
4/96 Deram CD London 844 583-2.
A slim-line two-CD set that comprises all the material released on Decca -- the official singles A's & B's, the essential and brilliant first album, along with the singles released without the band's OK, and the "From the Beginning" album, released originally in 1967 as retaliation by Decca to compete with the first Immediate LP. The nice booklet contains some photos provided by co-author John Hellier, and liner notes by Paolo Hewitt. The two discs comprise the entire contents of the 1988 "Small Faces" Decca CD on London/Polydor, and the 1989 "From the Beginning" Decca CD on London/Polydor, along with four bonus tracks, it contains two solo singles: Steve Marriott: "Give Her My Regards"/"Imaginary Love" (Decca 3/63), and Jimmy Winston & His Reflections: "Sorry She's Mine"/"It's Not the What You Do (But the Way That You Do It)" (Decca 6/66). This is an absolutely fabulous batch of songs, really, with at least a dozen that are essential and not contained on the Charly box below. The box does not contain

the rare Decca alternate versions contained on the French EP's (5 tracks available nowhere else), which would have been nice to have in place of the solo stuff which had previously been released on the Repertoire CD.

2. "The Immediate Years"
10/95, Charly CD IMM Box 1,
a 4 CD box set with a nice booklet containing all but one track previously released by the Small Faces on the Immediate label. Includes all the Decca single A-sides, all the Immediate A-sides and B-sides (in stereo and in mono, although only "I'm Only Dreaming" and "Afterglow" are different takes), the complete first Immediate album (14 tracks), the complete "Ogden's Nut Gone Flake" album, cuts that appeared on "The Autumn Stone", and all the accompanying oddities, the five live tracks from Newcastle 1968, various "alternate" takes, the first Marriott solo single (see below), and all but one of the unfinished backing tracks that appeared anywhere on an unauthorized releases from the Seventies, Eighties, and Nineties. Not a bad value for the money, and the best collection available on the market today, containing all but about a dozen or so of the band's most essential songs. As a bonus, it contains Steve Marriott & the Moments: "You Really Got Me"/"Money, Money" (World Artists 10/64), Steve's second pre-Small Faces solo single.

3. "Small Faces Boxed - The Definitive Anthology"
10/95 Repertoire 2-CD set, REP 4429-WO.
This deceptively titled rip-off contains the best versions (they mixed mono and stereo versions) of all the singles A's and B's on the first disc. The version of "I Can't Make It" is unique to this set. The second disc contains 9 tracks that aren't even the Small Faces: both pre-Small Faces Steve Marriott singles and the two post-Small Faces Jimmy Winston solo singles (the second is Winston's Fumbs: "Real Crazy Apartment"/"Snow White" RCA 7/67, available only on this CD), an otherwise unavailable alternate take of the Jan. '68 P.P.Arnold/Small Faces Immediate single "(If You Think You're) Groovy", the five live tracks, a dozen "alternate/rare" tracks found elsewhere, and one other "true" oddity, "Take My Time", an unfinished instrumental track that does have the novelty of featuring Ian McLagan on guitar! The booklet is rather nice, and contains an interesting Marriott interview. With only 5 actual "rare" and interesting tracks on it, this should be considered only by truly hard-core fans.

film and TV appearances (marriott only)

"Night Cargoes" (November 1962)
A 'Film Producers Guild/Children's Film Foundation'
Production.
Produced by Cecil Musk.
Directed by Ernest Morris.
Screenplay by Angela Ainley Jeans.
Adapted from a story by David Villers, Molly Border and
Cecil Musk.

Starring:

Waveney Lee	*Nell.*
Jones	*Richard Merivale.*
Stephen Marriott	*Mr Cooper.*
Pauline Letts	*Mrs Cooper.*
Ian Curry	*Mr Howard.*
Neil Wilson	*The Cobbler.*

An 8-part (15 minutes each) childrens serial, set in Devon,
where youngsters help a rich orphan expose his adoptive
parents as leaders of a smuggling gang.

Part one:
"The Wounded Stranger".

Part two:
"The Smuggler's Pony".

Part three:
"The Secret Panel".

Part four:
"The Mystery Of The Ruined Valley".

Part five:
"Trapped In The Tunnel".

Part six:
"Richard Knows Too Much".

Part seven:
"The Escape In The Coach".

Part eight:
"The Last Cargo".

Certificate (U).

"Heaven's Above" (April 1963)
Directed by The Boulting Brothers, John & Ray.
A 'Charter (BL- Romulus) Film Production'.
Produced by Roy Boulting.
Directed by John Boulting.
Screenplay by Malcolm Muggeridge.
Adapted from the story by John Boulting and Frank Harvey.

Starring:

Peter Sellers	*Reverend John Aspinall.*
Cecil Parker	*Archdeacon Aspinall.*
Isabel Jeans	*Lady Despard.*
Eric Sykes	*Harry Smith.*
Bernard Miles	*Simpson.*
Ian Carmichael	*Rev. John Smallwood.*
Irene Handl	*Rene Smith.*
Miriam Karlin	*Winnie Smith.*
Eric Barker	*The Bank Manager.*
William Hartnell	*Maj Fowler.*
Roy Kinnear	*Fred Smith.*
Joan Hickson	*Housewife.*

Stephen Marriott *as an uncredited young urchin.*
Plus cameo appearances by Malcolm Muggeridge and
Ludovic Kennedy.

A prison chaplain, mistakenly appointed to a village church,
causes chaos with his Christian charity.

*Black & White- Running time 118 minutes. Certificate (A).

In between takes at Pinewood Studios in Iver, Steve used to duet with Peter Sellers on guitar. As a footnote, in an adjacent studio at Pinewood, July Garland was in production on her last cinema film entitled 'I Could Go On Singing'. With her in England was her daughter Liza Minelli, who would wander over to watch Steve's duets with Peter Sellers. It was the first time that she had met Sellers, some ten years before their short, intense affair.

"Live It Up" (July1963)
(Alternate American title: "Sing And Swing")
Produced by 'Three Kings' (RFD)
Produced & Directed by Lance Comfort.
Screenplay by Harold Shampan.
Adapted from the story by Lyn Fairhurst.

Starring:
David Hemmings ....*Dave Martin.*
Heinz Burt...........................*Ron.*
Joan Newell ....*Margaret Martin.*
Veronica Hurst ....*Kay.*
Ed Devereaux.....................*Herbert Martin.*
Stephen Marriott ....*Ricky.*

A Post Office messenger forms a beat group and stars in a musical film.

With contributions by Heinz, Kenny Lynch & His Jazzmen, Gene Vincent, Patsy Ann Noble, Kim Roberts, The Outlaws, Sounds Incorporated, Andy Cavell & The Saints, Nancy Spain, Peter Haigh and Peter Noble.

*Black & White- Running time 74 minutes. Certificate (U).

"Be My Guest" (February 1965)
Produced & Directed by Lance Comfort.
A 'Three Kings- Harold Shampan Filmusic (RFD)' ' Production.
Screenplay by Lynn Fairhurst.

Starring:
David Henmings.................*Dave Martin.*
Avril Angers ....*Mrs. Pucil.*

Joyce Blair ....*Wanda.*
Marriott ....*'Ricky'.*

A family try to run a guest house at Brighton and make it popular. Dave Martin (Hemmings) meets American entertainer Erica Page (Andrea Monet) and let's her stay in the guest house rent free, while a teenage reporter exposes a producer's attempt to rig a beat group contest.

With musical contributions by Jerry Lee Lewis, The Nashville Teens, The Zephyrs, Kenny & The Wranglers, Niteshades and The Plebs.

*Black & White- running time 82 minutes. Certificate (U).

TV APPEARANCES:
Steve made four appearances on BBC Television. The first being:

1) "CITIZEN JAMES"
(BBC Television. Originally transmitted on Monday December 4th 1961 between 7:30 and 7:54pm)

Steve (in an un-credited 'bit-part') makes his television debut opposite 'Carry-on' star Sid James. The series also starred Sydney Tafler, Hugh Lloyd and Patrick Cargill. This episode, titled "Teenagers Of Today", carried this synopsis:

"The redoubtable Sid turns his attentions to the problem of the teenager of today. Doing some socioloigical field-work down at the local 'Palais', Sid and his research assistant Charlie, (played by Tafler), find just how knotty the problem is!".

(Steve was naturally one of the teenagers in the 'Palais' sequences, and spoke only two lines of dialogue).

2)"MR. PASTRY'S PROGRESS".
Episode two (of six) entitled "One Bob, One Job". (BBC Television. Originally transmitted on Saturday April 21st 1962, repeated on Monday February 7th 1963).

"Mr. Pastry's Progress", was the spin-off series to the highly successful series "Mr. Pastry" starring Richard Hearne. The details for the recording of the programme are as follows:

MONDAY APRIL 2nd 1962

BBC Television send the script of "Mr. Pastry's Progress" episode entitled "One Bob, One Job" to Steve, c/o "The Italia Conti Stage School & Agency", at Avon Dale Hall, 72, Landor Road, Stockwell, London SW9. He is commissioned to play the part of Harry Scroggs.

MONDAY APRIL 9th 1962

After accepting the part, Steve arrives for the start of four days of rehearsing at the 'General Suite', in Bloomfountain Road, London, W12. The session lasting every day between 10:30 and 5:30pm, where he works, for the first time, with #BBC producer David Goddard.

TUESDAY APRIL 10th, WEDNESDAY APRIL 11th & THURSDAY APRIL 12th

Three further days of rehearsing at Bloomfountain Road in London.

FRIDAY APRIL 13th

Operations move to Studio D at the BBC studios of Lime Grove, where rehearsals take place before the cameras for the first time. These sessions subsequently lead to the taping for transmission. (The day begins again at 10:30am).

The final 'run-through' before the cameras begins at 4:45pm. Then between 5:25 and 5:50pm, the programme is recorded for transmission on BBC Television on Saturday April 21st between 5:25 and 5:50pm. A repeat screening of the recording occurred on Thursday February 7th 1963 between 5:25 and 5:50pm. Steve was paid 13 and a half-guineas, this included his performance, rehearsal and costume fitting fee.

The synopsis for the show was:
"Scout Master Pastry is determined that this year's 'Bob-A-Job' week will break all records- and 'sweeps' on to success'.

3)"DIXON OF DOCK GREEN"

(Transmitted on BBC Television on Saturday February 9th 1963)

Two days after Steve (or rather Stephen) appears on BBC Television in a repeat showing of "Mr. Pastry's Progress", he reappears as Clive Dawson in the long running Saturday night 'cops & robbers' show "Dixon Of Dock Green" starring Jack Warner as P.C. George Dixon. The episode was called "The River People", a story by Ted Willis.

Steve's mother Kay remembers that he filmed his scene, where he had to jump in a cold river, at 6am on a Saturday morning. The episode was transmitted on Saturday February 9th 1963 between 6:30 and 7:14pm.

4)"WILLIAM THE PEACEMAKER"
(Transmitted on BBC Television on Saturday March 28th 1963)

THURSDAY DECEMBER 20th 1962
Steve, again through the 'Italia Conti Stage School & Agency' recieves an offer to appear in the programme "William", where he is requested to play the part of Bertie Franks.

MONDAY JANUARY 14th 1963
The first part of "William" takes place, with location filming.

TUESDAY FEBRUARY 5th to SATURDAY FEBRUARY 9th 1963
Work continues with more filming of "William". During these days, (Between 10:00 and 1:00pm) shooting takes place in the 'Student Movement House', Hanover Street, London.

SUNDAY FEBRUARY 10th
The conclusion of shooting on "William The Peacemaker", takes place at Studio D at Lime Grove, where between

10:00am and1:00pm, then later between 5:15 and 6:15pm, final work is completed. The show is transmitted on BBC Television between 5:25 and 5:49pm on Saturday March 28th 1963. The episode would be the first show in the new series.

For his part, Steve was paid:
* £7- 17 shillings- 6 pence = for rehearsals.
* £3- 3 shillings- 0 pence = for filming.
* £7- 7 shillings- 0 pence = performance fee.

Small Faces In Their Own Words interviews by Kent Benjamin, Ken Sharp & John Hellier

Words of Winston interview by John Hellier

All other research by Keith Badman and Terry Rawlings